Irish at Heart

Irish at Heart

MARIE GRAY

914.1504
406

HarperCollins*Publishers New Zealand Limited*

To David

The author would like to thank Malaysia Airlines for their support,
without which this book would not have been possible.

By the same author
Irish in the Blood
About Time
Tamu

First published 2000
Reprinted 2000

HarperCollins*Publishers (New Zealand) Limited*
P.O. Box 1, Auckland

ISBN 1 86950 344 9

Set in Aldine 721
Designed and typeset by Chris O'Brien
Printed on 79 gsm Bulky Paperback by Griffin Press,
Netley, South Australia

contents

map of ireland   6
acknowledgements   7
family tree   8
preface   11
1. preparation   16
2. the beginning of the search   23
3. land of lake and legend   34
4. the fact and the fantasy   40
5. ballymuck   53
6. the pilgrim way   75
7. searching for roots   85
8. new money and old   94
9. dear old killarney   102
10. peninsular people   111
11. to hell or connaught   126
12. in the steps of saint patrick   139
13. a lucky mistake   151
14. precious people of donegal   167
15. a different drum   177
16. a step too far   198
17. the search for irish blood   208
18. washed by the irish sea   217
19. the fun of cork   231
20. over and out   249
epilogue   253
bibliography   261

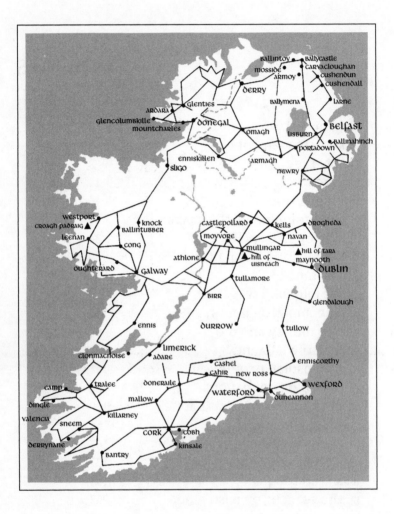

acknowledgements

My special thanks to Dr Linde Lunney of Trinity College, Dublin, who researched the family tree, and to Leonard Quigg of Ballycastle, who helped with local knowledge. Special thanks to Faber & Faber for permission to quote *The Cure at Troy* by Seamus Heaney.

Ireland: To the following people, whose hospitality made our journey so much more enjoyable — Michael and Pauline Simms, Christine and John, Drs Linde and James Lunney, Sam and Toye Black, and the many friends at the self-catering cottages who shared their experiences with us and made us welcome.

New Zealand: To my cousin, the late Brian Magill, who encouraged me to make the trip; and to Lambert Jansen for his generosity. Without the help of my husband, David, this book would not have been written. He drove me round Ireland, kept the peat fires burning and enhanced my perception of the country with his artistic gifts and historic interest. *Sláinte*.

family tree

James	Archibald	**Patrick**	John
m	m	m	m
Martha Reynolds	Mary-Jane Campbell	**Mary-Anne McGowan**	Mary Getty
To New Zealand	*Stayed in Ireland*	*To New Zealand*	*To New Zealand*

John			James
Mary Jane			Robert
Jim			John
Wilson			Mary
Willie			Kathleen
Martha Anne			Bessie
Archie			Francesca
Emilie ⎫			Archibald
Francis ⎭ Twins died			
Fred			
Bessie (Posy)			

James	Mary	**Robert**	Annie 1
m	m	m	Died 2 years
Ramari Ratana	Fred Hunt	**Jessie Manins**	
No issue	No issue	**Patrick Marie**	

8

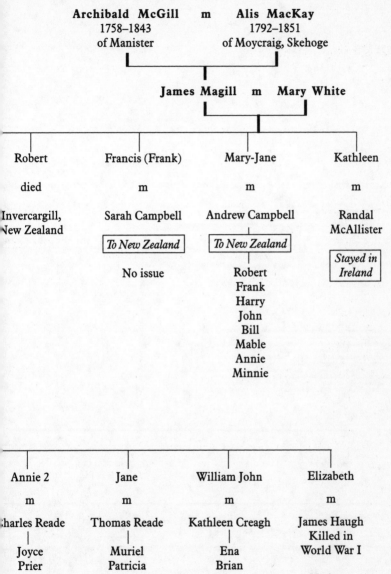

Archibald McGill   m   **Alis MacKay**
1758–1843   1792–1851
of Manister   of Moycraig, Skehoge

James Magill   m   **Mary White**

Robert	Francis (Frank)	Mary-Jane	Kathleen
died	m	m	m
Invercargill, New Zealand	Sarah Campbell	Andrew Campbell	Randal McAllister
	To New Zealand	*To New Zealand*	*Stayed in Ireland*
	No issue	Robert	
		Frank	
		Harry	
		John	
		Bill	
		Mable	
		Annie	
		Minnie	

Annie 2	Jane	William John	Elizabeth
m	m	m	m
Charles Reade	Thomas Reade	Kathleen Creagh	James Haugh Killed in World War I
Joyce	Muriel	Ena	
Prier	Patricia	Brian	No issue

preface

FOR SOME STRANGE REASON *Irish in the Blood* found its way into thousands of homes and hearts, awakening lost memories, pulling at heartstrings, sending waves of nostalgia throughout Australasia.

'Aye, you've said it all. You've told our story, so you have. Write some more.' Eyes filled with tears. 'We'll never go back to Ireland now, and anyway, you know, the Troubles. It's not so safe, if you get what I mean.' Heads nodded knowingly.

Write another book about Ireland? What did I know, really, except from books and letters and photos, and all my research findings. I *had* said it all, anyway — from my limited perspective in New Zealand. The crowded shelves of Irish books looked down at me accusingly, as if they too still had something to say, as if packing them away would close the Irish chapter of my life for ever. Did I want that? Was it just sentiment? Eight years of nostalgia, and living in the past?

But, as people talked, I knew it wasn't the end; it couldn't be. My love affair with Ireland and its people was really just beginning. And now the children and grandchildren of Irish immigrants in New Zealand were begging to know more. How could I let them down?

Maybe there would be a grant or some other kind of assistance to help such a project, either in New Zealand or in Ireland? I would try anyway, write a few letters and test the waters — Gwen Reiher, the enthusiastic wonder woman of Auckland's Genealogy Society, would be the first to contact. A human encyclopaedia with Irish in her blood.

11

'How did you get on tracing your rellies in Ireland, Gwen? Did the Historical Foundation in Belfast help you out with grants or accommodation or something?'

'Talk about the Irish telling you nothing — they won't even answer letters. I found five of mine sitting on top of their fridge when I finally made it back.'

'Were they embarrassed?'

''Course not!'

'Had they read them?'

'Aye!'

'Maybe I could try faxes.'

'Faxes? I've tried that too. Look, if you want to communicate with the Historic Foundation or any other literary society, ring at eleven at night and you'll get them sober at their desks at ten in the morning.'

'It can't be that bad!'

'Try it!'

So I did.

'My then, fancy that. The author from New Zealand. Your buke? It was here right enough, but, I've been travelling — to America — and lost touch with the office a bit. Try tomorrow will ye now? You say you want to write another? Gude! A grant? We're struggling ourselves, to be truthful. We could do with a few grants from somewhere. Ring tomorrow.'

Which I did.

'It's you again from New Zealand? I'd know that voice anywhere, sure I would. How's the weather down there? Great? Well, it's starting to lift up a bit today. The girls say your book was here on the desk, but they can't just . . . Look, Maree, tell your publisher to send three or four and we'll get it on our list. It's a good book right enough. A grand story.'

'Look, I want to come over and follow it up. Go back a bit further, do a kind of pilgrimage when I'm there. Is there some way you can help me? Do you have access to accommodation for travelling writers, or contacts we could use round the whole island?'

'Can't say about that exactly, but it's a grand idea of yours. Look forward to seeing ye then. No grants, Maree. Try the gude people in New Zealand. Good luck, see ye soon!'

A few old hands threw in their advice:

'You want to be careful going way back there to your father's people. They might think you're after land or old money or something. They might back off. Like the time I went. The rellies in the first five places were a bit cagey like, and the head of the house didn't appear. I said to myself, that's strange, I said. But I found out later they were scared I'd face them up with the ownership of the land, and put in a claim or something. You don't know what they're thinking over there. Not till I got on a pair of wellies and made them show me the graveyard did they thaw out. You know, me in wellies in the long grass? Just like themselves if you know what I mean. No airs and graces from the other side of the world.

'If you do go, take it easy. They might not take to you at first. Think you're rich coming all that way from the other end of the earth on a plane. May pretend they don't know who you are even, or like what happened to me — told me the old home was miles away, far too far to see it in a day, and then I found it was just a step away. They wouldn't believe you if you told them you'd sold those rings and watches and stuff to get to them. Anyway, they didn't ask you to come. It's kind of your business if you sell off the family jewels and heirlooms, like you told me.'

Should I go? What if there was no one at the old farm? What if the old landmarks of *Irish in the Blood* had disappeared under the auld sod? What if?

The oldest cousin, Brian Magill, phoned unexpectedly from Wellington. In a strong, vibrant voice he came to the point.

'You're dithering, aren't you? Go there, or you'll regret it forever. Don't wait for the right moment, there won't be one.'

How did he know, a very sick man in a wheelchair, with no idea of my dilemma? He knew because he had that touch of Irish in the blood, and that canny insight of a Magill. You could call it second sight.

It was 86-year-old Elsie Rodgers who nailed it. One of the Archies, the last to come from Carvacloughan in 1923. A squeaky old voice spoke in telegram style from a neighbour's phone in Hastings.

'I'm reading your book again. I like it, although the print's too small. I want you to look back further, right back to James and Mary White and further. That business about being related to the Kings of Munster and Field Marshall Sir George White. I'm almost certain they came from the South. They're pure Irish, not Scottish. Kathleen knew the origins and I heard them talking about it. No one passed it on. You know who Kathleen was, don't you? The one that stayed behind. Old Patrick's sister. Ivan McAllister should know more. I'd like you to see to it.'

It could take months to 'see to it'. But at that moment I knew I would try.

The sun shone on that decision. I could feel a great surge of excitement, of adventure, of doing something on behalf of the whole family. The 'storyteller one' was going over on behalf of them all — to 'see to it'. The Magill family rellies in England and Wales followed me around Ireland by letter and phone, and I'd never even met them. They wanted to be part of this pilgrimage too — from a distance. Always from a distance, even though it was only across the Irish Sea for them. Strange that. One day I might tell them so.

No one mentioned money, ever, and some of them had pots of it. Storytellers are expected to live like Gipsies, I learnt. It's what people like to dream about in moments of fantasy — battered old car, soup and spuds for six months, sleeping in sagging monstrosities called beds. Little did they know that we had to sell some precious paintings and heirlooms, that the jade set we all imagined would take us round the world and back turned out to be worthless venturine, that the New Zealand dollar was the lowest it had ever been against the Irish punt, that in desperation we allowed our house to be rented by a Great Dane and his family . . .

'Get yourself an Irish passport — you never know,' the voices said menacingly. 'If there's a punch-up or anything, you can produce it. Make a will before you go. You could land up gettting a bullet up your backside.'

On and on! I was sick of ignorant people and their timeworn one-liners — 'bog Irish', 'fighting Paddies', 'Murphies' and the rest of it. Sick of the pathetic documentaries on the New Zealand Irish, with strawberry noses and missing teeth, all throwing back jugs of Guinness. No one seemed to have told them that five of New Zealand's prime ministers had been Irish.

We left New Zealand at Easter as the Good Friday Agreement was being agonised over at Stormont Castle in Belfast. At the door of the plane in Kuala Lumpur, passengers were grabbing at a huge pile of newspapers. They disappeared in a flash. What had happened? Something tragic? Voices rose and fell in excited discussion as hand luggage was shoved and pushed into overhead lockers. Would we take off at all?

IRISH EASTER MIRACLE

Big bold letters spelt it out on the front page. Peace had been signed on a cold wet day in Belfast. Would it last? I was crying now, and David blew hard into his handkerchief. It seemed we were coming back 'home' on the most historic day in centuries.

1. preparation

'WE'RE ALL NEEDIN' A BREAK,' the young woman at the airport confided, looking over her shoulder furtively. 'My wee nieces are being brought up knowing nothing but *this*.' She pointed to the newspaper on her lap. 'This peace has *got* to last — we've had enough. Thirty years of bombs and soldiers and fear.'

We hurried into the crowded lounge, waiting for the call to board the plane from London to Belfast. No way would we miss this one.

'They searched through our bags for a harmless old pocket-knife and made us late.'

'Not harmless here,' the young woman said seriously.

On board, Easter Monday holiday-makers opened their papers, faces mirroring a thousand feelings. Dare they hope for peace? Bill Clinton's words showed up clearly in large print:

HOPE INSTEAD OF HATE
PROMISE INSTEAD OF PREJUDICE

'God help us,' my neighbour mumbled, his mouth closing over a big soggy bun. 'They've got a long way to go to get these Irish to agree on *anything*.'

A few seats behind, a young mother was busily preparing her four-year-old son to meet relatives in Belfast.

'Och, James, say Jesus Christ.'

'Jeesus Chriist,' mumbled the lad.

'Say it again, and properly.'

'Jesus Christ,' he yelled loudly.

'That's better. You'd better be a good boy when you meet yoar aunties in Belfast. They'll be lookin' to you. No feuterin' about.'

'Jesus Christ and all the saints.'

'Aye, that's better an' all. Now, can ye see it boy? Just look down at the coastline of Larne. Larne it is, James.' Her voice rose with unaffected excitement.

I wondered what a four-year-old in New Zealand would know about Jesus Christ? Some didn't even know what the cross on an Easter bun meant, let alone an Easter egg. One little girl told me her egg was Jesus' tomb and the two Marys had eaten all the sticky stuff inside and that was why it was empty!

They were selling 'footy eggs' when I left — Easter eggs in the shape of footballs with profiled faces of rugby heroes. That was the Kiwi religion. No mother in New Zealand would be preparing a child to meet the aunties in this way. I had entered into a different culture, a different mind-set, a religious country teetering on the brink of peace. I knew it in theory, but the reality? My heart sank. Was this whole trip to be clouded by politics and religion? I wanted to find out about other things — family, the new Ireland, changing values, pilgrimages, today's women, remnants of the ascendancy (the English landowning colonials), and a dozen other things. I wanted to see the beauty and history of this whole island. I looked out of the window too, catching the mother's excitement. There was Belfast, so close, and I hadn't had time to *feel* anything. It was all too fast.

We were in the airport now, and I could see the little boy shaking hands nicely with his aunties, his mother's face flushed with pride. I wanted to say 'Jesus Christ' myself. Say something anyway. Feel something! Here I was in Belfast, rooted to the spot with a pile of luggage at my feet. The nice Irish girl at the desk did the trick.

'Would you have ye tickets handy now?' She smiled with her eyes. 'Having a wee holiday, arr yez? Jest you enjoy it then.'

I was home.

My mind went back seven years ago. Not to a jet over the Irish Sea, but to a ferry from Stranraer to Larne. My first glimpse of Ireland on a grey morning. I cried then. Cried because the man opposite me thought I was English and ignored me. Cried when he found out I was from New Zealand and asked me whether I was coming to look for my 'daddy'. Cried when he bought me coffee and gave me his hanky. Cried when I heard the Irish lilt in the voices around me. For seven whole days I floated round in a mindless euphoria looking for the old farm, leafing through telephone books for the name Magill, finding dozens, achieving nothing, driving through places I had heard my father mention — Ballymena, Armoy, Ballycastle, Coleraine — asking here, asking there, knocking on doors — 'Do you remember . . . ?'

'Aye, there were Magills way back, I mind the time. Can't say I've met any these last fifty years. Try the old man down the road, he's been here nigh on seventy years. A few went over the Antrim hills in the famine time . . .'

Looking back on that first fleeting emotional search on Irish soil, I realised that if I had a chance to come back one day, I would have to know exactly where to go. No more feuterin' round!

Now, after seven years searching, I was back here knowing the exact address, knowing the road back to the old places, and knowing the name of one living descendant — Ivan McAllister. What would he be like? Would he think we had come back to claim a bit of land? Dig up some family skeletons? He hadn't answered any of my letters, ever.

No one had prepared us for the beauty of the rolling countryside in the drumlin belt of Northern Ireland and the pattern of country roads that wind endlessly round them. Teardrop-shaped humps up to half a mile long and a hundred feet high, all lying in the same direction. 'Providing pasture for cattle and crops,' the people said nonchalantly, but they loved their green drumlins too. 'But do ye not see Mourne over therre, with a wee sprinklin' of snow? That's Mourne, so it is.' Surely not the Mourne we sang about in 'The mountains of Mourne sweep down to the sea'? The very same. A wave of nostalgia choked me. I could hear those Irish tenors and the plaintive voices pining for their native land. It must have been hell to leave these fields for the crowded streets of London or any other foreign city.

A snowfall in spring in County Down. Gentle white flakes dancing across the daffodils and crocuses, covering lawns and shrubs and fields with thick white magic, leaving dusted hedgerows to form a quiltlike pattern. We crunched about in delight.

'But it's cauld for Easter, cauld. And think about our roses an' all. Gone! Finished! Oor fruit and vegetables. Gone! Finished!'

We stood spellbound in Lisburn's shopping mall, just listening and looking. Soft voices rose and fell all around us as if singing a lullaby. People in restaurants talking to each other so so seriously, their faces almost touching. The food didn't really matter, the 'crack' did. We would get used to the importance of conversation and atmosphere. Now, however, it was all new and intriguing.

A hairdresser is a good place to ask questions for starters.

'Aye, it's cold outside, so it is. Sit ye down a wee moment. Before the snow came it was mild, so it was.'

'Do you ever go to the South for holidays?'

'Never been to the South in me life. What would I want to go there for? You're only a few hours away and then you'd be back. That's not a holiday. A holiday is when you get in a plane and go four hours. Two hours isn't a holiday neither. It's four hours you have to be. I like Spain or Florida.'

'What do you do in Florida?'

'Take a time-share. Be a child again. Have fun! Ride the wheels in amusement parks and swing around. I couldn't work here like I do without a holiday like that every year. My head wouldn't take it. I'd be crazy right here!' She put her hands to her head.

'I like the big stone houses round about Lisburn and Ballynahinch. We have wooden houses in New Zealand.'

'Aye, I know that. You live in shacks.'

'But wooden houses can be really nice — spacious and modern.'

'Aye, I know that, but they're shacks right enough.'

The voice lilted as her wet fingers made furrows through my hair.

'Tell them in your book that Ireland's a grand place. It's only a few of them . . . You know well enough what I mean.'

'So, you don't know any addresses of anyone in the South? We might go there later on.'

19

'I can't say I do. You'll have to look up the books at the tourist places. But why go there?'

We needed a car. A questionable character shuffled up to David in a dealer's yard. A dark, tubby little man with shifty eyes like a bandit. He looked over his shoulder suspiciously as he spoke, then fixed David with a scary stare.

'I've got the car you want, so I have. VW Polo, hatchback. Come to my house and see it. Needs a bit of work done here and there, but I'll have it for ye — when? Just give me a couple o' days will ye? Insurance an' all — jus' leave it to me. David's the name isn't it? And you've got eight hundred pounds. Is that all? Now, David . . .' Blah, blah, blah.

How could David trust this con man, this rogue, this dealer with eyes like quicksilver? He could be from the IRA. David was a fool!

'He's OK. He won't let us down,' he told me. Oh yeah? With an odometer reading of 177,000 kilometres?

We landed 'Trixie' and I was never to say a nasty word about her. You would think David had had 'the guidance'. I hadn't! We would be pounding along the roads for six months. Could she last that long? Nah!

The Honorary Consulate for New Zealand in Northern Ireland would be sure to give us some information about the South. We'd go there.

Imagine a piece of New Zealand hidden in the countryside outside Belfast. Ballance House appeared unobtrusively out of the quiet Glenavy farmlands, a brave link between Ulster and New Zealand. The restored birthplace of New Zealand prime minister John Ballance and brainchild of Dr Jill McIvor, it covered everything from Maori culture to pioneer life and the impact Irish people had had on the new colony. It's all there in the exhibitions and video, and in the old orchard replanted with nineteenth-century fruit trees by the 1989 All Blacks. Irish prime ministers from Ballance to Bolger stare proudly from the walls. *Irish in the Blood* is in the library with other books of similar genre by Kiwi authors — Patrick O'Farrell, Anna Rodgers, Dan Davin. What better place to locate the consulate? Not in busy Belfast, but on home ground in Ballance House.

Addresses for the South?

'Sorry, can't help you there,' said the nice attendant, 'but you can have tea in the nineteenth-century tea barn.'

I had tea with Jill McIvor too, in her charming home in Newcastle, where kowhai and clematis flourish in strange surroundings. A lady dedicated to marrying New Zealand and Ulster.

The road from Downpatrick to Strangford Loch is a journey back in time.

We would discover that Ireland is just that. Two steps forward and one back. Massive cathedrals, abbeys and castles come out of nowhere, blowing the mind with their historic associations and antiquity.

'Saint Patrick was buried there,' our friend Michael says nonchalantly, 'and you can take a pilgrimage walk along the stations to the top of the hill. If you turn around now, you can just see him standing there.'

Then he's gone, this Saint Patrick who would follow us on our journeys. I would like to take this pilgrimage walk, but we are already speeding on to the ferry, watching the yachts fighting an 8-knot tide as they race close into the banks of the narrows of this huge lough. Further out is the Irish Sea. Pretty exciting stuff.

Portaferry had an information office. 'Walk through that tower-house castle and you'll find it,' they said, as if it had been built yesterday, not in Anglo-Norman times. The office had never had a New Zealander sign the book, and the girl there seemed surprised we spoke English. But they didn't have anything on the Republic. Why couldn't we find someone who had contacts? It seemed like a different country altogether, and we simply had to get there before European tourists shot the prices up to glory. With our dollar striking rock bottom, we would have to move, and soon. But it was fun to eat afternoon tea in a café at Portaferry, stuffing down the hottest, soggiest, most cherry-laden scones that only the Irish can serve up.

We sped home through the majestic cathedral town named after Saint Patrick. There would surely be more pilgrimages to honour the amazing patron saint of Ireland.

Along the street in Ballynahinch, the Union Jack fluttered from lampposts and houses, curb stones painted to match — red, white and blue. We could have been in England. An open red hand loomed before us on the street wall. Our friends must have detected our confusion. 'That's the way it is here,' they said. 'Not always done appropriately.' What did it all mean? This was Ireland, wasn't it? Perhaps we would find a different story further north, at the old farm at Carvacloughan. Impossible to go south without a quick look up there. I could barely wait.

The garage attendant at Ballynahinch looked at our luggage suspiciously. Backpackers in a car.

'We're going south tomorrow and we'll need all that stuff for self-catering cottages. Any contacts down there?'

'What? In the Republic?'

'Yes.'

'Whatya doin' around here then?'

'Writing a book.'

'A buke? What about?'

'Ireland.'

'Aye. Tell them all we're a friendly lot, so we are. Tell them not to believe the papers. It's only a small wee few who are makin' the trouble. Aye, tell them that! Where d'ya come from?'

'New Zealand.'

A glazed look came into her eyes. 'Hmm. A bit before Australia. Play rugby there. Gude weather.'

'Would you like to go to New Zealand?'

'*New Zealand*?' Horrified. 'I've not even been to the South yet. Dublin an' that.'

'So you don't know anyone there we could contact?'

'Not *there*.'

2. the Beginning
of the search

'WE CAN'T GET MCALLISTER'S on the phone. They're not in the book. I'll have to look up my records,' Big John the policeman said. 'Are you sure the name was McAllister? Yours was Magill, wasn't it? How come McAllister?'

'The youngest Magill of our family stayed in Ireland and married a McAllister. Look, it's all here. Kathleen Magill married Randal McAllister, the rest went to New Zealand.'

'But that's a hundred years or more ago. You don't expect them to be sitting there waiting for you, do you? Get real!'

'Not *them*, but a generation or two down the line. The address is Moyarget Road, a few miles south of Ballycastle.'

'Moyarget Road? It's miles long. You'll never find it. Come in our car and we'll make an exploring day of it. Now, write down what you're looking for . . .'

Imagery, dreams and sentimental feelings were being replaced by cold reality on paper as we sped north. Couldn't we go a bit slower? Sort of cruise along savouring the fields, the peat, the atmosphere, adjusting to a different ambience? I'd waited half my life for this moment and it was passing me by.

'This is a typical Ulster day, three seasons in an hour.' A voice cut sharply through my reverie. It was Christine, Big John's wife. 'We'll be changing from jerseys to T-shirts, jeans to shorts, sun hats to woollen caps, then the reverse. Not like home.'

'Right, now we're passing Mosside,' said Big John abruptly. 'We'll stop at this store and ask about this church you're wanting to see. What's this you've written here?'

'Wee church on the hill.'

'That's it. Where the Magills went to church. A chap in Ballycastle wrote a history of it. We'll call in and see him later.'

Big John strode in — an Ulsterman oozing authority. Christine and I gossiped in the back seat. Our first private opportunity.

'Did I tell you my mother Jess was in love with your grandfather, William Lamason? Only from a distance, of course. That's how far it went in Brethren circles those days. Just little demure glances and longing sighs.'

'Strange how both of us were brought up in that conservative church in Napier,' giggled Christine. 'New Zealand seems half a world away now . . .'

The shopkeeper and John were chatting on the roadside.

'Can't say that I know it,' the shopkeeper mumbled, 'but there's a Drumtullagh Church of Ireland up the road and around the corner.'

I jumped up excitedly at the sound of Drumtullagh.

'That could be it!' I called out. 'Maybe they just called it the "wee church on the hill" in the old days — a sort of nickname.'

And there it was, sitting sedately on a ridge overlooking four of the counties of Ulster, like the book said. But that was on a clear day — now it was raining and the four counties had vanished in cloud. Doors were shut, morning service over. The newly varnished notice board had the names of both minister and sexton, and their addresses. The date — 1841. A humble belfry took the place of a spire on this simple, small granite church, stained-glass windows and a few scattered gravestones completing the perfect village setting. It sat cosily in the countryside, welcoming, without pretence. Easy to imagine Mary-Anne and the other wives walking up the track from Carvacloughan and Mullaghduff, children following behind. James Archie and Patrick taking their places as vestrymen, joining their brother-in-law Randal McAllister. No mention of the women. Poor things would all be pregnant anyway if you bothered to count. Pregnant most of their lives. And no mention of John either. Had he already made his own way to the Brethren in Ballymena? Or gone off to Dublin or America? Must have. But his wife, Mary Getty, would be at home — and pregnant. Brethren or

Church of Ireland, that didn't matter. Babies came the same way.

'Get the key and let's go in there!' Big John said loudly. 'No use coming all this way from New Zealand and not get to go inside, is it now?'

Willie McKellop was the sexton, the notice said. In Mosside, just down the road. But Willie McKellop was away, the neighbours called. 'Try Willie McKellop's friend — roond therr!' But Willie McKellop's friend was deaf and dumb, poor creature, and we couldn't understand his sign language. Best try the rector at Armoy. Armoy! Wow!

Imaginary countryside — so familiar in *Irish in the Blood* — became real at last. Not storybook fields, not thatched cottages, not horses and carts, but modern farms and green, green grass. Mosside to Armoy. This is where the families had trudged about. Buying, selling, digging, milking, working from daylight till dark. We were on the very path Patrick walked to McGowan's 'big house', courting his Mary-Anne. A road now, and a fast car.

'Slow down,' I called. 'There's the Presbyterian church at Armoy. Mary-Anne and Patrick were married there when it was just a meeting house.'

'Let's get this jolly key from the rector first,' Big John said. 'We can look there on the way back.'

We all stared down at another simple stone church, each of us busy with our own thoughts.

'Why were they married here, at the Armoy crossroads, and not in the wee church?' Big John wanted to know.

'Mary-Anne McGowan was a Presbyterian, so they had to be married in the wife's church.'

The old 1769 meeting house had been turned into a church in 1841, allowing them a steeple and a bell. How things had changed over the years. Once upon a time, nonconforming Protestants as well as Catholics were not considered part of the Established Church of Ireland, so were not even permitted to have the title 'church' let alone a bell or steeple. And the farmers' tithe went only to the Established Church. No wonder there was unrest in the country when Presbyterians and Catholics worked together against the Church of Ireland. Unbelievable today. Almost unthinkable.

But some things don't change. The old trees nearby, bowing their heads into the tiny River Bush running alongside; the graveyard at the back — these hadn't changed. Only people — people with different mind-sets who wrote horrible graffiti on the toilets opposite.

I wish I knew where your big house was, Mary-Anne McGowan. It can't be far from here. Who will tell me? Ivan? You must have been a smashing lady astride your horse galloping up the hills of Knocklayd, and Patrick found an engagement ring for you up there, didn't he? A wee bit of crystal. I love that story but it took me years to fnd out about it. I know you missed Ireland when you came to swampy Napier. My father told me you were wringing your hands in despair on Marine Parade, longing for a glimpse of it. You brave girl.

We would have to leave Armoy and its memories till later. Move on! Move on!

The wee church is open now. I move around the dark old pews, sitting where they sat, staring at the stained glass figures, fingering the prayer books. How did all those families pack into such a small space, Sunday after Sunday? And the white marble baptistry, in its special alcove. My father, big Jim, and the 'clever' aunts had been baptised here. Fancy that! And no one mentioned a thing about it. No one told us about this wee church. Strange lot, the Irish.

At last the sun is shining and four of the counties of Ulster are clearly visible. Big John says we have to move on, there's a long way to go. Always that.

'By the way, that cousin of yours, Ivan, won't be at Carvacloughan today. I meant to tell you. He's in England, but his wife, Mary, knows we're coming,' Big John said suddenly. Just as Tantallus put his hand out to grab the fruit, it disappeared; so with me. It might be months before I could come here again and meet Ivan.

I see Moyarget Road, and we are to look for number 182. The country road is quiet on this Sunday afternoon. The small field next door to 182 basks in the sun's warmth, with a few cows grazing down by the Moyarget Stream. Mt Knocklayd is changing its mood by the minute, one moment misty and grey, the next alive with light and shadows. Is this the farm then? Again I wonder why the grandas never mentioned Knocklayd when its presence dominated their fields and houses and peat bog. They would have lived with it from early morning till the night blotted it from sight. Would this whole scene have been so much part of their lives that to be torn from it was a living death? Perhaps two months in the cramped dark quarters of a ship changes people's vision. We know they were hungry here, and couldn't pay their tithes and couldn't pay to send the children to school, and the winter weather sent their babies to an early grave. Mountains and rivers don't fill hungry bellies, and that political pot boiling in the background created dangerous feelings in the air. We heard about that. Ivan would fill us in with the rest one day.

A piercing wind threw us back against the car as we opened the doors at McAllister's, but we could still see ruins of old sheds on the fence line and an old rusted hand plough. Dogs ran around and barked at our legs, jumping in excitement. Was anyone at home? At last Mary appeared, flustered and ill at ease, her cheeks red with nervousness or exhaustion. What was going on here?

We had come to a respite home, filled with intellectually handicapped people. Ivan was away so Mary was struggling to look after them herself. Her own little girl of twelve played with a patient in the yard.

'That girl could knock my Sarah to the ground anytime,' Mary explained. 'Yes, she looks adorable, but when she throws a tantrum, look out! The lounge is full of patients this weekend, and Ivan's in England.'

Two tall boys came to the door, anxious to see these relatives from New Zealand. Students on leave from a Scottish university, one studying engineering, the other medicine. Ivan's sons.

'But you're so near Queens' University in Belfast,' we said. 'Why go across to Scotland?'

A long silence followed.

'It's good to get away from home,' one laughed unconvincingly, shuffling his feet.

The other made it clear: 'We've got enough to do with our studies without all the hassles that go on at Queens'.'

'Do you mean political hassles?' we asked straight off.

'Yes.' Hesitantly. 'Look, one of our best friends is a Catholic —

we're not against him. He came with us to Scotland too, but you can get into trouble at Queens' if you say the wrong thing, or find yourself in the wrong place at the wrong time.'

'That's sad,' we murmured.

'It's sad right enough, but that's it. In Scotland they hardly know what's going on over here. Suits us. We might even stay there. Better than this place.'

Mary didn't know much about old places or people, and her patients were yelling loudly for her from inside. How could she stand such awful guttural noises?

'I do remember an old gentleman, a doctor from Harley Street, who came to visit about twenty years ago. The Magill house next door was still standing then. Come back and see Ivan whenever you like.'

Just as we were leaving an old lady appeared quietly in the doorway. Mary's mother. She put out her hand for a greeting and gave me a hug.

'Do you remember a railway line going through these parts?' I asked hopefully. After all, I might never see an old granna who minded the time so far back.

'Aye,' she said softly, 'there was a train from here to Ballycastle. It started at Ballymoney, went through Mullaghduff back there, passed us here and on to Ballycastle. The station was just down at the end of the field there, I remember that right enough. Called a narrow gauge feeder line.' This old woman was smart.

So that was one more thing I hadn't dreamt up. One bit of history that had come down through chance remarks and letters and I'd nailed it.

Mary came out to the car.

'Ivan sold a piece of land to build this,' she said proudly. 'They haven't many in the North yet. You'll see we called it Mountain View Respite Home. Took us two years to build.'

'Are there any in the Republic?' I asked

She looked mystified.

'I wouldn't know anything about the South,' she replied. 'They get grants down there, that's all I know. We couldn't get one.'

'You're pioneers,' I called back as we drove away.

When would we see Ivan? Would he show us round the farm and explain everything? And what about Randal and Kathleen? What about the McGowans and Sir George White?

What about the graves, the family stories?

We decided to go into Ballycastle for a drink and call it a day. At least we'd seen *something*, I told myself.

Cheek by jowl, old dignified two-storeyed houses lined the road to the coast, attempting a modern gaiety with hanging baskets of colourful flowers overflowing out of doors and windows. Beach houses of former gentry turned B & B. Dark inside.

Big John was humming a tune:

> *'Did you treat your Mary-Ann*
> *To dulse and yellow man*
> *At the Old Lammas Fair in Ballycastle?'*

'You won't know what he's singing about,' laughed Christine. 'They've had these fairs here since 1606 and still sell sheep and ponies each year. Ulster people are great horse-lovers. As for "dulse", it's a yukky seaweed stuff and you chew it. Some people love it. "Yellow man" is toffee, hard as a rock. I've seen people get a hammer to it.'

'Yes, I know about dulse. My da used to talk about it. Cured everything, from miscarriages to boils. They used to have a bag in their pockets to chew. Yuk!'

'I say, sorry about Ivan. And all the things you wanted to find out. Bit of a downer, eh?' Christine apologised.

'We'll be back,' I told her. 'Maybe we'll come up to see you and Ivan in the marching season. Should be interesting, eh?'

She looked doubtful, a worried expression on her face. 'Last year's marching season wasn't all that interesting. Frightening is more like it. But come and see anyway. Just down the road from our place.'

From Ballycastle we could see across the shimmering water to the Mull of Kintyre in Scotland, only 30 kilometres away.

'On a good day the Scots used to row over for church,' a man told us with a twinkle in his eye. 'Didn't take them long.'

♣

One man in Ireland answered letters — Leonard Quigg, a historian who lived in Ballycastle. Five years earlier he had written a book called *The Wee Church on the Hill*, and I had spotted it in small print in the Ulster Historic Foundation magazine. The words 'Grange of Drumtullagh' had jumped out of the page in huge letters as if someone had come back from the dead to tell me something. Leonard's book was the key that unlocked the door to the Magills of Carvacloughan. Now we were to see this gentleman in the flesh. I pictured a white-haired, bespectacled old man poring over yellowing manuscripts, deaf, forgetful, living in a grotty flat under the road. Would it be better if John and Christine had a walk along the beach and met us later? Poor beggars, dragging along, bored out of their brains.

'We'll come and see anyway,' said Big John protectively.

We drove into an old English garden. A profusion of larkspur, hollyhocks and delphiniums surrounded a manicured lawn, forget-me-nots and pansies peeping out from everywhere.

'How beautiful,' we all gasped. An old English garden in Ballycastle. Another world.

Standing at the door was a handsome man of about forty. Leonard?

'Come in,' he said warmly. 'You made it. I mowed the lawns at the wee church yesterday, just in case.'

'But . . .'

'I had the feeling you were somewhere about. You said . . .'

You don't cry in front of people, but looking at Leonard across the room made me scratch hurriedly in my purse for pencil and paper and pretend to be busy. How could anyone be so interested in my research and so thoroughly *nice*? How could a man like this put together a history of the wee church? He should have been playing golf or cricket in smart white gear or drinking champagne in his English garden.

'How come you knew how to create this garden?' we asked him.

'As a boy I worked as a gardener for an English family, and this is what they wanted. They taught me.'

We had just turned our conversation to history, and the Magill clan, when the sound of music and marching interrupted us.

Leonard shrugged his shoulders in despair. David rushed out with his camera.

'It's the Republicans,' he explained on his return. 'They're wearing black berets and there seem to be six different groups with the IRA insignia, tricolour and badges. Fifes, drums and whistles are leading, with a hundred or so people following. On the skin of the drum I could see the head and shoulders of an Orangeman, with a rifle pointing at him.'

'I wouldn't hang around taking too many photos, David,' Big John cautioned. 'You could be in the wrong place at the wrong time.' That phrase again.

'Oh, come on John,' we laughed. 'In Ballycastle?'

'John knows more than we do,' whispered Christine.

Had it not been for Leonard's wife bringing in a tray of tea, the atmosphere could have been ruined. Joan Quigg was as gracious as her husband, receiving four complete strangers with warmth and interest.

'You've just caught us in time,' she said with a smile. 'Leonard is taking me to Scotland tomorrow to shop. I want to go to England to buy a pair of shoes in the Lake District. There's a special place there. We'll stay a few days; we're both on holiday from school.'

To Scotland? For shoes? Our New Zealand minds did a flip. But Scotland was only 30 kilometres across the water, so why not?

With Leonard to guide us we looked round the old Ramoan graveyard dating back to the fifteenth century. Surely we would find Randal and Kathleen and Mary White here, the likeliest place. But the ancient, green, mossy tombstones looked back at us in defiance, their legends indecipherable. I bet they were hiding our rellies.

'Sorry,' said Leonard as we parted. 'But I'll keep my ears open for anything that might help you.'

I knew he would. No wonder the old cronies around Carvacloughan called him 'awful nice' and told how his mother had brought him up 'tarrible dacent'. He was and she had.

We left Ballycastle nestling behind Benmore Head and drove round the coast road to Larne. There is magic here, in the fairy-tale glens of Cushendun and Cushendall. Gaelic country, old and mysterious. No sun now on the dark green hills and woods, only memories.

'IRA country, this,' said Big John menacingly, but little did we know that these same glens would provide a place of refuge for us in the weeks to follow, IRA or not.

Cars were piling up along the road at Ballyclare. What was happening here? A hold-up? No. Another march. Grown men in bowler hats, dark suits and orange sashes were playing tin whistles and accordians with a big drum banging some sort of rhythm. I knew those tunes immediately. This was a dream, or some sort of crazy flashback. It must be a medieval show, or someone's birthday. They were playing 'Abide with Me' and 'Jesus Loves Me'. That would be it — a Sunday school anniversary. How comic. Unbelievable!

'Those are Orangemen,' John said loudly, 'upholding the Protestant faith.'

We waited for him to laugh with us, but he was dead serious.

'You can tell you guys are from New Zealand,' Christine said. 'It's just like the Aussie reaction. They can't understand it either. "Didn't know you grew citrus fruit here," one guy said to us. But *you* should know about Orangemen,' Christine aimed at me. 'Your father would have told you. He was probably one himself.'

Then I remembered all that fuss at the Brethren hall in New Zealand. The annual church parade of the Orange Lodge: Da's apprehension. And the storm over Pat's marriage to Catherine, and those Orangemen sounding off at the Napier hospital. It all came back with sudden force, and I remembered that certain tension and uneasiness when the subject was mentioned at home, and Da squashing it. The Battle of the Boyne, William of Orange, Drogheda.

'My father wasn't an Orangeman,' I announced, suddenly alert. 'I remember that now.'

'Well, he was an Ulsterman then,' said Big John.

'Look, he left here when he was eight years old. He was a Christian, an Irish New Zealander. That's all! He didn't agree with the church being mixed up with the Orange Lodge.'

Everything went quiet for a while, and it was then I realised that visitors to Northern Ireland have no idea what deep-seated grudges and antagonism still exist in the hearts and memories of the people who live there. Three hundred years of memory which they want to cling on to for security. No one born outside Northern Ireland can look at Orangemen marching and understand them. They are out of this world, from an alien culture. Bizarre. Fighting for the faith. What faith?

3. land of lake and legend

POUNDS STERLING TO PUNTS, Union Jack to tricolour, green mailboxes instead of red, road signs in Gaelic, Trixie's radio talking Irish. We were over the border now in the poor South of *Angela's Ashes*. Frank McCourt made it sound so depressing, so gut-wrenching, I couldn't read his book without crying. Dozens of children, and ever-pregnant mothers. Washing lines groaning with napkins, and scruffy, unkempt gardens. Perhaps that was to come, but right now we were passing large fields ploughed ready for sowing, grand old stone houses and magnificent churches, small stone cottages attractively upgraded and modernised, dividing fences removed for modern farming. At every turn of the well-kept roads there was this feeling of progress, of enthusiasm. And drivers waved to us — a little lift of the hand above the steering wheel.

New bed-and-breakfast signs hung proudly along the roadside. The outside spelt confidence in the interior.

'The EU sponsors B & Bs,' people told us. 'And if the owner can speak the Gaelic — extra grants. But they've got to pass the Tourist Board test — no slipshod standards here. You'll see the shamrock sign.' Our self-catering book used the same criteria, but the networking of mates in the trade led us to cheaper cottages and wonderful characters.

This must be it then: 'Whitewashed cottage overlooking a lake and the owner next door. Follow two white stones up the drive, and through a white gate made of welded horseshoes.' We were looking into the eyes of a woman of about fifty years of age, or was it a hundred and fifty? Finely chiselled nose set in an unwrinkled

34

face of parchment, long grey-blond hair hanging effortlessly down her back. If she was attractive now, what must she have been twenty years ago? Mysterious, alluring, unfathomable, she led us to the cottage. I hesitated, obviously unsure whether to stay. This place wouldn't have passed the Tourist Board test! Maeve looked vaguely out of the window.

'Germans like it,' she said dispassionately. 'It's the lake. So different from the busy streets in Frankfurt they say. I was born here in this cottage, so I don't really see the beauty any more.'

Germans? Way out here in this remote corner of Ireland?

'But there's no laundry, no phone, and it's kind of basic. Summer hasn't come yet.' Outside the cold wind whistled, and I pulled my heavy overcoat tighter.

'You will stay a week at least, and then we can discuss it further. There's plenty of peat in that basket for the fire, and this oil stove.'

She left, leaving us to explore the rest of the rooms. Her cats peered through the bathroom and kitchen windows, and yowled at the front door. The bedroom was the worst. Maeve said her father had died there and she had been born there. Ghosts of the past.

'Do what you like with the single beds,' she had said significantly. I wondered what the Germans did? An ancient, dark Chinese lacquered screen stood in front of a disused fireplace with two plaster lions looking sadly from the mantelpiece, their once-proud faces chipped and colourless.

My mind flashed back to the bedroom in which my Aunt Lizzie slept in Greenmeadows, New Zealand. Dark, sunless, creepy. Uneven dark wooden floors, curtainless windows. Not much different, except here we slept with our clothes on and a heated brick for warmth. Maybe Lizzie did that too. We had come in the worst summer Ireland had seen for sixty years. 'Last year we had marvellous weather,' people said. 'You should have come then. Grand it was.'

'O ya! We have four hundred people working in our factory. It is not far from here,' Maeve's husband said proudly. 'We make spare parts and fancy fittings for cars. I came here twenty-six years ago — from Germany, you know. Fell in love with, er, er — Maeve — ya, Maeve. And now, you see me!'

Maeve didn't move an inch or say a word, her lovely Irish face a mask.

Above the peat fire a dark oil painting of Napoleon looked down on us, and a huge gold-framed oil of *The Last Supper*. Another showed a peasant girl in a thin, soft green dress, one hand resting on her cheek. The artist had named her Ireland. She looked lost and pensive.

'We weren't allowed to print the word Ireland on our bank notes at one time,' Maeve told us meaningfully, 'so they painted this girl. She *is* Ireland.'

Weren't allowed to print 'Ireland' on their bank notes? When was this then? Maeve's unfathomable eyes spoke a thousand words. Clearly this cottage was clothed in mystery and meaning. We would stay a bit longer than a week and live on the view and the history.

'I heard you speak on the phone from the North,' Maeve went on. 'From a Belfast hotel was it? I couldn't work out the accent, but now you are here I can hear it clearly. It is not the English we are used to. Yours is much softer, and not at all like the lady in the big house down the road. She speaks high, and rather loud. And you got my name from a friend in the self-catering? We're not up to the standard to put in the book yet. One day, when Kurt . . .'

'We weren't in a hotel in Belfast, Maeve, so don't worry. We were with friends in Ballynahinch. Have you never been to the North yourself?'

'Never!'

We stood at the window looking across the lake. The sun had already commenced its slow journey down and would soon disappear, leaving the twilight to throw long shadows across the still water. Maeve continued.

'The owner of the big house used to come down and make friends with my father during the difficult times. No one else lived near here then, so if he needed help he could rely on us Irish. He owned all that.' Her arm swept across the hills and lake.

'Do those people still own it?' I asked carefully.

She nodded wistfully. 'They're ascendancy. Given the land as a gift for fighting with the English.'

'Against you?'

'Yes!'

By chance we were to meet the present owner as we tramped along the main road.

'You are welcome to walk anywhere you like on our private road,' she said regally. 'Go up the hill and see the stone relic on the top. It's centuries old. 'Tis said a huge bell hung there to call workers to the mill, but who really knows? We love it so much here now we've come back to start a timber business.'

The voice came from an English girls' school. Old stone relics of a huge flour mill littered the roadside, derelict, dark, sightless windows pulling a blind on the past. Did a bell really hang up in that old stone cave on the hill — or was it a watchtower? We would go up and have a look for ourselves. From there the 'big house' in the valley appeared almost hidden behind trees and surrounded by six-foot stone walls. It must have been a watchtower, covered now in twisted old roots and spooky vines. Dangerous days, with Cromwell about and, much later, the IRA. They would have needed someone on watch.

Stretched out in a huge circle beyond, a magnificent panorama of lakes and fertile fields, the Meath valley showed a patchwork of greens and clumps of orange gorse. Church spires pinpointed the villages of Fore and Castlepollard, and, further away, Navan and Athboy. Not a soul about anywhere; only the bleating of black-faced sheep and their lambs dancing about, eager to suckle. We felt very alone in this beautiful valley, empty now, its people long since emigrated. They should come back now and live on the land they loved. You could almost hear a plaintive voice calling them back — back to Erin. A solitary car sped off into the distance, and the dip of the anglers' oars was all that could be heard in the long twilight. Fishermen cast their flies near a lonely *crannog* in the centre of the lake, hoping for brown trout. We looked at the old fortress, built in 600 BC, and wondered. Bronze age man protecting himself from the enemy.

Inside the cottage the TV screen showed the Virgin and Child, the sound of bells tolling out the Angelus — three, three, three, twelve. Right across Ireland TV and radio reminded people to pause and pray for one minute. A hushed moment before the news at

6.01 p.m. The presenter gave the impression it was a minute wasted. A pity if they pushed the Angelus out, we thought.

'But they want to,' Maeve told us. 'To catch up with the modern world.'

'It would be tragic if modern Ireland threw away its religious heritage, its Celtic rites and endearing attitudes, in its drive for economic advancement,' I suggested to Maeve.

'We're progressing too fast,' she said. 'It's scary. We need longer to adjust to our new-found wealth.'

Signs of staggering growth met us at every turn of the country road. Enormous new houses were springing up everywhere; old houses renovated beyond recognition; great stones from derelict farmhouses lovingly reshaped into new structures; fences transformed into new art forms. From among the old rocks peeped primroses, tulips and bluebells. Were these holiday houses for the hunting, fishing and shooting season?

'All of those things,' Maeve explained. 'Even Canadians and Americans whose old folk emigrated last century are building round here. They've made money and come back to their roots, re-thatching old cottages and paying thousands of pounds for reeds. You'll see their barbeques smoking. And, of course, Germans by the hundred. It's a German invasion. Buying up the big houses and estates and commuting to Frankfurt. Dutch and French doing the same, although not so many.'

'And the Irish?' we asked, fascinated.

'They can get low-interest loans from the council, banks and building societies. Pay back over thirty to forty years. All dependent on a means test. You'll find some big estates were given to poor people from the west of Ireland to work. Remember how they were banished? To Hell or Connaught, by Cromwell? You can easily pick the west of Ireland people.'

'How?'

'Well, they have their own way of speaking and doing things. Perhaps not as, um, sophisticated as the others round here. Plain farming people. But they work hard. After the soil in Connemara this is heaven.'

Somehow, out of death new life was emerging. The auld sod was breathing once more. We walked back along the country road, passing old water pumps protected against frost with layers of clothing. Farmers had not forgotten that these quaint old pumps were once the sites of wells, so they dressed them up against the cold — in case. 'You never know,' they laughed.

'Old graves were dug up when they straightened the road out there,' Kurt told us. 'They uncovered human skeletons buried in the sitting position.'

'You mean they were pre-Christian? Bronze Age?' David gulped.

'O ya! Concerned locals insisted the council build a wall to prevent the bones from tumbling down the bank on to the road all the time. And that *crannog* in the lake there. When I first came here a friend had a metal detector and found a bronze scythe under some boulders.'

While we spoke, Maeve sat watching *Eastenders* on TV. She was away with the fairies. Twelve cats collided with each other round the room, their food in saucers on tables, sideboards and chairs. Two dogs fussed and scuffled. Lumps of bread lay scattered near the doorway to entice ravens, jackdaws, doves and other pet birds. Sadly they had no children.

Maeve was with us again. 'I could have kept my job in Dublin if I hadn't married. I was a sales representative, travelled to England and Europe. But the German boys came down to the lake one day and found us swimming. We couldn't even speak their language.'

4. the fact and the fantasy

Icy wind and rain lashed against the brave remains of an old monastery left to die in an unkempt field. Sloshing along the flooded path it was hard to believe that three hundred monks had once lived in this desolate place. Today a solitary farmer went about his daily work emptying water into a trough from a plastic bucket. If it hadn't been for the memory of these brave monks of the sixth century, I would have turned back and huddled in the car for warmth. But Saint Fechin had quarried this stone in all weathers and spent hours in supplication for the sick as he lay immersed in the open pool nearby.

> Fechin the generous of Fobhar loved,
> It was no hypocritical devotion,
> To place his meagre rib
> Upon a hard bed without clothes.
> John O'Hanlon, *Lives of the Irish Saints*

Guilty at my lack of piety and laziness, I gazed up at the notice.

---

seven wonders of fore

1. the monastery in a bog
2. the mill without a race
3. the water that flows uphill
4. the tree that won't burn
5. the water that won't boil
6. the anchorite in a stone (patrick beglan 1616)
7. the stone raised by st fechin's prayers

Along that slushy path modern pilgrims still stop and tie pieces of cloth to a small tree and hammer coins into its trunk. Fechin deserves this devotion. To have built that small monastery and lived in it during an Irish winter deserves recognition. It was still only spring, yet the wind ripped through my clothes like a knife.

It is a big ask to believe a prayer could raise 2542 kilograms. A sceptical scientist suggested levitation, but — you can stand and stare and make of it what you will — the seven wonders are all there scattered about as part of a modern farm. Water is flowing uphill.

> Safe from the impossible pressures of a society immersed in its seething cauldron of avarice and materialism, Fore's people still go about their business with a blessing for a friend and a salute for a stranger. Their serenity, their quiet pride in the rich heritage entrusted to them might represent Fore's eighth wonder.
>
> Padraic O'Farrell Mullingar 1984

It did! The postmistress presented us with a splendid book, refusing any payment, and it was selling in the shops at eight punts.

'You'll get a decent meal at Pollard Arms down the road, sure you will,' a by-passer said mischievously. 'Tell me if you don't!' And he vanished in the opposite direction.

Three young businessmen were having lunch at the pub when we arrived and they signalled us to join them at their table. A serious, softly spoken lad was sounding off to the others.

'You won't change centuries of tradition with a referendum — never! That's them believing that, and the others believing something else, and why shouldn't they? Believe what you want to, but get the British out. It's one island we've got. It's ours. I'm voting no in the referendum anywa'. The Scots have got their independence, yous have got yours' — looking at us — 'so why not us?'

The others listened patiently, smiling at their friend.

'He's always talkin' history like that. We're not really into it.'

'Don't you want peace?' we inquired.

'Sure an' all, but the referendum won't do it. Get the British out, even if it takes a while to do it.'

At least he was honest and said his thing, even though the rest of us shook our heads. It didn't seem to matter too much to any of them. They tucked into monstrous meals piled high with chips, while we enjoyed our soup and soda bread.

'Is that all yous are eatin'?' they asked incredulously.

The grocer next door had actually served us, taking down the items from the shelves one by one.

'No curry powder, I'm afraid. Don't get a call for it.'

Home-made marmalade took up a good space on his counter.

'My wife makes that,' he said, pointing proudly. 'She's in Spain at the moment, on holiday. Gets really dark over there, she does. Some go raw and red in minutes. Not her.'

'Why didn't you go with her?' I asked, genuinely interested.

'Me? Leave this shop? I've never been a day's holiday since I started here thirty years ago. You can't trust the young people these days. I've got to keep an eye on them at home too, but I don't care.'

I could hear my own da saying exactly the same thing in exactly the same way, sitting at his desk in the old draper's shop in Napier. Pity my mother, Jess, didn't get the chance to go to Spain and go dark. She would have loved that.

Multicoloured flags lined the streets and houses in Collinstown. Was this a political rally? Did every house need to show which side they were on?

'It's hurling teams. They're really keen on it round here. Everyone joins in. The boys gather outside the pub over the road there to sort out their transport and get their teams together. That village square there used to be for the maypole. Do yous know what a maypole is?'

'Yes, sort of. Do you remember them doing it here?'

'Me? I'm too young to remember that. I mind the horses and carts pulling up there, that's all. A bit of fightin' too not so long ago. You know what I mean . . . Anywa', how's ye Gaelic going? Learning a few words, eh? That's the way!'

The Book of Kells has an awesome ring to it. The name speaks of ancient monks and self-sacrificing devotion. Rewritten from parts of the New Testament, it has been fought over, stolen, buried and burned, and still parts of it survive. The little town of Kells has a copy, the original being safely locked away in Trinity College, Dublin.

In AD 804 Kells' tiny streets were silent paths inside hallowed monastery walls; now they bustle with cars and trucks, and twentieth-century shops and banks. It seems somehow irreverent to be drinking coffee and indulging in hot scones with cream in full view of a historic round tower just across the road, knowing how the monks were hounded by Vikings and the whole settlement plundered four times. But you eat anyway, and build up a violent hate for Vikings and a passionate love for monks.

Ninety feet in height, the tower's five windows face the five roads entering Kells. It is not hard to imagine the scene. Monks escaping for their lives up the ladder to the lower door ten feet off the ground, their arms filled with valuable chalices and vestments, or clutching parchments and gold paint. Then up with the ladder. From the window they could drop stones and other nasties onto the invaders, leaving them shaking their fists and waving their spears down below. These monks had something their enemies wanted. Gold!

Round the corner from the coffee shop, St Colmcille's House is accessible with a key from a small house nearby. The little guide had inherited the honour from her mother — now dead, God bless her — and she had learnt to repeat the history fluently and proudly.

'One of the buildings of St Colmcille's monastery, in the early ninth century, may have been used as an oratory. It is two-storey, with three upper chambers, and its corbelled stone roof is still waterproof. No restoration work has been done yet. Vellum was stored upstairs where *The Book of Kells* was written and illustrated. Started in Iona but completed here about 804.'

Determined to see the three tiny rooms on the attic storey, David climbed the ladder inside the steeply pitched stone roof.

'Hope he comes down back on,' she whispered hoarsely. 'Many of those kind of people get the faint head.'

How tiny it was, this stone doll's house where monks did their writing and painting. No windows or chimneys; cold stones on the floor. We followed the guide down the cobblestone street in silence.

Kells town hall was the proud protector of an impeccable reproduction of its famous book. A plump, dark-haired girl opened it carefully with a key. Yes, we were allowed to touch it. 'Sixty pages and the gold cover were stolen and buried,' she told us. 'Never found.'

Rotten Vikings.

We were looking at exquisite pen drawings and coloured text; intricate curves curling round old Celtic motifs in brilliant blues, reds and purples.

In the churchyard nearby stood ninth-century high carved stone crosses.

'The one at the Market Square has been knocked down by a bus and is away having repairs done, English soldiers sharpened their swords on the base of it,' the girl said in one sentence. A difference of a few hundred years seemed nothing in Kells. 'Now, look out!' she yelled. A huge tourist bus swung onto the curb, its occupants intent on seeing *The Book of Kells*. One American dame looked at her watch.

'We'll have to hurry. We've got to go to Sligo, then Dublin, and fly out.'

'Yeah, you're dead right! It's only some sort of a book, isn't it?' her friend replied.

The splendid old Church of Ireland in Castlepollard, built 1821, held an attraction. People sat waiting outside in their superior-looking cars, eyes fixed straight ahead. Maybe they were listening to the radio until the last minute. Pity Trixie was so limited in her repertoire and could only splutter out the Gaelic on her cheap radio. Better rush over and buy a *Sunday Times*. Desperate news perhaps?

'A week's reading to be sure,' the shopkeeper said. 'Good and heavy for a punt.'

Yes, OK, but what had happened?

FIRST IRISH MARATHON WINNER

That was the headline?

Casually but reverently, worshippers trickled into church, passing a trio of elegant lights on a polished brass stand. Despite the meagre attendance a couple pushed their way into our pew, sending us shuffling along towards the end. A lady sitting there grimaced.

'Have we taken someone's pew?' I whispered.

She sniffed eloquently. 'It's a christening,' she whispered back. 'I'm here for that. I don't usually come. Perhaps we *are* in someone's pew. How are we to know?'

Bespectacled noses pointed at the prayer book, reciting prayers and readings, then all turned round to watch the christening ritual.

'A first grandchild for many years, wearing a centuries-old gown and hand-knitted shawl,' the grandmother whispered to me, leaning back over the pew in front.

No prayer for the peace process, no sermon, no singing. The prayer book had two options: bless 1. (Northern Ireland) the Queen or 2. (Southern Ireland) the President. The priest opted for the president. The names of the Pollard-Urquhart families set in a cold stone memorial plaque on the wall looked alien now in this empty old church where once they were held in awe and respect.

Now we were out on the footpath, cold, wet and surrounded by a few unfriendly well-dressed worshippers. The pub opposite looked inviting.

'Listen to this,' the barman said as the radio blared.

What had happened now? Surely no more killings?

'Sean Fitzpatrick has retired due to knee injuries,' he shouted out.

Well, good old Fitzy, way back there in New Zealand. We smiled to ourselves. The All Blacks *were* New Zealand in many parts of Ireland.

'Weather's going to take up,' the barman predicted. 'Why don't yous go and have a look at Tullynally Castle, just a mile down the road.'

Another Irish mile? It was five to the keeper's cottage, then we drove sedately for another before reaching wide stretches of green arable land used now for a few sheep and cattle. Wide lawns and walking tracks appeared as the castle loomed into sight. Trixie definitely looked out of place parked beside a formidable array of classy cars — BMWs, Jaguars and polished Bentleys — an unkempt pony beside all those pedigree racehorses.

Where did one pay the entrance fee to go into this seventeenth-century Gothic Revival castle? The three-storey turreted mansion looked on to tennis courts and a Grecian fountain beyond. So many chimneys, so many rooms.

With some trepidation I opened a gigantic red door and walked in on an elite 'conference'. The company stared, drinks on hold.

'Who . . . ?' they said in unison.

'I'm so sorry!'

'But the family live here — have done for centuries. Packenham is the name. Earl of Longford, you know. You can view the garden over the-are, through the gate. It's not quite the season for garden parties.'

Should I back out, or bow? On closer scrutiny, I saw the speaker was tiddly — very tiddly — and the 'conference' had turned into a swinging party. I left them giggling round a large fire and viewed the garden 'over the-are' as a misty rain began to fall.

Woodlands gave way to walled gardens, splendid trees from

China and the Himalayas, a magic grotto and two ornamental lakes. Primroses and bluebells peeped through the dark browns and green around us. What splendour!

How grand was Tullynally in the good old days. Elegant dinner parties and dances; high heels and parasoles in the garden; tailored trousers and pleated white skirts for tennis; discreet lovemaking beside the fountain or in the grotto by day, not so discreet in the evening light; top hats, tails, chandeliers, champagne. Tiddly. Matey.

And the service tunnel! A tradesmen's entrance with a difference. Underneath the immaculately groomed lawn in front, servants pushed supplies through a passage three to four hundred metres long. In came the peat, the grog, the food, well away from aristocratic eyes. Upstairs, downstairs, yes sir, no sir. Just a memory, now. To the Irish they had always been part of their landscape, a harmless breed who lived different lives and gave them menial jobs. Ascendancy . . .

> For every hill and vale between us and the horizon is historic ground. There is scarcely a townland that does not recall some great fact in the annals of Ireland. There are memories of the druids and the high kings, memories of Padraic and Brigid, memories of battles won and lost, tales of the Penal Days, and there are legends of the fairy folk hanging around the names of a hundred raths and forts.
>
> William Bulfin 1907

For the first time since coming to Ireland we hit the tourist trail. There was simply no other way to see Bru-na-Boinne.

The main road swept down beside a ruined church to a long, narrow bridge, and beyond that, on a hillside, a well-planned eighteenth-century village. Looking north across the Boyne, Slane is a pretty sight. Above the village is the Hill of Slane, where the first Easter fire was lit by Saint Patrick in AD 433 to symbolise the arrival of Christianity in Ireland. It all looks so peaceful and normal now, but then it was a revolution. An enormous challenge to the druid high priests. We were now in an area steeped in history and mystery. At last I had met up with Saint Patrick again.

Dozens of cars and buses were packed into the parking area of the heritage centre constructed around this amazing Bru-na-Boinne. Backpackers, babies in prams, toddlers perched atop fathers' shoulders — an international hotchpotch of people all gathered for an amazing glimpse of the past.

Architecturally sensitive to the shapes of the passage graves, the restaurant and exhibition area acted as a gradual transition from ancient to modern, not an imposed twentieth-century creation divorced from its surroundings. How much Ireland is indebted to the expertise of the EU for these wonderful heritage centres.

Five hundred years older than the Pyramids or Stonehenge, Bru-na-Boinne is dated 3500–2700 BC. One can only marvel at the antiquity and complexity of the magnificent monument. From the outside it looks like an enormous mound of earth covered with grass. It is the internal construction which makes you gasp. Built when stone was the only material for tools and weapons, it consists of huge slabs of rock, each resting partly on the one below, creating intricate passages, with carvings on the roof and sides. How could men bring 450 giant boulders of granite from the Mourne Mountains, 40 kilometres to the north, and masses of white quartz from the Wicklow area, 48 kilometres to the south? Eighty-five of the boulders are decorated, some in spirals and tri-spirals.

Most fascinating is the roof box, which admits a beam of light on the winter solstice. At exactly 0854 BST, the top edge of the sun appears above the horizon, and at 0858 the first pencil of direct sunlight shines through the roof box and along the passage as far as the front edge of the basin stone in the end chamber. For seventeen minutes sunlight enters Bru-na-Boinne, not through the doorway but through this specially contrived narrow slit under the roof and above the door at the outer end of the 19-metre long passage.

Men laboured for forty to sixty years to build this. The questions go unanswered. Was it a memorial to the dead, life expectancy being only twenty-five years? Were the ashes of the dead placed in the basin stone for the sun god to bless? Was it man's offering back to the sun for providing such fertile land? Was the winter solstice a special moment in the year when they waited for the sun to reassure them that their offering had been accepted and to promise to warm their fields for another 365 days? All ideas are only suppositions as we stand in awe at man's ingenuity 5000 years ago.

A huge modern bridge spans the River Boyne, and buses wait at the other end to take tourists and pilgrims to the three tombs of Bru-na-Boinne, Knowth and Dowth, the last two of which are still being repaired. This beautiful fertile country enabled the stone workers to farm their land and still have time to work on their tombs. They chose well.

At last I had come face to face with the River Boyne, a part of Irish history so well known and controversial. I had no desire to go down those seventy-five uneven steps to the viewing point marking the stages of the notorious Battle of the Boyne. Here Protestant William of Orange routed the army of deposed Catholic James II, though the brave Irish dragoons put up a magnificent defence as they held the river for an hour in the face of raking fire. The losses on both sides were about a thousand killed and wounded. Some speak of the event with pride, others with resentment, but its legacy remains to this day a festering sore, a cancerous feud perpetuated down the years by bloodshed and hatred. I did not want to see the ford of Rossnaree either, where the Protestant troops cunningly overtook James.

Some people have seen the Boyne sparkling in sunlight. Looking down from the bridge I could only see a snakelike river writhing in the wind, rain sending ripples across the grey water. Calm and weedy, it runs on to the sea, remote from all passion, unconscious of the things men have done upon its banks.

King 'Billy' was not my hero. He had never appealed to me when I had heard about him in New Zealand. The story had a sinister ring to it, and it was sometimes told with a smugness I resented. My da never joined in the King 'Billy' tales — I always remembered that. He was a peacemaker.

Drogheda, just a mile away, was another battlefield, where Cromwell made clear his intention to subdue the Irish nation and stamp out its consistent demand for independence. He turned his cannon on the ancient town, battered down its walls, slew every tenth man in the garrison and sent the rest as slaves to Barbados. Drogheda was something Da would not discuss either. It divided people, caused dissention, and that wasn't his forte — nor mine.

We moved along with the tourist crowd.

'If I come back to the States without seeing Bru-na-Boinne and the Hill of Tara, they'll kick my arse in!' an American shouted to us.

Then a crowd of teenage schoolgirls from Kilkenny packed into the buses, their uniforms and medals a grand sight amongst the scruffy tourists. A Dutch couple looked on in amazement.

'But is not this obsolete?' they whispered to us. 'In your country also — this?'

'Yes, we have such schools in New Zealand, with uniforms,' we replied. The Dutchman put his hand to his head.

'It does not happen now, in Holland. They are free there.'

'Is there responsibility in that freedom?' David asked him.

'Na! Now you have the word — "responsibility". That it is! We have none and so there are drugs, like in Dublin. Did you know that the average age in Dublin is 27? We have a son working there in computers. O, ya, he earns well, but . . . !'

'I hope he keeps his driving licence,' his mother said wistfully. 'He needs that. But the lifestyle there is fast and dangerous.'

We enjoyed sharing coffee in the restaraunt with our Dutch friends.

'One quarter of our country have problems — up here,' the Dutchman said, pointing to his head. 'They have treatment for it.'

'Psychiatric problems?' we asked.

'O, ya ya, that one! We come here for a quiet holiday each year. We love Ireland. First visit is to see the beautiful places, then you come again because you like the people. That is it!'

'Do you go to the North?'

'God, no, what for?'

'Where do the others go?'

'Florida, or Canada, or to the Grand Canyon. This is too quiet for them, and you have only the small bit of water between us — the Irish Sea. People in Holland want to travel further than that.'

The smart girl sitting at the desk of the tourist office in Trim seemed quite oblivious to the presence of King John's castle and the ruins of a thirteenth-century Augustinian abbey two minutes' walk away. Oblivious, too, to the fact that she was sitting in an old gaol on the edge of the Pale — the perimeter of the English-controlled area in 1172. (She was almost beyond the Pale . . .)

People living and working in historic places must get used to drinking their coffee in ancient gaols, abbeys and castles. To New Zealanders it is incredible. We don't have these ancient reminders at the end of our gardens or over the road. The girl kindly drew a map of the route to the Hill of Tara but warned us not to expect anything as striking as Bru-na-Boinne.

'It's best seen from the air,' she explained. 'Some people are disappointed there's no great edifice there, or heritage centre.'

We followed her directions along winding narrow roads, across old stone bridges and past decaying stone barns. A few elegant entrances revealed avenues of trees leading up to splendid homes and estates. Stud farms, and posh hotels tucked away for those 'in the trade'.

Where is this Hill of Tara? Where do you stop?

A small unassuming souvenir shop serving coffee and scones in the back was the first sign of anything related to a sacred site.

'You can see an audio-visual up there in the old church if you hurry,' the scone-baker said, wiping his hands on an apron.

We watched without enthusiasm. Compared with Bru-na-Boinne it was less than exciting. Was this once, in the third century, the 'Seat of the High Kings of Ireland'? Was this pagan kingdom with its royal banquet halls and feasts now only a hill with a view and a few ditches and the mere outlines of forts? But then, pushing through the old wrought-iron gates, one walks up 100 metres above the surrounding countryside, and Lia Fail is there — the Stone of Destiny, the inauguration stone of the Kings of Tara. Over two metres high, stark in its simple phallic form, compelling against the leaden sky.

The Rath of the Synods (*Rath na Seanadh*) has been excavated and shows the once elaborate structure with four concentric banks and ditches. The statue of Saint Patrick commemorates the saint's legendary visit to the court of King Laoire before he began his mission to bring Christianity to Ireland. He stands between heaven and earth, hand raised in blessing.

Now something happens. There is atmosphere here — a strange presence. Not a sentimental, drummed-up new Celtic culture buzz, but a haunting empathy with the misty past, a realisation of standing on the actual ground where Saint Patrick confronted the pagan leaders, where sacred rites and rituals as well as political matters were discussed by priest-kings over thousands of years. You become one with the past.

History has become legend, and the name of Tara a talisman for Irish nationalism. We left the hill reluctantly. It was like leaving behind a holy place.

'Ireland is full of old unhappy things that strangely shake the heart; and this mound of earth is one of them, lonely, remote and withdrawn like something left on earth after judgement day.' So wrote renowned English travel writer H.V. Morton, sixty years ago.

A memorial cross to the United Irishmen from this area stands at a lower gate. Two hundred years ago almost to the day, they died in the Battle of the Hill of Tara. Please God there would be no need for more fighting on this hill, or anywhere else in Ireland. If there were, it would not be from forces outside, but within.

5. Ballymuck: priests, nuns, fairies and farmers

THE IRISH TONGUE IS A GENTLE, lilting tongue, and I hope it never dies out.

Not far from Mullingar a few shops and houses made up the small village of Ballymuck.* Cars drove through it in half a minute; we stayed for ages. Our front door faced a row of ten old two-storeyed houses, joined together and all exactly the same. Grey stone weathered with age, windows with white lace curtains or none at all. Inside, the rooms were identical in design — sitting room to the left, parlour to the right, hallway down the middle, kitchen and bathroom at the end, bedrooms upstairs. What went on at the 'backs' outside was the owners' business. Some had lovely gardens, some ugly farm buildings, some a jungle of children's play things or a barbeque. Washing hung at crazy angles, but never any babies' diapers. I was interested in diapers. With all the Irish babies you read about in books, the washing lines should have been groaning. That's what I thought at first.

The local store on the corner had a notice. 'Newsagent, Grocery, Fuels, Undertaker'. What more could anyone want? Adjoining it the Winning Post pub provided a popular watering hole for the locals, and had been going for ages. The old da was into greyhound racing, or had been once. Probably a hundred years ago, but they spoke about it like it was yesterday. You could use the phone or buy milk or call the undertaker anytime because it was all connected to the Winning Post, which didn't close till the wee hours.

---

* The name of this village has been changed to protect the identity of its inhabitants.

Oifig an Phoist was my favourite. I loved saying it, and hanging around in there, talking and listening. The post office was just one of the old houses, simply converted. A few dividers and a counter made the old sitting room into an office and the parlour a place for the boy, the dog and the granna, with a cuppa and a peat fire to keep the place warm for everyone.

'Why, they could be waitin' for hours for a call or somethin'. In the old days no one in Ballymuck had a phone.'

Nine in the morning was really too early for this *oifig an phoist*. I would soon learn that. Mother stood in while Bernadette took one boy to school and brought the other to 'play at the *oifig*'. Mother was undoubtedly a whiz kid in the old days, 'but is it a phonecard you're wantin'? God save us! All these new-fangled things. Wait for Bernie, she'll be comin', so she will.'

A four-generation post office, this, the youngest playing with a tiny dog near the turf fire.

'Shouldn't be doing that,' Bernie says unconvincingly. 'Will I be glad to see him at school come September, so I will. Took this over from m' mother — you can see her certificate above there. Forty years service, and her aunt before her. Lives upstairs. Shouldn't have a dog, that boy there. From New Zealand are you?'

Who was living upstairs? The ancient aunt? Couldn't be.

'Yes,' I answer.

'Like the way you speak. It's beside Australia you are? Got enough water there? If you can't make the phonecard go, give it a rub on yer pocket and dust off any wee bits. That's what I do.'

A customer came in.

'Have you found my pension papers yet, Bernie?'

'No, I haven't!'

'What are we going to do then? It's been a while.'

'I don't know at all. I'll have another root about. Come back in a day or so.'

'Otherwise?'

'Otherwise I'll have to do somethin' else, won't I?'

Posting the mail required a leap of faith. A green-painted slit in the outside wall, that's all. Did it belong to the house next door? Would they take it in to the *oifig*? One day David saw it happen while he was sketching — a few letters fluttering through the slit onto the floor near Bernie's seat. And one day I saw a green van collect something from the *oifig* and drive away, so it must have been taken somewhere.

I liked Bernie — dark-haired, modern Bernie stuck in a dusty old *oifig* while her husband followed soccer across Ireland and England.

'Gives me a break at the weekends,' she said blandly. 'Me and the boys can just kick a ball in the yard. They like that.'

The old Ireland — quaint, warm and deliciously homely. Twenty kilometres or so down the road in Mullingar was a swept-up post office — modern, efficient, clinical and deadly dull.

'Don't think this *oifig* will be around on your next visit,' Bernie said. 'It's the last of its kind, so it is.'

Our host, Tim, was on a 'ramble' when we arrived at Ballymuck.

'You know, men in Ireland go on a ramble and you don't see them for the day. He'll be back for his food no doubt.' Kathleen made it clear from the start that men were the pits. But what was a 'ramble'?

'Now, you'll be sleeping in separate rooms I've no doubt,' she repeated for the second time!

'No, the double one will be fine,' I said firmly.

'Well, if that's the way it is . . .' her voice faded off. 'But there's all those others if . . . But I'll leave you to make a home for yourselves. You'll be tired out so you will. I've got the fire going for you, and Tim will keep the box full of peat. I'll see he does.'

It had been a large bungalow in its day. A single storey, now divided into two flats. One, self-catering, was for us; the other was for Tim and Kath. A washing machine — at last — and a microwave. Oil heating and the lovely peat fire. A picture of the Sacred Heart hung above the TV, its red light glowing night and day. A few 'texts' too. I was used to 'texts'. We had them at home in Napier.

'All Catholic homes used to have that Sacred Heart,' a friend told me later, 'every one of them. Not now!'

'You'll tell us about church tomorrow?' I asked Kathleen.

'I'll ask Tim about the Church of Ireland in Mullingar, or maybe there's a Presbyterian somewhere. There's a place called the kirk just down the road, but no one uses it nowadays. It's empty I think, or maybe it's the village hall now. Someone called Saint Oliver Plunkett is written on the front. Someone shot him, you know, and they made him a saint. Tim will know — he's been here since he was small. I'm just a blow-in, only been here thirty years — since I married Tim.'

'It doesn't really matter,' I said. 'We'll just go to the nearest one in the village.'

David agreed, just as Tim ambled in sideways to make himself invisible and avoid Kath's gaze.

'That's what I say.' He nodded affably to David. 'All the same, one God and that.'

They were buddies, men together, and Kathleen was outnumbered. I was 'the writer' — genderless.

It was Vocation Sunday at the local Catholic church down the road. They needed young priests.

'The last priest to be ordained here was thirty years ago to the very day,' the old priest stated. 'And to quote another priest: "Go home and breed for the church." Encourage your boys to come forward. That's today's message!'

The church was full upstairs and down, old and young mingling happily together in the warm, homely atmosphere. I came out of the door to find myself face to face with a man waiting for his granddaughter.

'Hoya,' he said to me. 'Whereya knocking round?'

It seemed we had known each other for years, his face a replica of my father's. Exactly the same clothes, too, except for the knitted waistcoat. I don't think Da would have been seen dead in that.

'It'll lift up soon,' he said, referring to the weather.

'Hope so,' I said lamely, my mind in a forty-year flashback. Did my face seem as familiar to him? I had the feeling he considered me a local rather some blow-in from the antipodes.

After mass, families wandered round the graveyard nearby and we thought how fitting it was to have the family buried by the church as if they were all part of the worship, living or dead. Pity all that had to change.

'But we usually visit the other graves after Sunday lunch, if they're not too far away, and one day I'll get Tim to take you to the Mass rock and the Sunday well,' said Kathleen. 'Not far from here it is. Ballymuck has a history going back hundreds of years, some of it not too pleasant either. Murders and hangings.'

'Priest a bit doddery on his feet,' she said later, 'but this afternoon we'll have a lovely drive with the help of God.'

A handsome, comely woman was Kathleen. Efficient, hardworking and devout. I would like her as a neighbour, I knew that immediately. We could talk about all sorts of things. And retired farmer Tim, lean and spare, propping up the side of the house for a 'crack' and sliding across the road for a 'quickie' when Kath wasn't about. I liked him already. But what was a ramble, Tim? Lucky for him there was always his son's fields to see to over the road. Life could get hot in their tiny kitchen. He winked at us knowingly while pulling up a cabbage.

'No heart in them,' he sighed ruefully. 'That frost in April. Nothing's good.'

'What do you eat with the cabbage, Tim?' I asked him.

'A rasher when Kathleen's home, otherwise I have a cereal.'

'A cereal for tea?'

'We used to eat a plate of porridge at nine at night when I was working hard. All the farmers did that round here. Nothing like it. I tell you what, farming was nothing like it is today. Before the EU came I had about ten cows, twenty or so sheep, say the same about hens, and a few pigs around the place. I had to grow enough corn and hay in four months to feed the stock for eight months.'

'Corn?'

'Yeah, oats or barley or corn — whatever — and get it milled down the road. I tell you this, I miss the weekly market an' all. Kath sold her butter, eggs and buttermilk there and I had the stock. If ya saw butter for sale outside someone's house, you'd know they were on the breadline. Swallow yer pride to do that, I can tell you. By the way, we're sowing the potatoes tomorrow over the road if yous want to see. There was little else to eat in them days, but with a bit of cabbage and porridge twice a day we had a bellyful. We'll be selling most of the potatoes we put in today. Don't need all of 'em now for eatin' ourselves.'

Would we ever find out what a ramble was?

So, 'with the help of God', we sallied forth in Kathleen's car. It was hers, make no mistake.

'That black northwest has let up,' said Tim from the back seat.

'We're going through Goldsmith country. They call it Sweet Auburn round here,' Kathleen said proudly. 'They come from all over the world to Goldsmith country. You know his poem that starts "Sweet Auburn, Sweet Auburn"?'

Tim raised his eyes. 'And they take home branches of the hawthorn tree.' He smirked.

No wonder! Where would you see anything as beautiful as the hawthorn tree in spring? Mile upon mile of pure white blossom as if a heavy fall of snow had turned the countryside white. We could have been driving through fairyland.

Strange, that, I thought. Nothing much of the Irish countryside in Goldsmith's writings. The rustic poets, like John Keegan Casey, had caught the magic but had worked for a living as well. No money for frivolities in those days, and no one to promote them. Poets were all from the ascendancy class then. The real Irish poets would have to wait in the wings, but not for long. Today they were well on the way, their writings acclaimed the world over.

The countryside was healthier here than round Lough Bane. No gorse or scraggy cattle as in the run-off paddocks there. A certain care and pride told us that perhaps here the farmers owned their own land.

'Yarra, they do,' said Tim. 'And the EU are worried about the large paddocks with electric fences and no hedges anymore, so they subsidise those of them who will keep their hedges for foxes, badgers and birds an' all. And pay them for tree-planting on poor land. Keep the farmers on their own property, they say.'

'It's the environmental part of the EU, Tim, you didn't say that,' put in Kath. 'And it's because the ancient stone walls are quarried off to make larger paddocks for tractors. That's it.'

Tim ignored her.

Now we were passing over the River Inny and the Royal Canal. Old churches, castles, pubs and inns, even thatched cottages, handcrafted and real. For once the sun shone, and I thought was there anything so beautiful as this, where history rises out of the earth to mingle with the fields and touch the trees?

'Oliver Goldsmith's father was the first minister here,' Kathleen said, slowing down at Forgney Church of Ireland. 'They gave it to the people here when they left. It's used sometimes at three on a Sunday afternoon, but only about half a dozen come, I hear.'

But who would know there was a service at three? No notice board, and a heavily locked gate. The usual Church of Ireland set-up in country areas.

Tim was straining for a look at the house nearby. 'Wonder if Nora's in,' he mumbled.

We walked diffidently through the huge, intricate wrought-iron gates, gasping at the picturesque old English cottage covered in pink clematis, with ivy and 'all-round' sweet peas climbing the walls. Daffodils carpeted the ground. Would Nora be in? Thanks be to God . . .

'She's Church of Ireland,' Kathleen whispered. Her family used to live in a 'big house' in Ballymuck. 'Tim helped with the horses when they ploughed their fields. Good horses they had too, for riding.'

Despite pyjama top and jeans, straight hair and crippled knees, Nora was a lady. To the manor born. We had made no prior appointment, yet she behaved immaculately. We may even have woken her, but she was too well bred to hint at it, or to apologise for her attire. We were looking at a maiden lady of the ascendancy era.

'Oh, do come in, but don't look there,' she said quietly. 'There's nothing to see. Just come in here for a drink.'

Nothing to see! Plush Kerry green carpet in the dining room, crushed strawberry in the lounge. A polished rosewood table and antique chairs spoke of regal dinner parties, elegant and formal. A winter-garden fernery and daffodils set in embossed leaden planters created a unique diversion in the hallway. Nothing to see?

'They should have been pruned before Saint Pat's,' she apologised, 'but we haven't had a good spring.'

Then we were drinking our sherries and Scotch in the drawing room, sitting on beautiful green chintz chairs and resting our glasses atop antique carved tables. Nora's shaky legs and dim vision made no difference. She served perfectly.

'New Zealand? Your father went *there*?' she enquired, fascinated. Why '*there*'?

'Most of the people near here went to Argentina to make money on the ranches. Most never came back, did they Tim?' She looked warmly at Tim, happy he was sitting cosily next to her.

'To Argentina?' I asked, surprised. 'Why?'

'Thousands went to Buenos Aires in the difficult times. They liked it better than North America. Cattle ranches.' She was nodding with her memories. 'Horses.'

Suddenly I could see my Aunt Lizzie in New Zealand nodding in the same way. They could have been sisters when you thought about it. I bet Nora's 'smalls' weren't hanging on the line for neighbours to see either, and you could never imagine Nora going to the toilet. 'Poor Lizzie,' Da always said. 'Only married a week — never got over it. The war . . .'

Paintings of English soldiers in red uniforms hung on the wall, and two of Nora's sisters on horseback in dressage pose. Above the fireplace a huge oil of the Ascension looked somehow incongruous to our New Zealand eyes in this setting, but who were we? Mere colonials from 'down under' having 'drinkies'. This was Ireland, where walls were covered in holy pictures and some people drank themselves legless.

'She's failing,' Kathleen said on the way home.

'She likes you, Tim,' I joked.

'She was always very kind to me when I worked with the horses,' he replied with affection in his voice.

'Of course she was, Tim, you were *hands*, that's why. They kept to themselves — a tightknit little community. Didn't mix with us.' Kathleen spoke stiffly. Tim shut up.

'No coffee mornings with you, eh Kathleen?' I quipped.

'You can say that,' Kathleen muttered.

'I had meals there,' Tim tried again.

'Yes, Tim, with the *hands* you did, not with Nora.'

The atmosphere was hotting up. Better try another tack, I thought.

'Did they go to school?' I asked.

'No, an English governess lived in,' Tim spoke up. 'Nice ladies they all were.'

Kathleen lapsed into silence.

'We'll pass their old home soon and show you. It was burnt down and just left.'

We had been long enough in Ireland not to ask who had burnt it down. You didn't ask those questions in a small village like Ballymuck, but obviously Kath and Tim knew, and said nothing. The IRA wasn't a pleasant subject. From the road we could see vines and trees growing inside the old mansion, and twisting like snakes outside over the stonework.

'Well, that's it,' said Kathleen finally. 'And Nora's living in the gatehouse of the King Harman estate now. The gatehouse!'

'It's still pretty flash,' I replied.

'Small compared with the big house,' Kath said wistfully.

'After all those grand parties she and her sister Billy gave here. My, they were something.' Tim grinned. You could see him with the other hands slurping up the leftovers of the expensive wines. But those days were over . . .

'Did you notice Nora holding Tim's hand on the sofa?' David ask nonchalantly a few days later. I stared at him, mouth dropping.

'Don't be silly,' I said. 'Stop fooling!'

'Don't believe me then, but I thought it was rather nice. You know, mistress and old retainer — buddy-buddy.'

'Probably more than buddy-buddy went on at the big house in the good old days,' I mumbled. 'Anyway, Tim needs his memories, God love him.'

We learnt a lot in the country village of Ballymuck, living as we did next door to a family of devout Catholic intellectuals who treated us as friends. The charm of Ireland? you ask yourself daily. It is the charm of a country still living spiritually in the eighteenth century, and we were part of it at Ballymuck. In some ways I was back in my childhood Brethren home, where 'God willing', 'Praise the Lord', 'Journeying Mercies' and 'With God's help' were part of the daily lingo; where people 'going to Mass' was little different from 'going to the meeting'.

'The weather's a bit better today,' I'd say.

'God be praised, it is.' As natural as breathing.

Kathleen gave me little books to read in my spare time. They contained devotional poems, written by holy mystics or monks. Striking in their purity and devotion, they made me feel superficial and worldly. Just like the Brethren's little books, but I had no guilt now. Thanks be to God.

Kathleen was one of five, the only one not ordained or with a degree.

'Taken out of school I was, because I was the eldest and my mother wasn't well. Had to look after the younger ones. I've got the brains of the others, and I'm just as capable, but there it is.'

'Some intellectuals can't even boil an egg, Kathleen, but it's obvious you can,' I philosophised. 'And you're a pillar of your local church by the looks of things, so . . .'

'Aye, I'm not regretting it now, praise be to God, but . . . you know.'

A tall, handsome brother was a priest in a parish near Dublin.

'Did well at Maynooth, he did. Got his MA writing a thesis on Ballymuck. I'll let you read that. He liked his year in Australia and a holiday in New Zealand. Liked the freedom you have there. I guess that's where he'll retire. Who knows? Only God and himself, I suppose. I don't like him living alone in that big rectory near Dublin. It's a lonely life. Got his music for company, but what's a man to do of an evening? Tell me that. Look at that stupid box, that's what he does, and there's no good comes of it with all that rubbish. Twenty years is enough as a priest, I told him, and then find a girl.' She was dead serious.

'Another is a teaching nun in Ballymahon. Mary teaches German, French and Irish.'

'Knows everything, that one,' said Tim with a shrug. 'Travels everywhere too. Off to Düsseldorf next week to a conference; always at conferences in Europe, for something. Studied the Irish language extra for six months in Dublin or somewhere. She'll drop in and see yous tonight with her friend.' He winked.

'And my other sister, Nancy, she's a hermit in France,' Kathleen said quite naturally. 'Was a mother superior once in Dublin. At the top, you might say, and then suddenly gave it all up and decided to live on her own. Won't come back to Ireland except to be buried. Went into a convent at age fifteen.'

'A hermit?' I spluttered. 'What does she do all day?'

'Prays,' said Kathleen flatly, with a shrug. 'Some people say it's a cop-out. I mean, you and I could be prayin' and let someone else do the work, so we could, but she wanted to do that — and don't think it's a big sacrifice for her. Nothing's a sacrifice when you want to do a thing, is it now?'

'But . . . How . . . ? Did she have a broken love affair as a girl, or, um, when she was, um, a mother superior?' I asked without thinking.

Kathleen collapsed.

'At fifteen! Mother superior! Love! Why she's never been shown a bed in her life!'

I gulped at my own ignorance.

'But . . .'

'Well, she does embroidery and sells it, and the French village people bring her food, so she's happy.'

'I suppose she prays for them?'

'Yes, she's always praying — at her wee home and in the church nearby. She's a good cook, so I suppose she eats enough.'

'Does she write to you?'

'Four times a year we write to each other, but what has she got to say, I ask you? The weather and herself, that's all. I give her family news and she likes that. My brother visited her once — took him a long time to find her. Said twenty-four hours was enough with her and he wouldn't go back. Wants to be alone, that one. Let her.'

'My other brother's in the tax department in Dublin. Head of it. Didn't like Maynooth so came out after the first stage, you know. Went teaching and didn't like that, so now he's in business.'

'And . . . married?'

Kathleen's voice took on a different tone.

'He's married to an English girl. We give her a wide berth, don't we Timmy?'

Tim grimaced. 'She's way beyond,' he said, pointing to his head. 'Off.'

As Tim promised, Mary, the teaching nun, and her 'friend' came to visit in our parlour.

'You don't mind if Father John comes in too, do you?' Kathleen asked uneasily. 'He comes every Sunday night, just to relax and be himself.'

I offered Father John a drink. 'Tea, coffee or . . . ?'

'I belong to the Pioneer Society for Total Abstinence,' he said. 'Do you know about that?'

'We have a similar group where they sign the pledge not to drink. My parents were in the temperance movement.'

He smiled broadly, and we talked well into the night — about the Renewal Movement.

'A few in the church make a noise about it. I just let it go. There's too much else going on for me to say yea or nay, and I'm too old to make a fuss. It's just a few women.'

We spoke of Ireland and the pub culture, of fatalism and submission, of luck and superstition, of the Irish language and his love of it, of fairies, of his worries about his fellow priests and their behaviour, of materialism, and of his anguish about the church as a whole.

'That was a very interesting priest we had in the house last night,' I said to Tim next morning. 'You should have come in.'

He winked broadly. 'He'd visit anyone at any hour of the day or night, so he would. Works himself to death. Needs Mary to put a bit of reality into him. She tells him not to hit his head against the wall. All these crazy priests that worry him, Bishop Casey and the rest, and today's world going to the devil. He can't do much about it himself, and Mary tells him that. By the way, he left this note for you.'

Bail o Dhia ar an obair. God bless the work of your hands.

Tears pricked my eyes. I didn't care if Tim saw them either.

Kathleen came in very early.

'About Father John and Mary. Um . . . The family think the relationship is, um, not seemly, um . . .' She shrugged meaningfully. 'But they can't both be lonely, can they? I think they need each other. I told my brother in Dublin he should get a girl too, for friendship if you understand. He doesn't need to criticize.'

The state of this empty gatekeeper's cottage in Collinstown, County Westmeath, bears witness to the fate of most Anglo-Irish estates.

St Owen's Church in Ballymore, County Westmeath. Built 1827. Roofless and lifeless since 1890. A relic of the English Plantations' Established Church.

Cut by hand or machine, and dried in stooks over summer, peat remains God's sustaining gift to Ireland.

Sharing a crack with the Two Ronnies slows down their progress on the thatching. But in Ireland, who cares?

Ashes's pub; nostalgic watering hole for generations of Irish immigrants from Camp, Dingle Peninsula, County Kerry.

The sheltered crannies of the treeless Atlantic coast: heather-tinted in summer, colourless and bleak in winter.

A tomb of the Stone Age, this dolmen in Kilclooney, County Donegal, stands stark and mysterious in a wild, neglected landscape.

PATRICK MAC GILL
"THE NAVVY POET"
1889 - 1963

I'M GOING BACK TO GLENTIES
WHEN THE HARVEST FIELDS ARE BROWN,
AND THE AUTUMN SUNSET LINGERS
ON MY LITTLE IRISH TOWN.

A surprise meeting with notable relatives in Glenties, County Donegal.

'Your sister is quite brilliant,' I told her, 'yet she still has a mind to believe the fairy stories. She told me to listen to Brian Kay's *Sunday Morning Discs*, where people tell these stories, and she's given me some tapes of them. I can't believe it.'

'Did she tell you about her fear of magpies? In her early-morning walks, she crosses the road if there's only one, because she believes: One for sorrow, Two for joy, Three for a girl, Four for a boy, Five for silver, Six for gold, Seven for a secret that's never been told.'

I like to believe fairy stories:

> About the year 1915 Patrick McGann of Cooleen, Killare, was coming home from a music session at Johnny Conlon's of Rathskeagh about midnight. A full moon was racing across the sky and a terrible storm was blowing as Pat and a neighbour were crossing the fields. When they got to the main road leading to Killare, the wind got stronger, so they decided to take shelter under the gable wall of a house near Rathskeagh. They tried several times to move on but each time they were blown back by the force of the wind. About 1.30 a.m., as the wind was howling about them, they heard hoof-beats coming across the fields in their direction. They heard the creaking of saddles, and a chattering like thirty or forty children gabbling together. Suddenly horses about the size of small goats jumped onto the road, with their tiny riders all talking in a strange language.
>
> The two men huddled close to the wall in case they would be seen. The riders went about one hundred yards down the road and when they came to a low wall they jumped over into the 'Raheens' [a series of low stone walls around a fort] and disappeared into the night with shouts of 'Tally-ho! Tally-ho!' Then the storm abated until there wasn't a breeze, and the two men, badly shaken, made their way home. Pat McGann had lost his cap during the storm, so next morning he returned to the scene to search for it. He found it. And then, walking down the road he found a little shoe about one-and-a-half inches long made from one piece of leather without stitching or sprigs. He took the little shoe home and showed it to his family. After keeping it in the house for some

65

time they became afraid and gave it to their local doctor, and it is told that his family still have it.

When Pat Moran was out on his farm on the morning after the storm, he discovered a number of large bushes uprooted on the local fort. The belief thereafter was that it was the uprooting of the bushes during the storm that had disturbed the fairies, and that they had had to evacuate their old home and seek an abode in a vacant fort in Lower Rathskeagh. This story was related by Patrick McGann many times, and a number of local people claim that they saw the tiny shoe.

I wish I had seen it.

'A grrand day for a stroll,' the man opposite called across. So few grrand days there were for sure. We had chosen the River Inny.

You can learn a lot from little boys.

'Any track along the river?' I had asked them.

'Naw. You American?'

'Guess.'

The boys stood still and looked at us both squarely.

'Crocodile Dundee,' one ventured at last.

'New Zealand it is, but you're near enough.'

The boys look bewildered and fiddled with their worms and grubs inside a matchbox. Obviously never heard of it.

'How many worms have you got so far?'

'Only two, but we're after getting more.'

'For coarse fishing?'

'Aye.'

'And you'll throw all the fish back?'

'Aye.'

The sign of a walkway led to the banks of the Royal Canal, but cattle had been mucking about and it was slushy with poo. No one would want to walk there — a pity. Just then a familiar notice caught our attention. The EU had it in hand, together with the local works scheme. In a few months there would be a new poo-free walkway. Three cheers for the EU. Into all sorts of projects, small and large, it had kick-started Ireland into action, restoring historic sights, canals, locks — the list went on and on.

Leaving the smelly slush we walked along the road beside the Inny. Two young women power-walked in front, their swinging arms and wobbling bottoms giving an urgency to the relaxed Sunday atmosphere.

'Four miles in an hour,' they called out breathlessly. 'We usually walk at eight at night come spring. Get a walking mate and go. It's good for our brains and worries and keeps us fit.'

We caught up with them. 'You wouldn't go alone or with a dog?'

They pointed to their heads. 'They'd think we were out of it.'

'What about with your husbands?' The thought hadn't entered their heads and they laughed even louder, their foreheads red with sweat.

'We girls can talk to each other when we walk. It's great, so it is!'

Men were learning to play a different role in Ireland, and after the drudgery their mothers had endured, these women were finding their own space and had their own jobs. Ten years in the EU had given them freedom.

Back at the cottage Tim was ready in his padded jerkin and jarvey, waiting. 'A grrand night for the bog,' he said. 'I'll be plaised to leave this mowin'.'

Obviously Kath was out at her 'wee job'. She kept that a secret, always.

The three of us bumped along the narrow road in Trixie, missing potholes and puddles by inches.

'Be carreful now, David, or you'll get bogged down,' says Tim from the back seat.

Bogged down? Was he fooling?

'Not at arl.'

'Sit in the front and direct us then, Tim,' I said pointedly.

'Aw naw, I like to be chauffer-driven so I can hear the birrds sing.' And he meant that too.

'See those sheep over therr?' he called. 'Wouldn' give much for them, would yer? Scraggy. But I tell you, they're worth a lot if you're after selling them. The EU subsidises the prices.'

We gaped. 'Ours aren't worth anything much in New Zealand these days, and they're beautiful. Some farmers are almost giving them away.'

'A pity of yous down therr then, if that's what's happenin'. I'd stop now, right where I'm directing yer.'

At first glance the great expanse of dry, brown, treeless land looked dead and good for nothing. But after walking slowly and looking carefully, the dead came to life — hillocks and hollows, small pools and lakes, mosses, grasses, lichens and bell heather of green, russet and purple. Tiny yellow tormentil peeped cheekily out of nowhere, and brave miniature toitoi called bog cotton, pushed its way out of dark nothingness. A precious resource for plants and wildlife. Tim watched us thoughtfully, a pleased smile on his face.

There was something about this ancient Irish bog. It was like walking on a treasure from the past built up of layers of roots, stems, leaves and fruit which had died from lack of oxygen. Walking on 8000 years of built-up energy on bog butter and skeletons with clothes and hair still preserved. Eerie stuff, but I loved it.

'Cuckoo's arrived!' Tim announced suddenly. 'Must be summer it is.' His face beamed at the sound of it. He was over the moon. A grown man! But *we* hadn't slaved at that bog face in a biting cold wind like Tim, preparing the peat to keep the hearth warm in winter.

Great long furrows of turf a metre wide lay drying in the evening sun, sliced from the hill by bulldozers then belched out along the bogland to dry. Tim would turn them over by hand in a few weeks' time and dry the underside.

'We'll stack the sods up shortly and they'll be dry for next season,' he said proudly, for this strip of bog was his.

'What happens when it all runs out?

'They're building the modern houses with oil for heating. It'll be oil all raight,' he mused wistfully, 'but not the same an' all.'

'It must have been dreadfully hard work by hand.'

'I've seen eight men working along that cliff face for days, when a tractor does it in a morning now and spreads it out an' all. New Zealand isn't nearly so cold in the winter, is it?'

'You're ten degrees latitude nearer the pole than us,' David told him. 'It's tough on you guys and your cattle.'

'Write this in yer book,' Tim says on the way home. 'The peat shovel is called the *hoy*, and peat is carefully footed in mounds so it can let all the water dry out. It's clogged with it so it is. How about that?'

'You better write this book yourself,' I told him.

Peat is part of Ireland's energy. Part of Ireland itself. Its very existence goes back beyond the Bronze Age to the last Ice Age, and one feels a certain sacred respect squelching across its spongy surface. There were times when I felt more a part of Ireland walking in bog than I did gazing at decaying churches and old ruins. As Tim said, 'God gave peat for Ireland anywa', and churches were man's affair.'

'The cuckoo's arrived,' Tim announced proudly to Father John and Mary the next Sunday night.

'The cuckoo, Tim?' they repeated excitedly, and rushed out into the garden to hear it for themselves, just as they'd done as children, their faces flushed with joy. Thanks be to God. He had sent a good omen.

A small solitary yacht tied to the wharf was dwarfed by a 75-foot Dutch barge in Barleyharbour on Lough Ree. We 'kicked along' the wharf as yachties do to sniff for signs of sea life.

'Anybody about?' called David, giving the barge a kick.

The for'ard hatch opened in a flash, and Liam Finnegan's handsome face appeared. It was all on. Baileys Irish Cream and the 'crack'.

'They *love* it! We turn it on for them all. Irish coffee for starters, settle them down, then — look — three double cabins, en suite an' all, bar, the lot. The English? Good fishermen, put the fish back into the lough. The Germans? Fish for pike, freeze it and take it back to Germany — very expensive there. A boat load of Germans is no fun — no sense of humour. Strip the lough of fish. Too many around here. Americans? Demand a package deal. Fishing, claybird shooting, boy, do they love it. Off on coaches and touring all day, then back here for a meal and a crack. Has to be all organised before they come. I thought at first the American women would be a pain in the arse but they *love* it. My wife — the chef. And I'm on the bar. Wow! We can have fun here half the night.'

'What about the locals? Don't they like a trip on the lough?'

'Nearer the church, farther from God. Get what I mean? You

can't get farmers to enjoy sailing round on a barge, and they won't encourage their kids. No money in the sea for them, and who's going to organise it?'

'Maybe the EU could subsidise it?'

'Look here, I'm a bit scared of the EU just now. There's Greece and Poland needing help. Maybe we've had our turn, who knows? We're not a banana republic now. Sure we're not.'

We left Liam Finnegan of the Shannon Barge Line on Lough Ree, his voice following us:

'Send some New Zealanders over for a good time, and call in at Michael Casey's on your way home. He carves bog wood, sanding and buffing it to a silky finish. Lets the wood speak.'

Huge black flamingos and herons in graceful poses were grouped outside the pub when we passed. No wonder American tourists paid the earth to possess one of Michael Casey's creations. And although he was miles away from civilisation, in Barley-harbour, they found him.

'You better go to the art exhibition at the pub in Abeyshrule,' Kath suggested. 'See the local talent. Opens at eight-thirty p.m.'

We should have known better. At nine people were at the bar drinking or seated in little comfy corners having dinner. At ten the exhibition was officially opened and the drinks went on. Strangely, we seemed to be the only ones looking at the paintings.

'People will start to come in now,' said a chatty woman. 'It'll be full about twelve. We Irish like to enjoy ourselves, so we do. You become scintillating, and get some "nous" at nights. My son leaves Ballymahon at twelve-thirty at night in a bus, goes to a nightclub and is back at four-thirty in the morning. No problem. Weekends mind you.'

'Do you know any of the artists?' I asked.

'What artists?'

'The ones who painted these around here.'

'Oh no, I'm just a friend.'

'Which ones do you like?'

'I don't know as yet — I'm enjoyin' myself just.'

♣

'It's a pet of a day,' Tim announced. 'We're going to let the cows and calves out.'

After nine months lounging about inside, eating, pooing and looking at each other, it was a big moment for the animals. How would they react? Slowly and heavily they ambled out into the green fields, still in a mental claustrophobia, still punch-drunk in their swaying gait. And then — it clicked. They were *free*. Some ran round in circles, a few ambled to the wire fence, others gathered in a group to discuss the whole new world of green pasture. Some ate their hearts out, some waited. A few bulls looked on with renewed interest from the next paddock. At last! The girls had been let out.

Tim drove with us round the farm, now run by his son. We stood looking at it all in the long twilight.

'Couldn't do the book work mysel' with the EU an' all. Couldn't talk to the bank manager like the boy can and raise a loan. Not built for that. I'm good on the fields still, so I am. Just look at these barns, will ye. Twenty-five cows they take, with those huge slurry holding tanks, and those large, powerful tractors for cultivation and hauling the tanker trailers for spreading the slurry over the fields. See the plastic silage bales? No hay these days, and the dairy company calls every other day. Yous can see it passing by. Those electric fences come from down your way, in New Zealand, don't they? Someone said about that when they heard yous was here. EU it is an' all.

And then, on this 'pet of a day', the spring twilight lent itself to entertaining. The whole countryside took on a magic, a stillness, a timeless mood between day and night, when the sun stood still and work was forgotten.

'Come over about nine then,' said a neighbour. 'Michael's been a bit thick today so I'd like the company. Not thick like you mean in New Zealand — not stupid — just in a rage. I take myself to the other end of the garden when that happens. We're pulling the devil by the tail these days, if you get what I mean. Trying to make ends meet. Selling off the fields to live, really.'

Here we were again, meeting a remnant of the ascendancy, their wealth dissipated by death duties, the once gay 'big house' slumbering in the sun, splendid antiques gathering dust in a lonely sitting room, a lifestyle betrayed by the passing of time.

Caroline had come from New Zealand twenty years earlier, for the hunts and parties. You could see her in full swing, jumping over hedges and ditches, but only in paintings.

'Do you still ride to the hunt?'

'No, there's not enough people round now to make a club,' she sighed, and shrugged.

'Do you want to come back to New Zealand?'

'No, I'm Irish now, and Ireland has substance. I like that. Sure, my mother's in New Zealand, and that's my home, but I'm Irish.'

Huge flagons of home-made wine caught the afternoon light in the parlour, pretty as stained-glass windows.

'Take a bottle of elderberry with you,' Caroline offered. 'This is an old one.'

It sure was. The nicest ever.

She watched us pass the huge old farm sheds, stables and pebbled courtyard, the old water pump and stone outhouses. She was still watching when we crossed the road to Kathleen's bungalow. We turned and waved at our Irish-New Zealand friend, and although there was a sadness and longing in her eyes we knew she had found happiness in her adopted country.

'I could live here,' I said truthfully. 'Just like Caroline.' Then I remembered we had waited two months for this 'pet of a day', and winter in the big house could be dismal and sunless. But I liked the 'substance'. We didn't have that in New Zealand.

One spring twilight, at about eleven, we passed Tim on the road — starting out on a ramble! He tried to make himself invisible, walking sideways, head down under his jarvey.

'Visitin',' he mumbled.

There must have been a few on Tim's 'visitin'' list — a wee dram here, a wee glass there, and then the final leg to the Winning Post in the wee small hours. For Tim's sake I wish we could have pretended not to have seen him — become ghosts or fairies, vanishing into thin air — but there was no way out. The episode was never mentioned, but Tim's evening peregrinations were a secret no more. He still winked at us behind Kath's back, though; we were still friends.

'That's Tim's key just behind the door,' Kathleen told me once. 'I don't get up anymore.'

Back then I didn't know what she meant. No wonder he knew all the gossip in Ballymuck next morning. We often wondered about that, and no wonder Kathleen slept with her window open towards the pub. She could hear the goin's-on if the wind blew her way, and Tim knew it. The women of Ireland are a strong breed. They need to be. They could rule the country with one hand behind their backs. One day they might. With two presidents already . . .

Time to leave Ballymuck. A wee farewell with Kath and Tim. Sherry for the women, Scotch and water for the men. How would I ask Kathleen *the* questions?

'Your parents must have been amazing people to produce such a family.'

'Every spring my father turned the car towards Croagh Padraig and Lough Derg. He cleansed himself that way. Mother went when she could, too. Try it yourselves if you get the chance. Most of us have climbed the mountain.'

'We'll have to find out about it,' I replied with complete ignorance, but somehow Croagh Padraig haunted me. Perhaps one day?

'Hm . . . Young mothers seem to be out working these days. What about in your day?'

'Wouldn't think about it. We had to churn and separate the milk, look after the chickens and pigs and feed our men — as well as the children, of course. Most had dozens of them. Then we had to get the produce off to market. Now chickens and pigs are for the specialist and the milk gets collected. It's all changed, and I wouldn't like to go back to all that.'

The wives today?

'They had good jobs before they married, so why give them up? They need the money for mortgages anyway. We didn't have jobs like that to go to.'

'Who looks after the children?'

'The grandmas if they can, or sisters or aunties. Childcare or crèches are expensive but better than leaving your job.'

'So when the wife comes home tired in the evening, she has to get to and produce a meal?'

Kathleen looked amazed at my question.

'Oh, never like that. The father makes his own midday dinner and feeds the children when they come home from school, and mother has hers at the canteen or somewhere near work.'

'OK for farmers,' I kept on, 'but what about city families?'

'Eat at the canteen at work or a pub nearby. Cheap enough. The children go to their minders after school and get a meal, and the minders see to their lessons.'

'When do they eat together?'

'A wee fry or something before bed, and always Sunday lunch after Mass with an outing, a picnic in the summer or a movie. Mind you, it's not the same as in our day. Neighbours were much closer together then and maybe we've lost a bit of that. There's not the get-togethers and community spirit we had in our days. And that TV didn't take over like it does today.'

'Families don't seem to be big these days. I was expecting pregnant mothers everywhere and clothes-lines full of diapers. I've only seen two pregnant mothers in two months, and no diapers.'

'Ten years ago, that's the way it was, but life's changed. Disposable napkins, and contraceptives on the counter for all to see.'

'So what happens when they face the priest?'

'No guilt these days, eh Tim?' She smiled ruefully. 'Do what they like most of them. Not all, I'm saying. My daughter-in-law over the road — wouldn't ever. We're not allowed to mention the words "family planning" over there.'

'What do you think about that then?'

'It's the new Ireland we're living in now. Just like anywhere in the world, contraceptives bring good things and bad. All these unmarried mothers proud as you like, getting their benefits and someone else bringing up the kids. Looking at TV half the day. I had the Rh factor so could have only two. The rest would have been born cabbages.' She threw a few more sods of turf on the fire.

'So . . . how . . . ?'

'Abstain, didn't we Tim?' She said the word with a martyrlike expression. Tim looked out of the window. No wonder he had the fondness for the rambling.

Ballymuck. How can we leave you?

6. the pilgrim way

THE GARAGE MAN WORKED on Trixie for two hours.

'You'll have no more trouble with her now. Good as new. Had a Polo myself once. Tricky things till you know how.'

'How much?' we asked.

'Ten punts about. Going up Uisneach for a wee afternoon drive?'

'How do we get there?'

'Just over the back — not far. Right, left, right and left again. Be a bit of a mizzle at the cat stone. Watch the crossing.'

What was he talking about? Nothing made sense. We followed his directions, twisting right, left, right and left again on the narrow country roads, looking for Uisneach.

Weatherbeaten wooden slats made up a simple notice, startling in its plainness, like a Kiwi fence put together with number eight fencing wire. No heritage centre this, with the usual car park, tourist shops and upmarket café; only a lonely horse pushing its face over the wall for company.

> hill of uisneach
> site of celtic festival of bealtaine
> ancient place of assembly
> st patrick's church
> centre of ancient ireland
> twin of tara
> site of druid fire cult
> seat of high kings

Nearby a tiny old white notice said:

> aill na mireann sn155
> the 'catstone' 1/4 [1]

In the misty greyness of late afternoon, a sense of desolation pervaded the historic site, as if modern man had passed it over in favour of something more spectacular. Mounting an old turnstile and heading up an unmarked hill, we found it difficult to believe this was part of the Pilgrim Way. Surely there would be clearer signs, even footprints of other pilgrims in the cowshite or further up the muddy track. Mizzle turned to heavy rain just as a herd of heavy cattle emerged from higher up the mountain and lumbered towards us. I am scared of lumbering cattle.

At last, on the southern slopes of the hill of Uisneach, a huge, rugged jumble of stones came into sight. A cat? Not likely! But from higher up, looking down, the shape of the stones does resemble a cat looming over a mouse, and encircling it all is an attractive earthern bank. From this vantage point it becomes clear why archaeologists believe the site is almost certainly a burial place dating back to 2000 BC or earlier, and why it is called the Navel of Ireland — where all roads meet.

At the very top of the hill a few scattered stones and grassy undulations in a thistly meadow are all that remains of the hill fort of Saint Patrick's bed, a well and a church. This is not a faked tourist attraction, for there is no physical beauty or ornate decoration, simply a realisation that when Jesus Christ was walking the dusty roads of Palestine, hardy Egyptian traders were making their way up the River Shannon in the mizzle, finding a pathway across the swampy boglands, and bringing spices, silks and satins to be traded for fine Irish tools and golden ornaments. They were coming to the great feast of Bealtaine, held on the first day of May on this very hill of Uisneach. Local clans would be dispensing justice, sharing entertainment and competing in sports. Back then.

One does not need much imagination to feel the winds of history here in the month of May, two thousand years later. Standing on this sacred hill, the very centre of Ireland, looking across towards the Wicklow Hills 145 kilometres away, old stone fences and small plots have given way to new, prosperous and wider fields.

At the highest point, just over 200 metres above sea level, is a monument marking Saint Patrick's bed. But one wonders if Saint Patrick ever slept — his itinerary was unreal, his exploits godlike. He was everywhere, it seems; an omnipresence, leading pilgrims across Ireland in wonder and curiosity.

Ancient and modern mix so naturally in Ireland. Secular and sacred intertwine on the pilgrim quest. Pink and white hawthorn hedges form a wedding canopy with lilac shrubs in pastel mauves and rich puce, throwing out a delicate fragrance. This should be a perfect day, another 'pet'. If only. If only people could forget past wars, crippling sectarianism and bigotry, and vote 'yes' for peace. Today! Faces and voices of the main players flashed across the windscreen of our minds — Gerry Adams, David Trimble, Tony Blair. Roaring from the wings the angry voice of the past — Ian Paisley. Could people not see that an end to thirty years of bombs and bloodshed meant a 'yes' vote? Surely they wanted an end to the Troubles. Posters of the Taoiseach, Bertie Ahern, appeared on every second lamppost. *He* was voting 'yes' — with his left hand. Must be lefthanded. Silly to notice that when the whole of Ireland was waiting in suspense.

> The timing is no less poignant for being accidental. The counting of votes today on the Belfast Agreement will begin on the exact 200th anniversary of the start of the 1798 rising. It was on the night of May 23, 1798 that the rebels intercepted the mail coaches leaving Dublin giving the signal for insurrection.
>
> Never before have the British and Irish governments and the leaderships of both militant Irish nationalism and mainstream unionism asked the people to give the same answer to a question about their political future. Never before has that question been framed in such a way that it asks them to decide not what they are willing to die for but what they can live with. Never before have we been invited so clearly to decide however grudgingly that the one thing we have no choice but to live with is each other.
>
> Fintan O'Toole, *Irish Times*

Would they do it?

We passed the Elbow, where they would celebrate tonight; the Curl Up and Dye salon, where the women would dolly up; holy water in a square wooden box outside the big church, where others would be praying in thankfulness. The alternative was unthinkable. Desperate prayers of intercession would arise to Almighty God. And then — bombs again?

Two farmers propped up a traditional thatched cottage and Trixie stopped dead. Could *The Two Ronnies* be on location here? But one had a glass eye, and the other's nose appeared a trifle blue beneath the twinkling eyes. A sure sign of that certain fondness.

'Hoyea.'

'Hi. What are you fixing the thatch with?'

'Oat straw with rolled bales be OK. Takin' the auld stoof doon so I be.'

'I like your flowers.'

'Aye. Peewons [peonies] they be. Just planted in.'

'All these huge new houses going up around here. Why so big?'

'Cost a hundred and fifty thousand punts. Mortgage forty to fifty years to pay off. Four per cent.'

'*What?*'

'Just a wee interest noo — not like in oor day. Showing each other up, that's what they're doin'. One betters t'other. Both of em working, that's the way of it. Houses empty orl day. You back to have a look round?'

'My father left in the 1880s. Land ran out.'

'God save us, they were poor. We all were.'

'My da told us his pants were so patched he didn't know what was patch and what was pants.'

'Aye, thems were poor times when your da left here. Wonder he had any pants at arl. God save us. See that big house yonder? Americans paid over two hundred thousand punts for that one. Want to live back here now. Like the green of things and the slowness of us.'

'Got roots here have they?'

'Aye. Left to make the money and now they're back. Oor uncles never came back, you naw, none of them — the elbow, you naw what I mean?' He gave his elbow a great push upwards. 'Too much the likin' of it. You puttin' things down in a book?'

'Yes. For my friends in New Zealand.'

'Tell them we've got bloody acid rain and dust from the Sahara being stirred up with nuclears. Wipe it off our cars we can. Yous been to Clonmacnoise?'

'We're just on our way.'

'Had to put the crosses inside 'cause of the bloody acid rain. Make repleekus [replicas]. Just give 'em a tap and you can tell they're repleekus. Hollow. Clonmacnoise — sit in the bishop's chair and it'll cure ya backache, and ya headache. You'll get ya warts cured at Clonmacnoise. Know what warts are? Knobs on ya!'

The tall, glass-eyed man spoke now with utter sincerity and dignity.

'Them crosses. Pregnant women went therr when they couldn't have 'em right. A man needed a thin chest and long arms to stand behind her, and she with her arms round the cross and him like-wise — and the baby came.'

'Amazing.'

'Yous been to Uisneach?'

'Yes.'

'You know de Valera? God bless him.'

'Yes.'

'His wife was an Irish speaker and a dancer, you knaw. They used to bike from Dublin up to Uisneach and stay the night therr. Sing and dance and all that. Bike home. She was like that you naw.'

The crack would have gone on for the rest of the day. Regret-fully we ambled back to Trixie. These were precious people. One poked his face in the car window, a wicked look in his good eye. My notebook lay open.

'Ireland's a lovely country. Tell them that.' He grinned. 'Tell them a pack of bloody lies.'

The four of us laughed together — a real good gutsy laugh — which took us to Athlone.

Twin spires of the church of St Peter and St Paul at Athlone tower above a squat thirteenth-century castle overlooking the River

Shannon as if to mother it. With a neo-Renaissance interior and vivid, modern stained-glass windows, the cathedral is a stunning edifice, with its doors opened for prayer each day at 5.30 p.m. since the Peace Agreement on Good Friday. 'Peace and Reconciliation' the notice outside said. They were praying for that in Athlone. We hoped God would answer their prayers today.

On this very day two hundred years ago, Henry Joy McCracken and the United Irishmen began their uprisings, and earlier, in 1691, the Catholic forces of James I battled to defend the Line of the Shannon. We were standing on battlefields of the past. Looking down on the historic River Shannon from the castle is like looking down on the set of a movie where any minute horses and soldiers could come pounding across, up to their waists in water, charging the castle to capture that all-important Line of the Shannon.

Inside the remains of the castle, magnificent audio-visuals present a dramatic run-down of Ireland's fight for freedom. It is all sad — bloody, violent and tear-jerking. A folk museum in the keep brings light relief, but one needs to sit down and think. So many battles two hundred years ago — and now, today . . .

A man sat down next to me, his small dog nudging our feet.

'Hoyya.'

'Hi.'

'You been in that museum?'

'Yes.'

'It's just shit in there, isn't it?'

'Not all of it. A bit folksy here and there, but there's a great big lump of butter they found still fresh in the bog, locks of ancient gates, gear for rope-making and an old gramophone with John McCormack's records.'

'Bog butter, that's it. Did they make you pay to go in there?'

'Yes, but it's worth it.'

'Shit. You shouldn't have to pay to see that stuff. D'ya like that up there?' he asked, pointing to the church.

'Magnificent.'

'Aye, it is. American?'

'No. New Zealand.'

'Got rid of the Queen yet?'

'She's OK.'

'Took over the whole place, didn't they?'

'Not really. Not where we live.'

A big crowd comes out of the audio-visual room.

'Look at them lot. That there's drinking Paddy covered in a cloth.'

'I think it's Coca-Cola. They're a choir from Dublin.'

'Holy God and Pat!'

I sensed my neighbour had 'the likin'' for it.

Nearby, a large notice says it all:

> **European Regional Development Fund with Bord Failte**

Where would Ireland be without the EU and the assistance it has given the Tourist Board over these heritage sites?

'Go to Bonnie Broughs over the bridge. You'll get a snark [snack],' my friend said.

We got more. A first communion snark.

'John Boy' was dressed in a little dark suit and white shirt, his hair cut in steps-and-stairs style. In front of me in the queue a little girl dressed in girl-bride finery argued with her grandma.

'You've got a nice dress,' I said pleasantly.

'Hired it for a hundred and fifty punts just out of Athlone,' the grandma whispered in my ear. 'Not a bit grateful either is she, you can see that. Hasn't two brains in her head.'

The little girl shrugged and flounced about, unable to choose. Would she take a chocolate eclair or a sandwich? Maybe a Mars Bar? We were starving. Would she never make up her mind?

'Get your gran a cup of tea as well,' I interfered. 'She's been a good gran to you.'

'Won't!'

Grandma broke in. 'You've received the Blessed Sacrament this very morning. You shouldn't be playing up like this. It's a mortal sin you're doing and tomorrow you'll be layin' it at the cross. Now let the lady go first seeing you can't make your mind up.'

The girl frowned darkly and dropped back. Mars Bar it was and nothing for Gran.

John Boy was a big man of the day on his side of the restaurant. Ice cream for him and his friends, but Dad had counted short. Chaos broke out and a frenzy of outstretched hands threw him off balance. Mother would have to cut short her own tête-à-tête with her lady friends and help. What a pest. Another uncle, and yet another, arrived.

'Shake hands with your uncle, John Boy.'

'Here's a coin for being a good boy.' The look on John Boy's face said it all.

'Only 20p you rotten old sod,' he whispered, and ran with it to his mother.

The wee treat for first communion had turned into a battle for hand-outs, and the uncles were put on the spot. Modern Ireland had turned this homely celebration into a free-for-all at a restaurant.

'Much better when they had it at home,' a lady whispered in my ear. 'None of this carry-on in public.'

Flags fluttered from the cathedral of St Peter and St Paul as we passed by, and peeping inside we gasped at the magnificence of it all: the penny candles glowing, massive arrangements of altar flowers, ornate statues, and the stations of the cross. I wondered how much dosh John Boy had collected, and whether the old gran had got her cup of tea.

Clonmacnoise. There must be more to this monastic site than a place for curing warts and backache, as the two Ronnies had suggested, or havin' babies normal like.

Stepping stones are part of Ireland's history. Throughout the entire island nature has somehow made a way through the bog, and it comes as a kind of miracle to be driving along the old esker ridge — a deposit of sand and gravel left when an ice-age glacier melted away, dumping its stony contents as a high road between boggy lowlands. Early pilgrims made their way to Uisneach and Tara and founded the monastery at Clonmacnoise, tramping along the stepping stones.

Situated beside the River Shannon and close to the boglands, this unspoiled monastery was formerly one of the greatest ecclesiastical centres of Europe. Where old sail boats once brought pilgrims to the nearby wharf, fizz boats bring today's tourists with a roar of engines. Saint Ciaran is honoured here, the humble monk of lowly birth who founded the monastery in AD 545. Familiar as we have become with the tragic history of these monasteries and mankind's greed for gold and power, it still comes as a shock to see the results. Here at Clonmacnoise shrines have been attacked, exquisite carving on high crosses decimated, bronze engravings stolen, and the finest Celtic art and illuminated manuscripts trashed. The earliest known manuscript in the Irish language, written here in about the eleventh century, suffered the same fate. (Today it forms part of the design of the Irish one-punt note.)

Although the ruins echo the old, old story of destruction by the warring clans — the Vikings, the Normans, the English — as we pass the 1000-year-old Cross of the Scriptures, the grave slabs, the churches, the beautiful chancel arch with geometrical patterning all so lovingly preserved by both Protestants and Catholics, we have a certainty such vandalism will never happen again in Ireland. A certainty, too, that in time both religions will allow the other to worship how and when it wishes in a united Ireland. Clonmacnoise is now a national monument, where the two religions have together contributed to its upkeep and where large groups hold services on the feast day of Saint Ciaran. That says a whole lot.

Ireland is full of mysteries, and Trixie's radio was one of them. Without enthusiasm, and no knowledge of the time, I switched it on, hoping for some jaunty music to shorten the journey while prepared for static or the news in Gaelic. It was exactly 3.00 p.m. on 23 May 1998, and the vote was being announced in the North. In the clearest reception ever, we heard the news. A 'yes' vote. 'Yes' to peace. A majority. An overwhelming turnout. Now we would hear the losers congratulating the winners. Oh, yeah? Not in Northern Ireland. No one ever admits defeat. What we heard was the losers saying they'd won. Ian Paisley's voice bellowing from his primeval swamp, sounding off from his pulpit of doom.

'We've won the day,' he boomed. 'Fifty-six per cent of unionists have voted *naw!*'

'Do your sums, Ian, it can't be that!' the others yelled back.

'There's simply no basis in those figures for claiming there's a unionist majority against the agreement!'

And the country's leaders had their say:

– 'The war is over,' said the Taoiseach, Bertie Ahern. 'Put away the guns.'

– 'Michael Collins would be smiling down from heaven.' Dick Hogan, correspondent.

– 'Trimble's toughest task is to dislodge the word "no" from the loyalist psyche.' *Irish Times*.

– 'The resounding "yes" to the Belfast Agreement has made it clear that the day of the men of violence is over.' Mary McAleese, President.

– 'Northern Ireland has voted to take the gun out of politics, north and south of the border.' Mo Mowlam, Northern Ireland Secretary.

– 'The most important civic duty which most of us will ever be called upon to perform.' The Taoiseach, Bertie Ahern, again.

– 'The DUP leader, Ian Paisley, is claiming that he has really won the election. This is like King Canute trying to hold back the tide.' Ulster Democratic Unionist Party statement.

On this momentous day in Ireland's history, we travelled back over the Pilgrim Way, passing the old battlefields of Athlone and Aughrim, knowing that apart from a small group of gangsters, the people of North and South had chosen the way of peace for themselves and their children. It was a start. We wanted to cry.

7. SEARCHING FOR ROOTS

A BIG DIG IN DUBLIN.

The early-morning train from Sligo to Dublin rolls across Ireland in a misty haze, its occupants barely awake. If they are awake, they're grumpy, bored, and resenting the monotonous routine of commuting to the big smoke. It is not the time for 'crack'. Irish are not morning people, that's for sure. A cheap 'Irish breakfast' is available all day, but my stomach heaves at the glossy coloured leaflet: two fried eggs, six rashers, Irish soda bread, toast, black or white pudding, porridge, chips, tea or coffee. All day. Every day.

Visions of the River Liffey, the Poets' Walk and Trinity College and the castle fade into the background. All those Dublin names and places that once made you drool seem far removed from this moment. And what's out of the window? Nothing much. And who are these guys sitting so silently next to us? Dunno.

If searching for family information was the reason for this trip, it was going to take forever to sift through the relevant documents in Trinity College and go back a generation further to the late 1700s to find out about the original Magills. Old Elsie Rogers in New Zealand (God bless her) heard it mentioned that maybe they weren't what the unofficial but accepted 'Family Tree and Notes by RHB' said they were. 'Pure Irish from way back,' she always said. 'I was the last to come out, in 1923, so I should know. I heard Kathleen talk about it with the others. I wish I'd listened properly, but we were only kids running around. Kids don't listen.'

I looked down at the well-thumbed family tree. 'Archibald, descendant of the Kings of Munster, and his wife Alis Mackay of

Craig-in-a-she-oak, Giant's Causeway.' Then, in the next generation, the suggestion that 'James Magill had married Mary White,
an aunt of Field Marshall Sir George White of Ladysmith fame.'
Did we have proof of all this? Or was the original compiler of this
family tree trying to turn ducks into swans, or, in more modern
lingo, was he up himself? Name dropping? Yet one is inclined to
believe a Harley Street specialist. If he hadn't got this right, how
many of his patients would be suing him for another kind of mix-
up. But, honestly, how could anyone decipher 'Craig-in-a-she-oak'?
The New Zealand aunts loved the 'Kings of Munster', of course.
'The Magills are related to the Kings of Munster,' they'd say snob-
bishly. 'We go back a long way, you know.' I could hear their soft,
ladylike voices repeating it at every opportunity, and making sure
we all knew about it, and that our manners should be appropriate
to our ancestry. We would all do well to remember that. I could see
my da ignoring them completely. He knew *their* dicey money manners wouldn't stand up to scrutiny by the Kings of Munster *or* Sir
George White for that matter.

I looked long and hard at 'Craig-in-a-she-oak'. It could be a
clue to a cryptic crossword, but it just didn't make sense. An awful
smell of chips and tomato sauce filled the carriage — part of the
Irish breakfast. I wished I could see past the man next to me and
look out of the window. He obviously didn't want to talk — his
body language said that. The older, balding man opposite was giving David the same 'no speakee' treatment, until, tired of being
ignored and itching for information, David started in.

'We're from New Zealand and don't know very much. Is that
the Royal Canal?'

It worked immediately. We weren't English after all! The man
switched smartly into 'crack' mode. He knew lots — about gorse,
sheep, turf and the EU project on growing Christmas trees for
Europe. Wasn't far from here either. His own son had 'gone down'
on that one. The younger man beside me brooded on, his handsome, sensitive Irish face a study. Maybe something to do with the
IRA, or his girlfriend had ditched him.

'Would Ireland use solar when the turf ran out?' David asked
next.

Suddenly my neighbour swung round, eyes alight. He knew all about solar, and he knew all about being poor in Ireland. Here was my chance at last. When the solar conversation had run out, I asked him, 'Are there any poor people in Ireland these days? Seems the EU has made this place prosperous.'

'You'll see them at the O'Connell and Halfpenny Bridges in Dublin.'

'By choice?'

'Some. I was there once. It's hard to get up once you're down. I'm a woodcarver in Roscommon. Broke up with my girlfiend and landed there. Just on my way up. Going to Dublin to buy tools. I'm sick of people ripping me off. Businessmen promise me the earth, all smiles, and I never see them again. Those Maori people in your country, they carve beautiful bows on boats and other things. What are those people like?'

'Wonderful craftsmen like yourself,' I told him. 'Like the Irish, going through a cultural renaissance. Finding a voice in society. Using their own language again, like the Gaelic here, in schools and on TV. Resurrecting their dances and songs, like your *Riverdance*, and rewriting the old stories and legends. Just as your sacred sites and mountains are places to be honoured and respected, the Maori people have an empathy with their land and water. There is so much that is similar with the Celts and Maori. Living in Ireland for these six months, we feel it every day. That's why we love it here.'

Jim Chaman, the woodcarver from Roscommon, is a special man. I hope he succeeds. Before Dublin railway station swallowed us up in its impersonal jaws, he said humbly, 'You know, nature has done the carving. All I'm doing is shaping and polishing it up.'

How can a visitor cope with Dublin?

Today it is a gracious city with two faces, on either side of the Liffey. The north side of the Liffey has the wide boulevard of O'Connell Street, one of the grandest streets in Europe; the Custom House, a masterpiece of 18th-century architecture; Moore Street market, which rings with raucous Dublin cries; and unpretentious pubs frequented by real Dublin characters, so loved by James Joyce. Dublin's south side is the cultural and fashionable part of the city with its elegant Georgian buildings, two cathedrals and a castle, and Ireland's treasure houses, the National Gallery, National Museum and Trinity Library.

Illustrated Guide to Ireland

A cosmopolitan mishmash of people walk the narrow malls, some as smart as tomorrow, others making do in yesterday's gear. Academics in suits with walking sticks rub shoulders with down-at-heel, shabby tramps, while designer labels from all over the world match each other in this city where yuppies and businessmen from all over Europe and the UK find a common market for fun or work. A weekend in Dublin is the way to go. It's all on here — all-night dancing, music, crack, food and Guinness all rolled together in the switched-on aliveness of the place. No wonder, when the average age is 27. No wonder the oldies have moved out to the suburbs and beaches, where traffic is less hectic and the nights are quiet. As in every other city in the world, you could be happy here with dozens of wealthy friends, or lonely and neglected in a back-street dive. It depends on who you know and what's in your pocket.

A quick trip in a double-decker bus shows only the outside — the Guinness empire, huge churches, gardens bequeathed by the ascendancy now turned into parks, and, across the road, former ascendancy homes, with brightly coloured Georgian doors, now offices or élite apartments. The bus swerves to avoid tables and chairs sprawling out into the middle of the street from the dozens of cluttered little cafés where the coffee is superb and the people exciting. Now the driver is pointing out Dublin Castle and Trinity College. It is interesting that, with his coarse jokes about Sweet Molly Malone's bronze statue and cleavage, he also makes much of *The Book of Kells*. Not as a tourist must-see, but as something important to be kept safely inside Trinity College. As an Irishman he is proud of this, and says so. Next minute he's singing, 'In Dublin's fair city ... Crying cockles and mussels, alive, alive-o! She'll be selling those in the day,' he laughs, 'but what wares does she sell at night?'

Back and forth we go across the Liffey, past the statues of James Joyce, Dean Swift and Oliver Goldsmith, and the huge one of Daniel

O'Connell, the great liberator, with real bullet holes in its bronze. Close by is the historic post office of the 1916 Easter Rising with scars from British bullets in the portico. It is not possible to digest everything or choose where to go. There are artefacts from 3000 BC in the museum, and the art gallery has mainly Irish artists in many of its rooms. So you get off the bus with its jazzy Irish music and stand, shell-shocked, on the pavement, with no space left in your brain.

We are escorted round Dublin Castle by the perfect guide one would expect here. Educated Irish brogue, dark suit and tie, flashing smile and natural crack. He waits patiently while tourists lag behind and doesn't raise his voice. The tourists do it for him. We stand in the cobblestone courtyard where Republicans were once hanged, are taken round the bedrooms where Queen Victoria once slept but more recently Hilary Clinton. 'What about Bill?' someone whispers behind me. The vast Saint Patrick's Hall has a painted ceiling and a frieze bearing the arms of the Knights of Saint Patrick. (He's here too.) Former English viceroys look down their noses in amazement at the motley crowd below, and at today's Irish presidents being inaugurated on their patch — women at that. I felt proud of Mary Robinson and Mary MacAleese, these women of Ireland. The oval Wedgewood Room so typically English and delicate in its shades of blue and white that one has difficulty in imagining today's jeans sitting on the Chinese-style Chippendale chairs. We pass casually through the Throne Room, where English kings and queens received their subjects on a massive throne last used by George V in 1911. Only the Norman Record Tower survives as a reminder that this castle was built around 1250 as part of Dublin's defence system. We go down under the tower and see an underground stream and the rock face being excavated. 'All sorts of artefacts are still being found,' the guide says. Suddenly the darkness takes on a sinister feel and I need to get out. The set of *Michael Collins* has become too real.

What a privilege to have two Trinity College lecturers as our hosts in Dublin. Professor James Lunney of the Physics Department, and his wife, Dr Linde Lunney, a historian and part of a new EU research programme on famous people of Ireland.

There was nothing unusual about the Lunneys' home in the pleasant suburb of Rathfarnam. Two-storeyed and comfortable like so many in the street, it had grown out of a need to live out of Dublin city but near enough to commute to Trinity College, an hour away. What was remarkable, however, was the ditch which ran along the back of the garden.

'James is digging up pieces of pottery there,' Linde explained. 'It's part of the Pale. You'll have heard of that already?'

'Yes, we found a girl in the Tourist Office in Trim which is housed on the edge of the Pale. You should do a research project on your findings, Linde. It's amazing.'

'I've written articles on it already, and asked the people of Rathfarnam to report anything of interest they dig up in their gardens, but we need more money to really excavate the ditch and document it. I'm sure we'll get it done one day. Isn't it fun to be living on a historic site?'

We bombarded the Lunneys with questions when we met in the evenings. How patient they were, and how sensible. No prejudice or bigotry, no negative one-sided tongue-bashing about religion or politics, and yet here were two people from different disciplines, one a Catholic and one a Protestant. Their three children were being brought up to understand and be accepted in both churches and were being tutored by nuns and ministers.

'How did you manage to make this unusual arrangement?' I asked Linde.

'I looked at the position without prejudice or emotion, just as I would look at a subject in my work. I wanted the children to be at home in James' family at Fermanagh and with mine in Portstewart. To be able to take Communion in both. I have no great feeling myself for one church or the other, and neither has James. In fact, most Sundays we all go to the Presbyterian church nearby because we like the in-depth sermons the minister gives. James especially enjoys going there. The nun who taught the children is a friend of mine too. We have a lot in common.'

If this marriage could accommodate such an arrangement, there was certainly hope for the peace agreement and the future of a united Ireland. But would it have to be just the intelligentsia who could bridge the gap? People like the Lunneys and ex-President Mary Robinson? Surely more would follow. The *Irish News* said it all:

> Opponents of the peace deal are living in the past. They want to form a ring of wagons and keep the enemy outside. But the Agreement doesn't threaten the Protestant culture, religion or way of life. As a regular visitor to the Irish Republic I know it has changed. It is no longer a theocratic state.
>
> It makes sense for these islands to be integrated more closely. We are all part of Europe. Both sides of the Border must get to know each other better.
>
> Fintan O'Toole

'What kind of people are you researching?' I asked Linde.

'A cross section really. The founder of the Quakers, Henry Bewley, for instance, and John Gifford Bellett, a founder of the Plymouth Brethren. I know you have connections with the Brethren, so you'll be interested to know that John Bellett lived about a mile from here. A great man who became a barrister in 1821. I'll send you the paper I wrote on him. He was regarded as the best writer among the Brethren and his views greatly influenced their theology.'

'I see in the front of my Great Uncle John's Bible that he was "born again" in 54 Upper Sacville Street, Dublin, in 1868, so he must have been influenced by John Bellett.'

'That's possible. Can I help you with your family research?' Linde asked. 'Show me any papers you have with you.' She cast an experienced eye over the 'Family Tree and Notes by RHB'.

'Funnily enough I've been researching someone around the Moss Side area myself, so some of the names could be familiar. Hmm . . . Kings of Munster, Craig-in-a-she-oak, and they came originally from Rangally or Rankeilly in Scotland. And what's this about Field Marshall Sir George White? Do you mean the White's of Whitehall in Broughshane?'

'Yes, it's those Whites. And I believe they still have land in the Glens of Antrim. I plan to go and look for them next time I go north.'

'I'll do a bit of research myself at Trinity and let you know in a week or so. Where will you be?'

Linde Lunney's findings were astounding. With an ear attuned to Irish place names and a meticulous knowledge of the townlands round the Carvacloughan area, she traced the family back to the eighteenth century. Had we not met Linde in Dublin the mystery would never have been solved. I could hardly wait to get back to the North again and find these new places. What would Ivan say? Did he know already? And the graves in Ballintoy — they must be there. As for Sir George White, I'd have to comb the glens myself.

One fine day we lunched with James Lunney and the lecturers at Trinity College. What an experience to be eating with Dublin's academia in their olde-worlde surroundings. An ordinary meal of duck and vegetables for them, no doubt, but for us a peep into a historic past and an atmosphere perpetuated since the early eighteenth century. No paper cups and watery coffee here, no trash cans overflowing with old chips. That was downstairs in the student canteen. We were elevated to the lecturers' private lounge for after-lunch drinks, with a butler straight out of Dickens. In dress suit and cummerbund, with an air of pompous professionalism, he strutted his stuff, white napkin over his arm.

'Would you like your coffee refilled, madam?' he asked, with a flourish of the filter jug.

Of course I did. And I could have an *Irish Times* if I wished, or help myself to sherry or Scotch on the sideboard. Of course I didn't. A small Kiwi almost engulfed in a big leather armchair would much rather talk to Professor James Lunney or watch the passing parade in the rarified atmosphere of Trinity College.

'I don't need to go to church,' one researcher told me. 'One hour in the Long Room of the Old Library at Trinity is better than any church.'

I saw her point. Completed in 1732, the sacredness of its ancient books can be felt. It is spine-tingling to look up at the galleries packed with thousands of illuminated manuscripts and writings by ancient scholars and find yourself one solitary mortal gasping for a crumb of that vast repository of knowledge. God is surely here, in the minds of his scholars.

It was Exhibition Week at Trinity, a superb display of the history and construction of the original *Book of Kells*, in which every facet of the four famous volumes is featured in detail from start to finish. Parchment, dyes, Celtic motifs, quills. The exquisite workmanship from the mid eighth century, although magnified, is still perfect in line and circle. The idea of monks with limited lighting and tools producing such artwork is mind-boggling, and as people move quietly from one exhibit to another, there is a hushed reverence and an atmosphere of awe.

But you must escape from Dublin! Forcibly take yourself out of the wonders and treasures that the amazing city offers. You could dance to Irish music on the bar tables all night if you wished, and drink Guinness till you dropped to the floor. Some have to escape from that, too. To take in everything is to suffer from physical and mental exhaustion. Dublin has too many faces — too much history, too much emotion. No wonder H.V. Morton literally disappeared overnight and found himself in the Wicklow Hills, without even telling his friends. The pressure on a writer's imagination is overwhelming, and one must leave James Joyce's statue to face the streets alone.

Drowsy commuters lie about in the train on the way home. Students, businessmen, nuns — some munching left-over sandwiches or reading the papers. We pass Maynooth, its spire just visible in the distance, and I look down at the notes a Catholic professor at Trinity has given me.

'One of the finest Catholic seminaries, it now has full university status and lay and clerical students study here side by side. The seat of learning for thousands of priests, its rooms now empty, waiting for younger men to fill them. Which they won't until priests are allowed to marry,' he concluded, 'and I'm not interested in the church till they do.'

The train rumbles on towards Sligo. It seems we have been in Dublin for years. The cheap Irish breakfast is still being served, begorrah, and it's 10.00 p.m.

8. new money and old

'IF YOU ARE BRIGHT, WITTY and rich you will enjoy Kilbeggan Races, and if you're not, you will enjoy it just the same. Voted race course of the year in 1990 and pipped at the post by Listowel in 1995, Kilbeggan is a thoroughbred racing venue.'

Down the road a museum of whiskey distilling adds extra glamour to Kilbeggan, and even more money. One floats on the other.

Durrow Abbey is a virtual outsider in this racey area. No money-spinner or up-market heritage site, just a once great abbey founded in 553 by Saint Columba (Colmcille) and original home of the famed seventh-century *Book of Durrow*. Some of the pages are the first ever to have been completely covered with pure ornament, the rest exquisitely illuminated passages of the gospels. It is remarkable the book has survived at all through the plundering and burning of the Dark Ages, not to mention a local farmer who poured water on it to cure his cattle. Thankfully, it is now in the Trinity College library.

'Where is this abbey?' we asked in a small village nearby.

The man scratched his head. 'Somewhere up there about a mile, on the left, I think. Someone lives there now — it's sort of private — but you can try. It's got a gate and a long avenue, I remember. Look for a notice.'

Barely legible, an old insignificant notice printed on one side points to two large iron gates with 'Private' written in large letters. Just inside, the keeper's cottage is run-down and empty. Nothing spells welcome or even *caed mile failte*. But the iron gates yield to a push.

Assuming we were permitted to view Durrow Abbey, with its old well and high crosses, we strode along the shady avenue, bold and determined. After all, it was listed as a must. A huge kennel bearing the legend 'Guard Dogs' looked ugly under the spreading oaks, but it was empty and looked disused. How quiet and charming the old house appeared in the morning sun, covered in ivy with a touch of autumn red, until, a few yards from the entrance, the occupants of the kennel — three of them —appeared out of nowhere, barking madly, eyes blazing, fierce teeth bared. We stood quietly, assuming an outward nonchalance we did not feel. A tubby man in working clothes stood at the door of the imposing mansion. At first amazed at our cheek and temerity, then suitably embarrassed, he gave a curt order to the dogs and they slunk back with a dirty look in our direction.

'The sign,' we mumbled. 'Durrow Abbey?'

'Himself is in Dublin on business, but three pounds would be fine to see around,' he said reluctantly. 'I am helping to wire up the house. Sign the book.'

'Himself' was restoring the Tudor Gothic-style house into a lavish modern home, no money spared. A five-star hotel in the making, everything of the best; and 'Herself' had an open circular wardrobe taking up a whole room, its bright chrome chock full of gowns from the best houses in Europe. A peep of the stables was all we could see of the old abbey, but 'You can look at the old parish church and gravestones down by the gate. Don't fall into the holes near the gravestones, God help and preserve us. You could injure yourself.'

'The holy well?'

'Too dangerous now. The parish comes to see it on Saint Colmcille's Day — June 6 — but that's all in actual fact.'

The parish had been there in 1997 for the 1400th anniversary of Saint Colmcille's canonisation, we read. The only indication of care.

Awaiting the hunt and equestrian events, Himself's magnificent dappled horse and other beautiful thoroughbreds grazed nearby in the lush pasture, while acres of rolling green fields and hedges lent a wide vista to the whole estate. The simple grandeur of the old house had given way to the new wealth of an Irish landowner.

In 1186 the Anglo-Norman lord of Meath, Hugh de Lacy, was killed here by a workman. De Lacy was overseeing the final demoltion of Durrow Abbey, and the workman, outraged at such profanity, struck his head off with an axe.

In 1839 the Earl of Norbury was murdered here — believed shot by a tenant.

Darrow Abbey Fact Sheet

The history of Durrow Abbey warrants guard dogs.

Partially hidden in a spooky grove of great oak and beech trees, the now weathered and indistinct ninth-century high cross is carved with scenes from the Bible, including the sacrifice of Isaac, the Crucifixion and soldiers guarding the tomb of Christ. Neglected tombstones lie about in careless disarray, and across the field the old well sinks silently into the ground. A derelict little church is the last one sees of Durrow Abbey's glory, its stained-glass windows covered in cobwebs and vines.

The longest clothes-line ever links fifty tinkers' caravans on the roadside outside Birr, tattered garments spread in disorderly fashion from one to the other. My Aunt Lizzie in Greenmeadows would have been shaken to see such a brazen display of undies for passers-by to view. Unbelievable. Yet this travelling community, prohibited from parking in private fields, is allowed to live literally on the road, ekeing out a precarious living selling mats and jewellery, and jumping the odd fence or two after dark. To boost their meagre earnings, the tinkers will disclose vital information, at a price, on a variety of subjects, from IRA whereabouts to the latest Garda swoop. And all the while little children play outside the caravans quite happily, seemingly oblivious to the traffic on their doorstep. It would be bad luck to remove the tinkers, people said. They are part of Ireland's heritage, displaced persons from long ago.

What a surprise to turn the corner and find a superior town retaining its genteel upbringing. We were in old-money country now.

Birr Castle and township is real old ascendancy, a legacy of the Georgian past. Mr Parsons, an Englishman from Norfolk, was granted 1000 acres of land in 1620 and set about the task of making himself a town and a castle. But this family were not impractical, white-fingered dilettantes who rode horses and sat around partying; they were hard-working aristocrats who knew how to construct buildings and telescopes and oversee town planning.

One of their finest creations is the Great Telescope, the largest in the world for over 70 years and weighing about seven tons, for which a new 75-inch lens is being made costing £200,000. No wonder the Parsons were ennobled to the Earls of Rosse. Their descendants still live in the castle, surrounded by a superb ornamental garden, and although the public is not permitted to disturb the Earls, they can wander on foot in the garden and view the telescope, or trot round in a horse carriage — at a price. With no old ascendancy in New Zealand, nor aristocrats who gift estates, the concept is fascinating. We need wealthy people to donate large pieces of land for parks and recreation in our part of the world and stop the money-hungry developers filling up our beautiful hills and beaches with monstrosities for the rich and famous.

Our made-over Irish driver, Declan Cleave, hurried his greasy Chinese lunch to don top hat and tails and assume the role of English raconteur. We are ladies and gents for an hour, trotting past flowering magnolias, cherry and crab apple trees, hornbeam alleys and 11-metre-high box hedges, claimed to be the tallest in the world. Our companions are French, with little English. We are New Zealanders with little French.

'Nouvelle Zealandia,' we try. Madame shrugs and shakes her head.

Monsieur thinks very hard, and then mumbles, 'Blacks.'

'All Blacks?' we suggest.

He nods vigorously, peering at us curiously. It is obvious neither of them had ever met New Zealanders before, and both were fascinated we spoke English. The French, as usual, gave a substantial tip to Declan. We didn't.

'Nice couple, those French,' Declan says pointedly. 'Good crack. When you think of the Germans and Italians who come here — well, I cut their tour short. Americans are good crack.'

I wondered about the 'good crack'. The French hadn't said one word. Obviously driver Declan had his own way of translating 'crack' as 'tip' when it suited him.

After such pomp and circumstance, it seemed ironical to find just a lean-to for a ticket office at the gates, with homemade jams and touristy nick-nacks for sale. It could be 'Birr Castle and Demense' on a tea towel is a load of fun, and pure olde-English marmalade is a way of making ends meet, but such sentiments didn't gel somehow with mine host at the gates, who assumed the role of the Earl Rosse himself as he opened and closed with an affected flair. He was delighted my da came from the North and I was searching for more Magills round the place. He noted our accents and commenced a eulogy on the English and the 'good old days'. Looking over his shoulder for possible eavesdroppers, he was about to launch into a put-down of the South, and politics, but he had chosen the wrong people, and his attempts at comradeship fell on deaf ears. We pronounced him a Pooh Bah — to ourselves — and bid him goodbye.

Trixie came to a dead halt. A thatched cottage of straw (barley and oats) was definitely not to be passed. Neither were the two characters lounging in front, and their huge pig. By way of introduction we asked directions to Garry Castle — a good excuse to hang over their wall for a chat.

Tall and weathered, sporty jerkins and jarvey caps denoting their farming profession, they watched every movement of their prize pig whilst yarning to us. Mesmerised by its immensity, the four of us followed the big pink monster as it snorted round the yard.

'Yarra, New Zealand. You got sheep over therrrr?'

'Millions of them.'

'Paisley's a planter. He's no Irishman. Some say he's Scotch. Anywa' he likes to forget the likes of him put us down. Didn't have a say we didn't.'

'You can't talk to men like that,' the other farmer said. 'Don't want to understand. We're fine here.' Waving his arm over the fields. 'That neighbour's a Protestant, that's a Catholic, and there's another Protestant at the back. We don't think about it, just normal with each other. We go there, they come here. It's those in the North!'

'Hard heads,' said David. 'Your straw thatch is great.'

'Them reeds is too expensive. Everything has to come off if you have to do it over again. Have to sow a field of oats mysel' and harvest it with the old machines. High as myself, them bunches. See them there gattin' the sun?'

'What do you call that bundle?'

'Stooks. Ten sheaves made one stook. Then stand them up and lean 'em on each other. Those new machines munch the straw up too fine.'

The big pig moved slowly into his own house, suddenly bored with our conversation and resenting the usual loving attention being diverted to the visitors. One last snort in our direction said it all. The party broke up.

Some like to give the impression these countrymen of Ireland are simpletons. I'd say they were just as shrewd and far more love-able than any city slickers, despite the fact that Garry Castle was in the opposite direction to where they said it was.

– The *Irish Times*: CLINTON, BLAIR CALL FOR NORTH TO SEIZE CHANGE FOR PEACE

– 'If I were an Irish Protestant, which I am, living in Northern Ireland instead of the US, I would be thinking about my daughter's future and her children's future,' said Clinton.

– Boston: US college pays tribute to Ahern's 'inspirational efforts for peace'.

– U2's free concert: Bono raises the hands of Hume and Trimble before taking the stage at a YES campaign rally at Belfast's Waterfront Hall. Downpatrick band ASH's 'Don't let me down' was Bono's opening number.

– TV: Paisley and Trimble in impossible debate. Paisley yelling and paper bashing.

– The *Irish Times*: The Archbishop of Armagh, Dr Robert Eames, says: 'The churches, as part of the division, must also be part of the cure. They had to look into their own hearts and root out any prejudices there which would be an extremely exhausting process.'

– The *Irish Times*: 'Scare-mongering on the pact is fed by some who should know better. Sinn Fein has signed up to total and exclusively democratic means of resolving differences on

political issues and opposition to any use or threat of force —
for any political reasons. Gerry Adams wants an end to violence.'

President Bill Clinton told Frank McCourt of *Angelas Ashes* he'd
rather see the new Limerick than read about the old. He was right.
Fifty years is a long time, Frank — things have changed. Yet there
is still a heaviness round the back roads of Limerick. It is poor and
depressing, drab and grey. The detour sends you round and round
and round again where no one would choose to drive if road construction hadn't clogged up the normal route. Two-storeyed, sunless
dwellings squashed together on both sides give that Coronation
Street look. Which one would have been Frank's? you wonder, peering up and down. They say his old patch is gone now, and the new
movie has to mock up his slummy alleyway. Some say it didn't
exist at all, but Frank should know where he lived. I can see the
old church across the road, its windows peering inquisitively into
Catholic bedrooms, and at the crossroads a life-size statue of Our
Lady in blue and white plaster.

Solemn-faced pregnant mothers with pinched faces, prams and
pushchairs, and desperate men, ruddy-faced and angry, stomp these
streets. Doesn't look as if they have the money to enjoy this Bank
Holiday. Little children have runny noses and some are crying
loudly on the footpath. God help them — this must be the slum
part of Limerick. There *are* poor people in Ireland after all. The
EU can't possibly hand out enough for everyone.

At last the traffic eases and we join the flow of cars anxious to
leave all that misery behind and head for Killarney. There are gardens now, bright flowers, fresh air and sunshine. A very old lady
bent in half lovingly tends a planter by the roadside, and the little
River Brosna flows silently to Lough Gur. It is heaven. But there is
more, if that is possible, for round the next corner the 'prettiest
village in Ireland' appears out of nowhere, sitting in a bend of the
River Maigue, its main street lined with thatched houses, crumbling ruins and a Gothic-style mansion. Well-dressed women and
smart trendy men sit outside up-market cafés chatting amiably in
the sun. Is this a film set? We shuffle our maps. The coffee smells
divine. We are at Adare! How could anything be so different from

those back roads of Limerick? Poor and rich. Down-at-heel there, ever so smart here. Golf and fishing and music festivals each year drawing people from all over the world — singers and orchestras and dancers. Ah-h-h! There's magic here on the country roads, and plenty at Adare Manor, where Bill Clinton would soon be playing golf while Hilary looked out lazily on the spacious green lawns, thinking.

9. Dear Old Killarney

KILLARNEY'S LAKES *ARE* BLUE, but there's more than romance in this tourist town, more than sentimental crooning. There's money to be made. Kerry airport, 'Gateway to the West', is only 20 minutes out from the rush and bustle of crowded streets. As the summer holiday season kicks in, private houses turn B & B almost overnight, lining the approaches in their hundreds, while nearer the city big hotels and even bigger churches hit the skyline. Narrow main streets made for horse traffic seeth with a miniature United Nations. Well-heeled overseas tourists rub shoulders with backpackers, knocking into each other, scrabbling for food and bargains. Every second building is a restaurant displaying menus at overpriced rates. Crowds line up outside to peer intently at the small writing behind the glass, before moving on to the next. Then they're back, peering again. B & B people have to eat *somewhere*. That's the trick of B & Bs. Hand-knitted sweaters from the Island of Aran are piled high inside the small shops and outside on trestles. Hundreds of them.

There is a diversion from the people rat race in Killarney town. Horse-drawn hackney carriages and smaller jaunting cars for two stand at the ready, waiting to drive tourists round the sights — Muckross House, Ross Castle and the rest. A legacy from the ascendancy again — gifting their magnificent mansions and spacious grounds to the public. Without these parks and gardens, and the adorable horses, Killarney would lose half its glamour.

A horse's natural functions must be performed on the spot — loudly, and with characteristic fervour. A sudden rush of pee pours down the gutters, and small birds arrive to peck for undigested materials in the other stuff before it's even cold. Plenty of that, too. It is a sideshow without cost, in the middle of town, as are the horse guides or jarveys, albeit in a different way. The jarvey brogue in Killarney is almost comic in its broadness. Could they be having us on, you wonder? This is the brogue they give Irishmen in funny movies. A take-off of the inimitable Paddy of all those Irish jokes. But it is for real, and the earthy twist of phrase brings reluctant smiles to the satiated touristy faces of passers-by. The jarveys are experts at handling people and horses, touting for fares or flicking their whips as they canter down the highways and byways. Jarveys have the gift of storytelling, passed down through the generations, and the clip-clop, clip-clop of their horses makes fine music in Killarney. May they never be silenced, or replaced by motor noise.

Nightlife starts at eleven.

'Will there be Irish music with dinner tonight?' we ask hopefully.

'Depends how they feel, the musicians. Could be here or over the road. Their choice. Can't really say. Anywa', if they come they don't start playing till around half eleven. They might eat first, depends. Free meals wherever they go.'

There are times when you have to give things a miss.

About 10 kilometres out of Killarney, we are lucky to land a primitive self-catering cottage at this time of the year. (The neighbours tell us this.) It is really a trampers' patch. There is a bath, and electricity is 5p per unit. No clothes-line or pegs, so trampers must wash their clothes in the bath and hang them on trees, or rush into town to the laundrette. The bed lacks springs, and our view is of framed faded teddy bears on the walls. Thank God for a peat fire.

The German population spreads along the Killorglin Road around Aghadoe Hill, their fine homes facing the majestic outline of Macgillycuddy's Reeks, Ireland's highest mountains. They have a panoramic view from sunrise to sunset, watching the mist and cloud dance in and out the tops, changing colours from blush pinks to mauves and purples.

There are German industries here, acres of workshops turning out what Germans do best — machinery. Liebeg safety bolts, Liebeg this, Liebeg that. The name Liebheri stands out in gold on the huge gates, and Germans pour in to work — then out to play — in beautiful County Kerry. The huge international hotels are theirs, and a mass of B & Bs.

I knocked on the door of a German hair salon one Saturday morning.

'I am closed, but I will take you. You are not American, I see,' the plump *frau* said firmly.

'You live here?' I asked.

'We came for three years here to work in the industry. That was thirty years ago and look at us now. Nothing then but small cottages — nothing! Now hundreds of Germans come for holidays — they're mad on it. I let their houses when they aren't here. Whatever you want — B & B, full board, anything. I can cook dinner if they want, or we have the big Hotel Europe over there — that's German. Biggest in Killarney. A daughter of Liebheri is buying Dunloe Castle near the Gap. You know it?'

'Yes. And how long does it take to come from Germany?'

'Two hours in the plane to Dublin, then forty minutes to Kerry airport. We go to Germany when we like it — we have an apartment there too. Belongs to us.'

'Aren't you going to blow-wave my hair?'

'My girls do that but they are not 'ere. Sick. My husband wanted me to make this zalon. He zed it will make money. I told him I had no training, but he zed get girls in from Germany. I just do the phone and wash. Is it not good? Vait. Now I vill spray it.'

It was the worst hair-do I've ever had in my life. I came out looking a mess and feeling worse, but I'd got the gossip.

'You pay five punts, yes?'

'Do you mind all these Germans taking over round here?' I asked our Irish neighbours.

'It's no problem. They can do what they like. Someone has to do all this industry. We might not get around to it ourselves. Anywa', they bought the land and there's more jobs for us. We live here and they live here. We don't have to mix.'

'Bought it cheap thirty years ago, eh?'

'Yarra, but we didn't want it then. No good for farming it isn't.'

'And those Americans down the road in those mansions. They've got the best views in the world.'

'Aye, they're Americans, but they're Irish-Americans. Their roots are here and they're for retiring on Irish soil so they are.'

'Do you mind?'

'Why should we? We can build our own mansions if we want to. There's a few of oors at the crossroads if you care to look as you pass. They're Irish.' He laughed at my concern.

'We're in the Common Market now, remember that.'

Our neighbours have moved out of their house and into the garage.

'We do this for three months of every year,' Anne said. 'You can have our house for a week before the tourists start. Costs the same as the one you're in, but it's better.' It sure was — and immaculate.

'Do you mind moving out to the garage?'

"Course not. Everyone does it in Killarney. Make-money time.'

Anything was better than the boring teddy bears, but now we were actually living in someone else's house, with their choice of décor, not a near-empty self-catering outfit.

Holy pictures and statues crowd the room. It's chock-a-block. Every nook and cranny has a little nick-nack — a saint here, a cross there, a special plastic flower peeping over the Virgin's shoulder. A huge Sacred Heart of Jesus looks down sadly from the wall straight at the enormous TV with Sky. (We've never had Sky in Ireland.) The fridge is covered in prayers. Anne is very devout, I can see that. Perhaps I could learn something from these new kind of prayers. But I'm hundreds of years behind or ahead — I don't know which. It's a different language. I'm asked to touch my scapular and receive a partial indulgence. Next time I go to the garage and use the phone I'll ask Anne.

They're huddled in the tiny garage, set up as a miniature of the main house. More statues, more pictures, another Sacred Heart looking at the TV, and a dozen or so rosaries hanging on a hook at the door. Anne is saying her rosary as I arrive and Michael is smoking his pipe while watching *The Simpsons*. In an hour or so they will both rush out to work in a hotel in Killarney. It's not a problem. I haven't disturbed them. Saint Philomena is Anne's favourite saint, she tells me. Patroness of the Living Rosary. Anne loves her to death. A beautiful looking young girl looks out from a photo. I wonder how old she is and ask. She looks about sixteen. Anne's pencilled eyebrows go even higher.

'But she's hundreds of years old. Philomena isn't living *now*.' Obviously I'm out of my depth.

'You've got almost as many holy things here as in the bungalow,' I observe jokingly. 'I've never seen so many.'

Michael looks heavenwards. 'You won't either, just, it's desperate,' he mumbles sincerely, still staring at the TV. One has the impression that the religious side of life is a woman's domain here, her home a mini altar. Perhaps he'll go out for a 'wee strolley' later in the evening and talk men's talk at the pub.

'What's a scapular, Anne?' I ask. As a nurse, I wondered if it was related to the scapula, the shoulder blade. 'I've been reading your prayers on the fridge.'

'I'll get a scapular for you and David from the monks' shop tomorrow, and Michael will bring it in. Won't you Michael?'

Bring us a scapular each? How?

'Aye, I'll do it.' Still watching *The Simpsons*. Then the phone rang, and Michael stiffened.

'That's that girl Emily phoning our son Mike again. Only sixteen years old she is and phones him three times a day. Talking about nothing at all, just nothing.'

'Why doesn't Mike ring her for a change?' I ask casually.

'Once in a six month would he do that.'

'Don't you like her?'

'She's got no job and no dowry to bring with her either.'

'Do you still expect a girl to bring something with her?'

'Well — a bit of land maybe, or a house or something.'

'Why don't you do something about their relationship, then, Michael? Sort of say something to Mike?'

He heaved his large body into an upright position and focused his eyes on me — angrily.

'Say something to Mike? Look here — he might end up not marrying anyone at all and I'd get the blame for it all the rest of m'days. See that man across the road from ye with those six cows? Hasn't got a woman and now he's too shy to ask. And that one building the big house just a few doors down. Seen him? No woman either. That could happen to young Mike if I say anything. Desperate it is. And they won't go to Mass, these kids. The priests put them off, fiddling around with young boys. Disgrace for the Church and for us all. Put that in your book will ye, from me! I'm for wishing Bishop Casey back in these parts all the same. I like that man, despite all the fuss, but the others . . . !'

After throwing that one into 'the book' he launched into another.

'And put this too. The government doesn't help marriage. In our day you got married and then had your babies. Today they're giving these single girls the rent for their houses and seventy-five punts as well for their babies. No need to get married is there? They should do what they do in America and give nothing for the second. The first could be a little mistake, but the second? Well — and then the boyfriend moves in and no one can check on them now can they?'

Michael settled back into the depths of the sofa, exhausted, and

Anne nodded her approval. Next day Michael brought in two little packets of leather scapulars, already blest by the monks. We could put them round our necks if we liked when we prayed, or the accompanying small metal medallion could be a substitute and worn all the time.

'The people in the garage next to you are Carmelites,' another neighbour told me. 'Very religious Catholics, so they are. Good people.'

They were too.

Obviously it was a strange request to ask the *Borde Failte*, or Tourist Board, about churches. The sight of the majestic 1855 limestone Catholic church should have been clear enough, or the eighteenth-century Church of Ireland right in the city near where the horses did their thing. The girl in the information centre looked at me with impatience. I was pathetic.

'Don't know anything but the Catholic one,' she mumbled and stomped off. The boy at the next counter scratched his head. 'At the end of the horses there's another one — Methodist or somethingorother.'

We tried our luck at the 'somethingorother'. Stepping over a gutter full of amber liquid we met with a brave little congregation meeting on the day of Pentecost, the plain brick interior in stark contrast to the ornate edifices elsewhere in the city. Visitors spoke up from the Netherlands, the United States and England, together with locals from Killarney and Cork. When our turn came people gasped audibly at the foreign-sounding name of our home country. 'New Zealand? Well, we've never had anyone from as far away as that in here!'

Another visitor from behind said, 'Magherafelt.' I'd heard that name before. Wasn't it near Carvacloughan, in the Ballycastle area? I wished I could turn round, but my mother, Jess, had always taught us that it was rude to turn round in church, so for her sake I would wait. Strange how little things like that cling to one's persona. 'If the Queen can sit for hours without showing any boredom, so can you,' she had insisted.

'You're from Magherafelt?' I asked the man later over a pink marshmallow biscuit. 'Um, well — my father came from around that area and I'm looking for family. It's near Moss-side.' I could have been looking straight into my da's eyes right then. It was weird and squeamy.

'Aye, I know it. They say "Mosside" as quick as lightning there, but don't you try it. They don't expect it from visitors, and they might think you're being smart or something. Not that you would, but people are touchy in the North.'

'And what about Ballintoy? The old folk are meant to be buried there. I'm looking for them.'

His friendly wife joined in. 'Ballintoy's a pretty little place by the sea. We drive there on Sundays and have tea at a lovely café. Scones with cream.'

Scones with cream, and graveyards. A strange mix. But people still had to enjoy themselves and not everyone was digging round for roots in another country. Not everyone realised I had taken eight years to get this far.

'We're staying in Portadown over the marching season to have a first-hand look. They'd never believe me in New Zealand unless I could say, "Look, I was in Garvaghy Road and saw them beating those Lambeg drums myself." '

What was I doing? Should I be saying things like this in Killarney, or anywhere else? The two from Magherafelt looked over their shoulders and lowered their voices to a whisper.

'We were both in the Royal Ulster Constabulary. My wife thirty years. And there's two sides to this. It had to come, this Agreement. Some Unionists had two votes — one as landowners, and the normal one. Two votes, one man — excluding those who didn't own land — kept the Catholic votes down. That's not right! And the way the Unionists gerrymandered the electoral boundaries for the same reason. We're scundered with the whole thing — both sides have to change. In our day the RUC wouldn't have Catholics on their staff, now they have to. A token gesture really, but at least the Catholics have a voice and the RUC can't be accused of racism.'

They did Paisley over in good style.

'We would all be damned to Hell in his eyes — all of us in this wee church. Women in jeans, lipstick, perms, hats — *nevah!*'

'We're just *scundered* with it all,' they repeated, 'and we've got such nice Catholic friends.'

'Should we be scundered too?' I asked mischievously.

'Aye, ye should. It means fed up!'

High above us, stained-glass windows pictured Scotland's thistle, England's rose, Ireland's shamrock, and was it a leek from Wales? Bibles and hymn books a donation from the States. All countries had participated in building this simple brick church, and somehow, after intermittent and irregular times of service, they were now able to keep the doors open every Sunday. John and Charles Wesley would be smiling down as we sang their grand old hymns and the minister read from their journals. They had preached in this part of Ireland often enough. We felt privileged to be part of the service, and the Irish minister gave a grrand message, so he did. 'Methodists in the States would always see them right.'

10. peninsular people

'ARE THERE ANY LEPRECHAUNS in Killarney?' I asked a jarvey.

'Leprechauns?' he said, taking a good look at me. 'Why this is the most terrible place in all Ireland for them! You could not stir a foot in the old days for them.'

Washed by the Carribean warmth of the Gulf Stream, three mountainous fingers jut out into the Atlantic Ocean — the peninsulas of the west coast of Ireland. Semi-tropical, fascinating, different.

'Wait for the weather before you go,' the locals advised us.

Suddenly, unexpectedly, the sun appeared out of grey cloud, and it was time to move. It could be another week or two before it happened again.

'The worst summer for sixty years,' they said. 'Yous should have been here last year.'

'Have you done the Kerry Ring?' they said flippantly. 'Get there before the big buses start pounding the narrow lanes. It's one-way traffic.'

Despite the orchestrated tourism, this Ring of Kerry has a magic beauty of its own which is indestructable. Nature has made in this place a paradise of seascapes, cliffs, mountains, lakes, adorable villages and rhododendrons rioting over stone buildings and hedges. There are memories of monks and political leaders from the past, and the bizarre characters of today. No place is complete without people, especially if they are Irish.

It was at the village of Sneem, with its gaily painted cottages and rocky river, that I fell into a coma. A prize-winning sculpture

111

by James Scanlon stands at the crossroads, called 'The Way the Fairies Went'. I looked for a notice left, or perhaps right, but there was neither. Which way to go? The sound of a river brought me to a small stone bridge, beneath which the boulders were whipping the water to a creamy foam as it thundered its way to the sea. A dark, swarthy looking man and his wife sauntered up beside me.

'So romantisch?' he mumbled to himself in German, his eyes glazed. 'Do you know where . . . ? I am Austrian. This place is . . . ' And he gazed heavenwards.

'I'm from New Zealand,' I replied simply. They both stared, obviously shocked.

'But so far away. Near Australia, I think?'

'Yes, that's right.' They shook their heads in disbelief, clasped my hands firmly and walked on in silence, looking for the fairies.

'This place,' he mumbled again. 'So romantisch.'

I bought an Irish coffee at the pub and sat down outside in the sun next to a Dutch couple. They seemed to be in a coma too, their light beers untouched. Suddenly aware of my presence the woman stretched herself and mumbled, 'It makes me forget everything, this place. I would live here but for my Dutch pensione.' She sighed audibly. 'I come here many times, already four, and always it is the same. The magic. You will understand.'

What on earth was she talking about?

The sun shone warm that day in Sneem, and sitting there drinking coffee outside the pub, I felt like Alice about to go behind the looking glass. Strange. At that moment I'm certain I heard the gay laughter of fairies and leprechauns as they danced on the river rocks nearby. I had taken the right road after all. An hour later the woman and her friend were still there. She looked at me knowingly.

'You see what I mean?'

A small deviation from the Kerry Ring is the island of Valencia at the south-western end of the peninsula. The atmosphere is different here, remote and historic. A perfect harbour for smuggling in the past and a sly wink from the boaties in Port Magee suggested it could still be a perfect place for today's sophisticated smugglers. Once over the bridge a road winds along the cliff edge to an old slate quarry at the top. There is no one about, only a notice pointing to a cave in the cliff face. In the dark grotto sacred figures peer out of the gloom, as if enticing people inside. It's spooky and not the place for an evening picnic. But at the next turn in the road Dingle Peninsula and the Blasket Islands rise out of the blue sparkling sea, with Dingle Bay taking a wide sweep inland. It is breathtaking. We could almost be sailing round the Hauraki Gulf with the Hen and Chickens and Little Barrier Island. Catching the late sea breeze, a small yacht inched its way out of the harbour, and we were engulfed in a wave of homesickness.

It is another group of islands, the Skelligs, further out to the southwest, which really casts a spell. On a clear day they are just two jagged shapes rising out of the Atlantic Ocean, inhospitable, rugged and exposed. Uninhabited today except by birds and seals, from 800 to 1400 the larger of the two was home to a community of monks. We could get there in two-and-a-half hours by boat, but the swell even on a good day is scary, the boatman said, and he doesn't put to sea lightly.

'Then you would have to face a five-hundred-foot climb up an old stairway of thousand-year-old stones if you wanted to see the monastic sites and holy wells.'

We give it a miss, reluctantly. But how could all those monks have lived in stone beehive huts on the cliff edge and scratched an existence out of the barren rocks with so little soil? And then to come and go in small boats when the sea would normally be bashing ferociously against the rocks below. It is all a mystery.

Down below, at the very end of the peninsula, Ballinskelligs Bay stretches in a wide blue circle. It became the new dwelling place of the island monks. All that is left of these brave Christians is a collection of old stone relics, *clochans* and churches on a small beach. What made them leave their island home to return here to the mainland? That is another unanswered question. Little Barrier Island has a few kiwi and other protected birds, but monks in AD 800?

Derrynane House drew us like a magnet. For years we had heard about the 'Great Liberator' Daniel O'Connell, who broke through the yoke of religious persecution to bring emancipation to Ireland. We had read about his amazing contribution to Catholic civil liberty, and now here was the big chance to see his house and memorabilia. Pushing Trixie to the max we drew in at the large National Historic Park. A quick look at the brochure. Whew! The audio-visual should be on in five minutes.

'Last showing four p.m.,' the snappy receptionist said. 'You are one hour late.'

'Look heaar, we've come all the way frarm Connecticut to see this. You should keep it rolling till six,' a huge American woman said loudly.

'We'll come back tomorrow and have another try,' I said, also loudly.

'Why, where do you come from?' the American asked.

'New Zealand.'

She freaked out.

'You're not coming back from theaaar to see Daniel O'Connell are ya?' she asked seriously.

'No, Killarney!'

'Well, there'll be no coming back from Connecticut for us!' And she stomped off with a grimace at the receptionist.

We came back. For naive colonials, Derrynane House gave us a taste of what liberation was all about. You can *feel* it there. Daniel O'Connell's presence lives on in this great house, in the grounds, in the historic harbour and the beach nearby. He was a barrister of great distinction in London, and the china and period furniture echo to the sound of good living, as befitting a man of his class, but looking at his portrait one senses more than a love of material possessions. It is the face of a determined man with a purpose. A feeling he is wanting to say something more to *this* generation.

The audio-visual is dramatic and nerve tingling, filling the tiny theatre with a presence larger than life. People file out silently, absorbed in their private thoughts. They take their mood into the state room, where a carriage is housed, designed in the old style of a Roman chariot. It is not hard to imagine O'Connell driving through Dublin streets after being released from gaol. Drama, danger and excitement fill every square inch of the room, because the man's spirit is there, compelling yet wistful.

A glance at the little chapel nearby, with its sacred writings and private letters, tells all one needs to know about the soul of this deeply spiritual man and that of his wife, Mary.

PEOPLE OF IRELAND
Merrion Square 11th February, 1844

FELLOW COUNTRYMEN,

Once again I return you most heartfelt Thanks for the Peace, Quiet, and good Order you have observed; and I conjure you by the Country we all love and even in the Name of God we all adore, to continue in the same Peace, Quietness and perfect Tranquillity.

I tell you solemnly, that your Enemies and the Enemies of Ireland, are very desirous that there should be a breaking-out of Tumult, Riot, or other Outrage. Be you, therefore, perfectly peacable. Attack nobody. Injure no person. If you respect your Friends — if you wish to gall your Enemies — keep the Peace, and let not one single act of Violence be committed.

You are aware the Jury have found a Verdict against me. But, depend upon it, that I will bring a Writ of Error, and will not acquiesce in the Law as laid down against me until I have the opinion of the Twelve Judges in Ireland, and if necessary, of the House of Lords.

Be you, therefore, perfectly quiet. Do no violence whatsoever. You could not possibly offend or grieve me half so much as by any species of Riot, Assault or Outrage.

It is said that the great Question of Repeal has been injured by this Verdict. Do not believe it. It is not true. On the contrary, the result of this Verdict will be of most material service to the Repeal, if the people continue to be as peaceful as they have hitherto been, and as I am sure, they will continue to be.

Obey my Advice. No Riot. No Tumult. No Blow. No Violence. Keep the Peace for Six months, or at the utmost Twelve Months longer, and you shall have the Parliament in College-green again.

I am, Fellow-Countrymen,
Your affectionate and devoted Servant,
DANIEL O'CONNELL

What would Daniel O'Connell say to these words in the *Irish Times* of 1998?

– SHADOW OF TERROR HAUNTS UNIONISTS It will remain to be seen if voters will embrace the concept of new political partnerships; if this were to happen it would transform the political landscape! Tactical voting could shape assembly elections as much as decommissioning and prisoner releases.
– Gerry Adams, chirpy and upbeat, insists Sinn Fein is ready for government.
– Orangeman calls for dialogue with nationalists on parade routes.
– Nationalists remain sceptical of Trimble's position as he battles for advantage over Paisley.
– Paisley says any more re-routings not on.
– Trimble urges Mowlam to use Bill to decommission.
– Ian Paisley canvasses Ballymena for Thursday's Assembly. DUP stands for 'Don't underestimate Paisley.'
– Not everyone in Ballymena is impressed with Dr Paisley. 'How are you?' he says to a mild-looking middle-aged man. 'None of your business, you big shite,' comes the reply.
– UUP leader [Trimble] hopes for a new accommodation of peaceful co-existence and mutual respect.
– Trimble commits himself to era of change in North.

And All must need
in tolerance combined
A steady purpose to achieve,
extend employment bodily
nature, peace of mind,
When each may grasp his neighbours' hand as friend.

John Hewitt

What is it that makes these Killarney lakes so different from our own in New Zealand we ask ourselves on the way back. Ours are just as beautiful, our mountains equally majestic and unspoiled.

There is no overcrowding in either place and people are free to row a boat or fish as they please. So ...

We are looking with different eyes at a countryside steeped in history and legend. We have our own Maori legends, but here is a certain maturity and innate knowledge; secrets from the misty past are woven into every stone and patch of earth. This land has seen warlike invaders plundering its shores, and maybe a certain melancholy still hovers above the beauty.

Yet on the surface you see no melancholy. The jarveys look you in the face and tell the same stories about the lakes handed down from their fathers and grandfathers all in good faith and marvellous humour.

'The wather's so deep in it, that there's no end to it at all.

'Two young men wint up the mountain to bathe and afther a while one of them noticed that the other was missing.

'"Now what shall I do?" sez he, "for he's surely gone and drowned himself?" So down the mountain he runs, and a rescue party goes up with ropes and they drag the Punch Bowl for a week includin' Sunday. But divil a bottom can they find to it! Three weeks afther comes a postcard from New Zealand from the drowned man sayin' he'd arrived quite safe and sound and would they please send his clothes. That's how deep it is.'

The sound of horses clip-clopping along the road is our wake-up call. They are on their way to the famed Gap of Dunloe, a few miles up the road. At a more civilised hour the big hotels and B & Bs will load their patrons onto buses. Later still, BMWs, Mercedes Benz, and American left-hand drive glamour cars will swish past in style. Jaunting cars and their jarveys will be waiting to escort them through this 'grim and terrible valley, between the great wall of mountains — Macgillycuddy's Reeks on the right and the Purple Mountains on the left.' If there is nothing else to talk about over the Guinness in Killarney's eating houses, there is always a tale about the Gap of Dunloe.

'See that man on the fine horse in the photo there,' said Anne next door. 'That's Michael's grandfather, one of the first to take guests through the Gap. Isn't he a fine figure of a man?' He was too. 'You know the story of Kate Kearney at the cottage up there,

117

and the three jarveys who disappeared too, just near the Black Forest? Some years ago there were bandits running out from behind the rocks offering milk to the tourists. Tell you what, it was a dhrap of poteen in those bottles. They don't do it now.'

'Do you think Trixie could make the trip? we asked.

'That thing?'

'Yes, Trixie.'

'Go very early or very late. You might do it. You know it's a six-mile mountain pass don't you? What's the matter with the horses?'

H'm, well, how could we say it? How do you say money is thin and you're strapped?

'Nothing the matter with the horses. Just thought we'd give Trixie a go.'

Not a wisp of cloud smudged the great mountains as we left for the Gap. Even the horses and jarveys were barely awake. Two sat up suddenly and waved us back in menacing style, but they couldn't stop us, we knew that. Down we went, taking Trixie slowly over the rough path, stopping for breaks when the warning smell of rubber got up our noses. Sick with apprehension and wonderment mixed, we beheld a magnificent grandeur open up before us, and felt dwarfed and insignificant, crushed between two giants. Slowly they parted from their morning embrace and we were free to move carelessly into space, still reeling from the emotional feeling of otherworldly beauty.

Out of nowhere, it seemed, a trim-looking tweedy gent walked his dog along the road. No bandit or highwayman this. The dog stopped on command.

'Give him a wave as you go by,' the tweedy one suggested. 'He's trained to do that on this narrow road.'

'American?'

'Yup, Irish American.'

A few hundred yards on a tweedy lady was taking the air.

'Great day,' we called.

'Uh-ha!' She grinned through her lipstick.

So where on earth did these people come from at the end of a remote mountain pass? Americans didn't usually live in baches or primitive cottages, walking dogs as if on a country road in Florida.

Round the next bend a large, coloured stone house appeared. New, beautiful, spacious, romantic, with a small burn across the road and a fishing dinghy pulled up. And there were more, and more and more, until we reached Moll's Gap. Architects' delights, Irish-American dreams for retirement. And the blue faint heat haze of the far-off Killarney lakes gleaming like the Promised Land.

Good old Trixie!

'Did you ever hear the story about Moll? Well, it's the truth I'm tellin yez . . .'

A year previously, to the very day, my brother, Pat Magill, had visited relatives on the Dingle Peninsula, and they were still 'getting over it' when we turned up.

'Look — within minutes his suitcase was open and the bedroom a complete mess! Papers everywhere, clothes thrown in heaps. He had a *ball*,' Mary Jo Slattery reminisced.

'You could never find him in the morning,' Paddy, her husband, went on. 'Then someone would call round and say he was sitting outside Ashe's pub in the sun reading the paper. At seven in the morning! Waited for the shop to open, they said. God help us!'

'And the time when the tourist buses full of Americans were sitting in Ashe's watching Irish dancing and having a meal, and this voice comes out of nowhere: "I can see you're all crying with emotion at the music and dancing in this old pub. The atmosphere's great, isn't it? Why don't you tell all your mates in the States and in those tourist places to come here twice a week?" '

'My God!' said Brid Dunne. 'It was Pat in the bus using their mike, and he'd just arrived. We hardly knew him!'

What else was coming? It's a wonder he didn't speak in Gaelic, I thought wryly.

Brid continued: '"Tell me where old Mago O'Donnell lived," he wanted to know. "He and my dad kicked up a big stink when Catherine and I got married. It's a wonder you didn't hear the noise over here." He winked. "My old man didn't even come to the wedding."'

'We heard it all right,' said Mary Jo.

'He really wanted to know,' said Brid. '"Anyone around now who knew old Mago?" he asked. "I'd like to have a yarn with them.

They tell me that Ashe's pub was his watering hole.'"

'Brid knew an old pub mate of his,' Mary Jo remembered. 'And they went looking for him.'

'It wasn't long before the two of them were on the stools in there having the longest talk ever. You'd think Pat had been there all his life, and the locals loved him.'

I could almost feel Catherine looking down from Heaven at the scene — her father's birthplace — in the small village of Camp, near Tralee. She would have loved the big, old, two-storeyed stone farmhouse with thick walls, and green pastureland right down to the edge of Tralee Bay. It would have been her sort of place.

'I'd love to walk the Strand one day,' Catherine said to me once long ago. 'My father always talked about the Strand.' But it wasn't to be. Pat and her daughters walked it for her, and I followed a year later. She wasn't far away . . .

Walking the Strand is no big feat of physical strength, it just has a feel about it, like walking the beach in New Zealand where the family has walked for generations. Children's children have played there, and it's *yours*.

'And do they swim here?' I asked.

'What, in the water here? Mary Jo gaped. 'Not in the water, really, just dabbling our feet on the edge. It's really too cold in Tralee.'

'And old Mago took the train each day to work,' Paddy went on, 'to Tralee or Killarney. It used to run the whole length of the peninsula in the old days. The government thought it would help the poorer, isolated areas around Ireland — taking produce out, bringing people to work. Pity it folded. Not everyone has cars or trucks round here yet. Strange, isn't it, though, the famine didn't touch us here. No one suffered like they did in other places. I guess it's the soil — it's different from Connemara or Donegal. Sheltered, good land. And today it's a Gaeltacht peninsula — an area where the Irish language is preserved,' he added proudly.

We had taken the hard, lonely way to Camp. Because it was there.

A steep, narrow unmetalled road climbs up from Aughils on the south coast through the Slieve Mish Mountains to a high pass. It was not really a sensible thing to bring old Trixie so high in a howling gale, with misty rain lashing the windscreen and no other cars around, but the sight of hardy sheep nestling in the heather and the amazing views over Inch seemed to inspire her to keep going.

'Did you come that way?' Mary Jo asked incredulously. 'Well, you'll not go home that way, for sure. So, you've seen some high views of Camp already? Let's have apple pie then!'

James Ashe's old pub is a small, white, plastered-brick one-storey antique, brimming with history and Guinness — a watering hole for the old boys of yesterday and for today's locals and tourists. It looks ageless. Saint Mary's church (1826) next door is a strange bedmate.

'Look, they can drink there all Saturday night, climb the fence and read the lesson at first Mass on Sunday,' someone told us.

'They must be kidding,' I said to Mary Jo.

'I know it happens,' she said wistfully. 'I belong to the Pioneers for Abstinence, so I'm against all that. Paddy does the gardens at the church and the new rock work is his.'

'It's beautiful!'

'He does it instead of going to church. Lots of people have given it up, with the priests misbehaving and all that. I'm the only one that goes in our family.'

Saint Brendan, the navigator, had his origins near Tralee, and just as Saint Patrick follows the traveller to most parts of Ireland, it is Saint Brendan who has the limelight around Dingle. The stories of Saint Patrick's adventures on land are almost as improbable as Saint Brendan's on the sea. What is not improbable is the Ogham alphabet or cypher system, which bears the oldest known inscriptions in the Irish language.

> These stones may well have acted as memorials to those whose names are carved on them. [The alphabet] is made up of anything between one and five notches which are engraved on diagonally across or on either side of a central line providing a total of 20 signs (19 letters of our own alphabet and the diphthong ng). Where comprensible, the text says something like 'son of B' or 'X descendant of Y' and little more.
>
> Peter Harbison

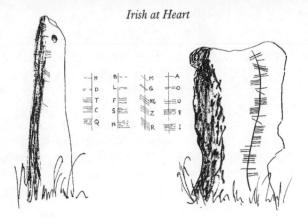

Atlantic rollers pound this most westerly point of Ireland, and it is not at all surprising to round the wild coastal cliffs and come across a grotto with the Virgin praying. Any sailor would need prayers on such a coastline. It is genuinely frightening. The coves echo with waves that hit the black rocks and rise — foaming, perpendicular — at the fleeing gannets. And the long Slieve Mish Mountains, and every valley — miles of them — are, most weirdly, without trees.

The fishing village of Dingle is grim in the rain. Fishing boats had obviously remained anchored in the harbour for days because it was too wild to set sail. Dead seagulls, splayed out like old-fangled ladies' hats below Clogher Head, testify to the furious winds. Shops appear artificial, dusty, some full of old memorabilia, yesterday's newspapers, crucifixes, and curios for the tourists. Brandon Mountain takes you over the dizzying heights of Connor Pass down to Brandon Bay — a hairy, almost one-way road like the old Napier–Taupo road, where drivers are polite, back down, wait, and on you go again. But from the heights of Brandon the whole peninsula is spread out like a topographical map, path and road, cove and headland. Down there is the Gallarus Oratory (ninth century), and out at sea is Great Blasket Island. The views all over the peninsula are dramatic and unlikely, as anyone who has seen *Ryan's Daughter* knows.

On the shores here, Saint Brendan decided to build his boat and with fellow monks sail away in a quest for eternal youth. The

whole voyage is a strange legend of epic and mystical adventures, of whales, demons, spirits and birds — the stuff ancient sailing yarns are made of. At Ardfert further north, a massive cathedral is being restored commemorating the fifteenth century of Saint Brendan's birth.

At Clonfert, near Clonmacnoise, another monastery founded by Brendan in AD 563 still stands, its sandstone doorway decorated with elaborately carved grotesque faces. Inside the abbey, the chancel arch is decorated with relief sculptures of grinning angels and a mermaid holding a mirror.

A busload of Germans followed us into Clonfert, their high-powered cameras focused on the well-rubbed mermaid.

'Amazing, isn't it?' I said to one of them, innocently enough.

His eyes squinted at the lens and he grinned. The mermaid had the largest and most polished bosoms of any sculpture in any church I'd seen so far.

A group of girls came in after us to practise their songs for a wedding.

'The acoustics are marvellous,' they told us. 'This church is still used for services every Sunday.'

An early-medieval church still in use. Remarkable.

We farewelled Dingle Peninsula and our relatives from Camp at the Ross Hotel in Killarney.

'Let's not stay here in the Aghadoe Hotel,' they said on arrival at that establishment. 'It's too clubby, too restricted, too formal. They'll be making us drink Pimms and their own fancy cocktails. Let's go!'

So we followed them to the Ross Hotel.

'This is us,' they all decided, sitting in a cosy corner of the bar. 'We'll get the snack.'

'The snack,' at 9.00 p.m. — toasted sandwiches, dessert, coffees. And to round off, Irish coffees at 10.30 p.m. The crack was extra good that night. The lights dimmed for last orders at 11.00 p.m., and we were saying our farewells around midnight on the still crowded streets of Killarney, where the nightlife was just beginning. Fiddlers were tuning up in the restaurants as people walked in for a meal, music, dancing and crack. How old does one feel in Killarney at midnight? Too old to start on that game.

These *Mná na hÉireann* — Women of Ireland — are a new breed of Irish. Mary Robinson, the former President, addressed them separately by that name in her speeches. Strong, liberated women who are able to make decisions of their own and choose their own professions — a big change from the lifestyle of their own mothers — house-bound, priest-ridden and husband-dominated. Let their husbands 'ramble' or go on 'wee strolleys' to the pub, let them spend their leisure hours in men's company. These women have their own groups and interests, and despite the heavy leaning towards 'the dhrink' and the pub culture in Ireland, they recognise it as the 'Irish Virus' and make their own lives. And they are loads of fun!

Mary Jo Slattery, Mary Lucas and Brid Dunne — I salute you. *Sláinte!*

Beara Peninsula is not for the fainthearted and those easily upset by heights, but if you can stand the twists and turns of the narrow cliff road and not look down, the ageless ruggedness of the great mountain faces is stunning. They lie like pages in a book, or as if a glacier has suddenly stopped moving and turned to stone. Maybe that's what did happen. Strangely, at sea level all is tranquil. Glengarriff, where lush tropical woodland flourishes in the inlet at the top of Bantry Bay, is a Mecca for gardeners who enjoy planting exotic flowers and leading a Mediterranean lifestyle. Life is either rugged subsistence or a garden of Eden on Beara.

We did not wait to gape at red and gold sunsets over Bantry Bay, but as we neared the tiny northern village of Ardgroom, an extraordinary mixture of people were walking the one narrow street. On lampposts and shops, leaflets announced the name Michael Dwyer. A pop star? Only one pub seemed to be the gathering point, so we followed along for a bowl of soup and some bread. Obviously they had all come from a Mass of commemoration for their hero and were in need of drinks and somewhere to play their guitars. Learned men from Dublin, alternative lifestylers, old patriots and young people from all over Ireland.

'And Michael Dwyer?' we asked.

'A Wicklow rebel who was transported to Australia after the rebellion of 1798, and who lies in a grave in Waverly cemetery in Sydney. Two hundred years to the day.'

Today the air is full of stories and legends about Michael Dwyer.

'One day British soldiers were looking for him and he hid behind a ferocious sow in a sty. As the soldiers approached the sow, Dwyer agitated its hind legs and made it grunt fiercely at the soldiers. No one could occupy the same sty as the sow, they figured, and left.'

We waited half an hour for our soup.

'If you wait an hour more there'll be a roast meal for all,' the barman announced to everyone.

I suppose they had waited two hundred years to celebrate Michael Dwyer's part in the rebellion. What was an hour? They had their instruments — and Guinness.

11. to hell or connaught

'I KNOW NOW THAT THE STRANGE beauty that flies like dust through Galway is the spirit of Gaelic Ireland, something that is a defiance to time, something that is like a declaration of faith. Galway must be almost too beautiful to an Irishman.' H.V. Morton once again.

Sixty years later he would be saying wistfully: 'Galway has outgrown itself. Where has that "strange beauty" gone?'

I wish Galway had never grown up. I wish I had visited it when the Claddagh people were still living outside its city walls, huddled together in their Gaelic fishing village, neat, whitewashed thatched cottages planted at haphazard angles, with no regular roads running to them, and where one man's back door opened on to the front of his neighbour. All that is left is a small museum at the back of a jeweller's shop where people buy the Claddagh ring as a souvenir and peer at old photos. Galway had to grow up, and Claddagh people had to 'get a decent life'. We know all that, but it's sad all the same. It would have been exciting to pass the time of day with a few handsome Spanish merchants and watch their galleons unloading the best wines for the exclusive families of Galway. After all, the galleons of Galway were as accustomed to the ports of Spain as they were to Irish waters.

'But they would have only spoken to you in the Gaelic,' a woman told me. 'They used to say, "If you talked English you would be a wiser man than I; in Irish it is not that way the story is."'

The sun wasn't about to go down on Galway Bay the day we passed. Biting rain swept the up-market city, forcing us into the museum and then through the 1584 Spanish Arch to Kenny's Bookshop.

'Kenny's Bookshop *is* Galway,' say the academics of Ireland. Two hundred thousand volumes about Ireland in every genre stack the shelves, the staircases and the upper floors, in baskets and crates, out the back and across the road. Signed portraits of authors fill every inch of wallspace, from James Joyce to Frank McCourt — new and old, first copies and antiquarians. Seven Kennys have run the shop over the generations. I saw two — a fat one and a thin. For five years I had been searching for William Carleton's book *Traits and Stories of the Irish Peasantry 1844*. Would the thin Mr Kenny know . . . ?

'Up the stairs, first landing, to the right,' he said without hesitation.

'And *Irish in the Blood*?' I asked, as a joke.

'Ground floor, second shelf, under Colonial History,' he said without looking up. Wow!

I didn't have the nerve to say I was its author. Not in this overwhelming tower of books and famous authors reaching to the sky. It was like David facing Goliath.

'I saw your home page in an Air New Zealand magazine,' I told him.

He looked up and smiled. 'That's us,' he said proudly.

Well-heeled Americans sat round waiting for their books to be wrapped, parcels like small mountains piled up on the floor at their feet, and orders for every new book to be sent to the States each quarter. Ah-h-h. Kenny's does that. Americans love it and demand it.

Our lunch table was propped up against an old stone wall.

'Original sixteenth-century city wall?' asks David, wide-eyed.

'Yup,' replied the waitress. 'Scone or roll?'

The waitress couldn't care less about sixteenth century walls or the fact that glamorous Galway was once cut off from the Irish and Spanish living outside. She just served the clients while we pondered Galway's history at our elbows.

So who will tell us about today's Galway?

The smart sophisticated lass in the bus takes up the practised commentary.

'Big apartment mall on Eyre Street to your left, and the statue of Irish story-writer Padraig O'Conaire to your right in Eyre Square. The River Corrib washes the western side of the city and upstream a salmon weir stems its flow. Only four fishermen are allowed at one time. If you see five, one is illegal. To our left is Poor Clare Convent with only ten nuns left. It is an enclosed order and the nuns ring a bell when they need supplies. God love them!'

It didn't take long for the guide to drop her professional voice, discard the speaker system and become one of the bedraggled group around her. After all there were only four of us huddled together in this dripping monster of a bus — driver, guide, and us — and we are all wet through to the knickers. Best be chummy and wet than put on a show to an empty bus.

'Bit of a disappointing drive at the weekend, so it was. My dad has a sister in Poor Clare. Drove from Dublin, so he did, and all he got was a handshake through the grille. Brought a box of chocolates and couldn't even hand them to her — they went down a chute, God love us. He never even saw her.'

'What do they do all day?' I asked.

'Make communion bread and pray. A bit of gardening here and there.'

Now we are passing Salthill, a fast-growing, élite suburb. New, modern hotels, glamorous B & Bs, flash restaurants.

'Tourists love it,' she said with pride. 'Rich people even come across from Dublin for the weekend and holidays. Pubs are open till one a.m. You can eat and sing along and dance and then go on to a nightclub. The crack is good in Galway. Grab some lovely big chips and fish on the way home to your bed — no worries at all. You've had a great night — no problems. Galway University on our right has a mixture of Irish and European students — they're mostly from Germany and France, over here on Erasmus grants. It's all EC money. We get the same grant. I've just come back from eighteen months in Germany. Plenty of tech. grants too.'

We stepped down on to the flooded pavement.

'Where do you come from?' she asked suddenly.

'New Zealand. They don't know much about Ireland there.'

'I'm surprised at that. What about Tim Finn from Crowded House? I know him. I sing in a band at nights myself but my voice is gone today and I'll not turn up at all.'

Her voice lilted prettily. She tripped off down the street, long thin legs in black tights disappearing under a mini miniskirt, heavy black heels clack-clacking a staccato rhythm.

We left the once historic city to a strange mixture of humanity. Poor musicians slouching around in long coats carrying their fiddles, and rich tourists roaming the malls, seeking antiques or jewellery. There is much more in Galway to be sure, but it was time to drift into the traffic like gormless corpuscles in the bloodstream pouring out of the city. We didn't need Trixie to throw a coughing fit and stammer her displeasure in the middle of it. Commuters were in a hurry and their body language told us so. Time for them to get out of Galway too and into the country where living was cheaper.

'Only the rich can live in Galway,' our smart girl had said.

But those Claddagh rings with two hands grasping each other over a heart. 'If you wear it in a certain way, you're looking for a man; if you've got a man, turn it the other way,' the shopkeeper said mechanically. I wanted to buy twenty-three right then for my children and grandchildren. Damn that New Zealand dollar.

The Gaeltacht along the coast of Galway Bay is a step back in time where old ways survive.

Only two cars pass us on the lonely road from Oughterard to Spiddle. Nothing but bog all around. But as the sun at last breaks through the grey clouds, brave clumps of white bog cotton wave a cheery greeting.

Even at low tide Spiddle pier has an attraction — its yachts lying on their sides in the green slimey mud. No one is awake.

'It takes an extra hoor to shake off the Guinness,' a lobster fisherman says later.

Dragging thirty heavy lobster pots 30 metres up from the bottom of Galway Bay is no joke. It's hard yakka, and he's lucky if he gets ten lobsters a day. He's not complaining, though, for the bay is blue today, covered with liquid diamonds dancing in the early-morning sun. He might sit awhile and think and let the warm sun sink into his weatherbeaten body, then he might clean up the mess.

Then again, he might just think.

On the coast road to Carraroe all signs change to Irish — suddenly. No explanation, no dubbing in English. Traffic signs, shop signs — everything! Our road maps stay the same and are useless in this new world. Slowly a few words start making sense — *siopa* is shop; *oscailte* is open. We won't starve. The B & Bs have a loose translation so we will have a bed if we need one:

> an feadó's
> Brialann
> Briefeasta. lon Beile

Mr An Feado's ancestors must have been Spanish, that's for sure. 'Food and Drink' change their spelling to *Beal an Daingin*. Easy to remember. At Casla another straightforward notice warns us to *Sruthan!* Underneath is a picture of a car falling off a pier into the water below. It probably means 'Struth! Don't drive on this pier.' So we take a wee strolley, for it's a grrand day anywa'.

A Galway hooker lies sideways on the hard like a beached whale, and tucked into a cosy corner of the harbour a 32-foot Weatherly bilge-keeler sloop. The front hatch is open so we make a few appropriate yachtie noises and a girl's head appears. She's ready for the crack.

'How did you get this boat here?'

'Built in the UK in the sixties, taken to America, shipped to Ireland. We sailed it here from Dublin. I'm blobbing out. Just finished exams in Dublin. My husband is teaching Irish in the special school nearby. Children come in the holidays for intensive tuition in Gaelic and this area lends itself to that.'

'Gosh, it's just like our kohanga reo in New Zealand, where the Maori people are discovering their own language and culture again.'

'*Daolne gan teanga Daulne gan croi*. "A people without a language is a people without a heart." That's what these Gaeltacht schools are teaching. Gives people a new confidence.'

'So many similarities here to our New Zealand scene. *Ko te reo te ha o te Maoritanga*. "The language is the heart of Maoridom." That's what they say over there. Anyway, what are *you* studying?'

'A masters in computers.

'And then?

'We'll go to England for three years. My husband wants to work with wood and learn to make luxury yachts.'

'To sell in Ireland?'

'Yes, Dublin.'

'But why England?'

'Look, the Irish get on OK with the English in England. It's those in the North. The English there aren't the same. You'll have heard about that already. We know more about France and Athens than Northern Ireland and get on better with them over there. Strange thing is my mother lives in Donegal and I've never been to Belfast or Derry. Why don't you give the North a miss in your book? Do you have to go up there and hear all that stuff?'

'I want to give the full picture. After all, my father and all his family came from Ballycastle way and I'm tracing the roots right back to the seventeen hundreds. Some parts of the North are very pretty, and there's a certain loyalty.'

'I guess so, but all that suspicion and bigotry — I'd give it a miss.'

'Will you get a good job in Dublin when you get back?'

'Two years ago I'd say we wouldn't be back but now there's jobs. After graduating we all went to America to get the jobs, but now all my friends are coming back home. It's booming, with international firms setting up here.'

'Thanks to the EU?'

'Yerra, but I think theyrr going a bit too far, and it's scary. Once they pull out, then what?'

'I hope the Celtic tiger keeps roaring for a while yet. It's great seeing these fine new houses and factories springing up. There's a buzz about the place.'

I leave her throwing sleeping bags out in the sun.

When Cromwell banned the Irish 'To Hell or Connaught', this land was part of the Connaught deal. Hell was the immigrant ships to America and the convict ships to Australia. A great choice!

On this Lettermullan peninsula, landscape has suddenly turned to moonscape. Rocks lie strewn for miles — huge monsters, like

dinosaurs, rising up from their rocky beds, with hardly a blade of grass between them, maybe enough for one heifer in the summer. It's like a whole outer-space movie gone mad. Turf sods lie drying on top of rock fences, for a bit of extra cash. Brave people open their eyes in the morning and look out at a sea of rocks, jump in their cars and head for Galway. Mothers hang their washing in rocky back yards devoid of flowers or trees, go inside and turn on the TV.

'I would go mad!' I said to one mother.

'Some do,' she replied without a smile, 'and there is free counselling — anytime.' Don't mention rockeries here, or fancy rock pools. Mention the sandy seashore, fishing, the church, the pub or a trip to town.

Back of it all the Twelve Pins range of mountains shuts them in to live as best they can. A hundred and fifty years ago their grandparents walked out of this godforsaken place, starving to death in the Great Hunger. Their tumbledown cottages are now just a graveyard of memories. The ruins are there still, some grafted on to new houses, others a heap in the back yard.

No one is starving here these days — there's a fisheries co-op and wheels to escape.

'The EU is always there for subsidies if we kick off an initiative,' they tell us.

One doesn't expect a crowd on this deserted coast road, but suddenly, without warning, gaily coloured flags flutter from a large pub, breaking the monotony of grey stone, and people are sitting at outside tables, drinking in the sun. A certain buzz of anticipation and activity is in the air and a constant stream of mothers and children crosses and recrosses the road. What luck! *Curragh* races are in full swing on the harbour. Narrow canoes of traditional design, worked by three oarsmen, are sitting ready for the gun, their narrow six-foot-long oars at the ready. Semifinals. They're off! And these magnificent men are rowing in perfect unison, their curraghs whipping like darts through the water.

'How long should it take to do the course?' I asked the girls sitting next to me.

They giggled at my English.

'Twenty minutes — the first one home,' they answered.

We were sitting on a natural grandstand made of enormous flat rocks sloping down to the water's edge. All around us spectators spoke in Gaelic, their voices rising and falling with the progress of the race. There is nothing more wonderful in Ireland than to hear the Gaelic spoken like this, in a natural setting. There is that uncanny feeling of a language perfectly suited to the people and the place. It belongs here. English is superimposed and sounds stilted. An occasional 'Jaysus Christ' as the winners neared the finishing point provided the only two words I knew.

'Looking the guys over?' I suggested to the girls. 'Got your eyes on any of them?' They looked at each other knowingly and smirked.

'I've got six daughters like you at home in New Zealand and they would be blown away at these handsome men.'

They smiled into their hands. Sure they were handsome. We chatted about their black fingernail polish and other girlie things, then they asked if I would buy a raffle ticket to 'help the boys'. Giggle giggle.

We exchanged a punt for a *ticéad* but when I looked at the range of prizes on the ticket they were all in Irish. Out of the ten I could only understand two — 'Bodywave' and 'Brandy'. The rest would be pure guesswork, and I was really only interested in chatting with the girls anyway.

Dark shadows made grotesque figures of the rocks as we headed home across lonely moors and bogland. Should we take the turning to *Ros an Mhil* or *Scrieb*? No one can tell us that. The road is empty.

Oughterard is a charming quiet village sitting a mile back from Lough Corrib, its narrow main street a mix of olde-worlde Georgian and thatched houses, hotels and restaurants. The names of leading thirteenth-century Irish clans live on here. You can eat Connemara roast lamb and mint sauce at O'Flaherty's or O'Connor's, and James Joyce is the toast of this beautiful Joyce's Country. A few miles out of the village tourists stop at Joyce's general store, an up-market antique shop, and gaze about as if it was holy ground. The atmosphere makes for a certain wistfulness and curiosity, as if any minute people expect James Joyce himself, or his grandchildren, to step outside and greet them as they throw down a beer at the tables opposite.

This day was Bloomsday — held on 16 June every year to celebrate Joyce's Leopold Bloom in *Ulysses* — and was being marked in an attempt to end the censorship faced by other famous authors.

'What is it about?' I asked

'It's a long story but has to do with advocating the unnatural prevention of conception or procurement of abortion or miscarriage. Some of Joyce's books are still banned because of his views on that, but the Amendment of the Censorship of Publication is having its first reading in the Dail today.'

'Poets and artists are revered in Ireland, you know. They don't have to pay tax. Goes back hundreds of years, to the Behan law.'

The coverage of Joyce films and works filled our TV screen for a week; even the Taioseach took part in an international reading. How warm is a noncommercial reading of famous works in a non-bigoted presentation.

'But you must see Clifden,' people told us, 'the capital of Connemara — or of Boston, in America.'

'Do they call it that?'

'See for yourself. Best golf courses, best hotels, best B & Bs, best food, best cattle markets, and best views across the Atlantic.'

Indeed. This 'little Boston' had replaced the once 'pretty little Clifden' where a few donkeys roamed the streets, cattle changed hands for a pittance and people starved in the famine.

The real 'old Connemara' boasts no up-market glamour. Black-faced sheep wander about this near-empty country round Kilary

Harbour, and cattle graze above the purple flush of heather. No one about. No one in charge, only an old man fixing a two-strand fence which wouldn't keep a cow in. A hundred ruined stone cottages tell the old story of The Hunger and the desperate trek to America, but out of the ruins a new generation is springing up with bigger and brighter houses. Out on the coast third-generation landowners are doing up their old stone farmhouses and renting them out in the summer.

'Don't you want to live out here?' I asked a young woman on Omey Island, near Claddaghduff.

'My grandparents left me the land, but I've got my own job in Galway,' she said proudly. 'The EU helps the other farmers round here if they want to stay. We're just checking on our herd. We use it as a run-off in the summer.'

Unexpected glimpses of the old Connemara flash into view — a clutch of roosters flapping noisily on the window ledge of a cottage overgrown with vines and cobwebs. Separating crops from grazing land, walls of loose stones cross half-acre and quarter-acre fields. We look for Connemara ponies, but they are pets now for children and tourists, not the workhorses of the past, underfed beasts of burden. We are grateful for that. As I looked at these remnants of old cottages rotting into the ground, horror stories of the Famine clouded my vision. Some of the dead had been left unburied; other people walked along the road like an army of living corpses. Down these very roads.

The man in charge of the spinning and weaving centre at Leenaun on Kilary Harbour has been to New Zealand and knew Godfrey Bowen.

'Stayed nearby here, he did, and gave a demonstration of hand shearing. Passed on now, so he has, and wrote a little book about wool with religion in it. Over the road they shot *The Field* — you know, with Richard Harris and John Hurt. See those pubs and shops? That's where the scene of the battle for land between Bull McCabe and the Yank was filmed. Hasn't changed.'

The Boat Club pub and restaurant in Oughterard is full on tonight, overcrowded and loud. Latecomers pour out onto the footpath and across the narrow street, the noise of their steel chairs and tables graunching on the metal as they push and shove. Not the place to gather local news tonight.

A few yards down the road, hidden behind huge, sinister trees, the historic Protestant church is dark and silent in the evening light. Is it alive or dead? Open or shut? Not a notice, not a person — only deadies under gravestones. I ask three times along the tiny street, go mad, then try to buy a newspaper.

'Ten o'clock,' said the lad behind the counter.

'Are you sure it's *every* Sunday?'

'Yerra, ten o'clock. And they're having a stall or something in the Corrib pub after. Funds for the church. Nobody much goes there.'

He was right. Half a dozen locals, and a few visitors from Salt Lake City come over to be with their old granda who was a member there. We left them trying to have a singsong round the old organ and rustle up a bit of pizazz!

'They're used to lots of singing, the Mormons,' a man told me. 'What d'ya think they'd be thinkin' about this place?'

'The melancholy of a passing era,' I told him.

The church was very beautiful inside, and we bought some home-made marmalade at the stall in the Corrib pub. Not the place to gather local news either.

Moura is in charge of the simple hair salon. But she is certainly not simple.

'Whatya doing around here?' she asks.

'Writing a book about today's Ireland, I hope.'

'Most women these days go out to work, you know that? We pay baby-sitters to look after the kids after school till we come home.'

'What about breast-fed babies?'

'Oh yes, breast-feeding's coming back in again. The mums gave it away for years but there's a health scare on and they're back on it. They express and then if the baby-sitter runs out she gives them SMA from a can, already made up. Straight from the can into a bottle.'

'But that's expensive, like Pampers.'

'Aye, it is that, but it's easy if you get what I mean. Pampers have been in for ten years. No one uses cloth napkins, we haven't time and that — well, get what I mean? And the baby-sitter won't use anything but Pampers and SMA. We wouldn't expect them to either.'

'Those beautiful homes round Lough Corrib there. Just like our Lake Taupo in New Zealand. Owned by Americans and English are they?'

'They're Irish, so they are. The Irish are coming up you know. You can commute from here to Galway if you want that, or have it as a holiday home.'

'I don't see any pregnant women about here.'

''Course you don't. Contraception's been in for years. We're not backward you know.'

'What about the priest?'

'Go to Mass on Saturday night here in Oughterard and you'll hear him give a little nudge about it. Nice priest we've got in Oughterard. I was at a house Mass last night. Just forty of us you know, to put a blessing on the house. Had to pay the priest. We've got to watch the drugs for young people. Keep them busy is what I say, but if anyone round this village gets an inkling of who's selling it, we'll get them. We pull together. Mind you, *I* wouldn't take the pill if we want to talk about that again.'

'Why not?'

''Fraid of cancer, that's all. Not guilt — not me! Some seventeen-year-old kid came in here four weeks ago to the day and asked me where to go for a morning-after pill. I'd never heard of it truth to tell, but my sixteen-year-old daughter was helping out and she told him. Fancy that! Me not knowing and her knowing and him doing the business the night before and coming in here asking me while I cut his hair. God help him! You know some of these young things don't read that book that goes with the pill, and are still scared to go to their doctor and ask. But then, here's me not knowing too. I mean, the "after" one! If your husband likes painting tell him to go round the corner and look at Aughnanure Castle.'

'Thank you, Moura, thank you very much. You're brilliant.'

Round the corner to a castle? Moura was out of her depth there, surely, but I passed the message on with a giggle. No harm in going 'round the corner'. She was right!

A six-storey tower house stood among trees on an outcrop of rock that had been sculpted and pierced over centuries by the stream curling round it. Built around 1500 by the O'Flahertys, the most powerful clan in the region, it was now a beautifully restored heritage site.

Stories of love and hate and murder were written on its walls, about the sixteen-year-old wonderwoman Grace O'Malley, and the terrible Donal O'Flaherty raiding and plundering County Galway. An ancient horror story just waiting to be made over into a modern movie, the script already written. Even the title is there, inscribed over the west gate of Galway town:

'From the ferocious O'Flahertys, Good Lord deliver us.'

12. in the steps of saint patrick

> In 500 BC Ireland was already recorded as Insula sacra [Holy Island].
>
> Ora Maritima, Festus Rufus Avienus

IT IS A BIG STEP FROM AD 441 to 1998. It is also a big step for New Zealanders to grasp the meaning of time in this very old country. Many saints and monks lived and died here leaving so much wisdom and visible proof of their devotion and spartan living. We don't have any of that.

When Saint Patrick first entered Galway Harbour to make his pilgrimage to Croagh Padraig (Patrick's Mountain) and Ballintubber, he used the waterways of Lough Corrib and Lough Mask to get there, then built his first church near a much smaller lake — Lough Carra. It's known today for good fishing rather than the abbey.

Between the two big lakes lies a neck of land and a town named Cong, where we started our pilgrimage to Ballintubber and Croagh Padraig. Cong was full of travel-type pilgrims. Extraordinary travellers who came by helicopter or road to revisit a movie — *The Quiet Man* — partly filmed here in 1952, starring John Wayne and Maureen O'Hara. Cong had been taken over by Americana: an authentic thatched cottage with mock-up scenes, videos, T-shirts, tapes. You could stay at a QM B & B or a QM hotel, have coffee at a QM café, get untold information at a QM info centre, and gaze at a picturesque bridge over a river where the QM hero and heroine had made love. Yet, separated from all this hype by an old tin fence, was Cong Abbey.

'Cong Abbey? Well, I don't rightly know — I've come to see *The Quiet Man*. We're not into abbeys.'

Strategically placed at an east-west, north-south crossroads, Cong Abbey is a hallowed place. It was founded in 1120 by Thurlough O'Connor, High King of Ireland, on the site of a sixth-century church. Most of the surviving ruins were destroyed by Cromwell, but the famous Cross of Cong was salvaged and now occupies a prime place in the national museum in Dublin, highly treasured by Irish people.

> ... 30 inches tall and 19 inches wide it has gilt-bronze plates over an oak base, richly ornamented with interlacing stylised mammals tussling with serpents. Some say it originally had a piece of the True Cross enshrined in it, but this relic was lost in the passage of time.

Set in scenic woodlands of oak, chestnut, cedar, pine and American redwood, with a river winding lazily in their shade, the abbey itself is not especially beautiful but has some fine carving and a pretty cloister overlooking the water. Despite all their religious devotion, the monks were shrewd and practical. A small stone fishing hut juts into the river, complete with a fireplace, under-the-floor eel traps and a bell-rope communication to the cookhouse several hundred yards away. Somehow the message would get to the monk on dinner duty: 'Prepare for fresh trout or salmon for dinner and an eel for entrée.'

I walked along a shady path with two worried grandparents.

'The kids told us to bring back a couple of fairies,' the grana said, looking round seriously.

Granda pursed his lips. 'Our family is always away with the fairies, so it shouldn't be hard.'

I could see the kids' point. Cong Abbey, in the woods, was one of those 'fairy places'. No one would have been surprised if at the next corner one or two had been sitting grinning on the path.

Dubbed 'the Abbey that refused to die', Ballintubber in County Mayo is the next stop on the trail. There is a certain agelessness about the history of this place which haunts the visitor and creates a special aura. The abbey becomes not a building but a person. A notice directs us across the fields to *Tober Padraig* — Patrick's Well. Are we really looking at a place dating back to 441? Has a part of the date been chipped off or worn away over time? No, it is 441, and this is where Patrick baptised his converts and where the imprint of his knee is clearly visible. Something inside tells you this is legend, and not to get carried away, but the whole rock enclosure and bubbling clear water is strangely moving, as are the words set into the stone:

> i bind unto myself the name
> the strong name of the trinity
> by invocation of the name
> the three in one and one in three
> of whom all nature
> hath creation
> eternal father, spirit, word
> praise to the lord
> of my salvation
> salvation is of
> christ the lord. amen.

This is not legend. It is truth. I look at the indent of Patrick's knee again.

Around the grounds are stations of the cross in natural settings — beside rocks, bushes and waterfalls. For the passion play performed each year by the local community is a life-sized wooden cross and a sepulchre carved out of natural rock — part of the permanent outdoor scenery.

Inside, the awesome simple beauty declares itself even more in the original altar and chalice, worn and stained with age. Free from intricate filigree or silver or gold, the medieval stations are small, unadorned plaster models, almost childlike in their quaint simplicity. Tiny candles burn bravely in a small alcove. Nearby, in a special room of its own without any candles or adornment, sits a cleverly crafted wooden representation of the Virgin and child. It appears almost life-size and could be that of a Maori mother with a three-month-old babe on her lap.

This abbey is obviously not meant to be a modern showpiece or an architectural wonder, but a witness to the living, protecting hand of God and his people who have kept it alive since 441.

A young, enthusiastic guide steps in, full of zeal and humour even for two people. The history has to be read over and over again before it sinks in:

441   Foundation of church by Saint Patrick
1216   Abbey founded by Crovdearg O'Connor
1265   Nave burnt
1542   Suppression of the abbey by Henry VIII
1653   Partial destruction by Cromwellians
Penal times
Worship continued in roofless abbey on grass-covered ground
1889   Restoration of the abbey
1994   Restoration of the chapter house.

780 years of continuous use — despite all that!

The old carved chancel is there, and the font and baptistry of 1200. It is all weathered and cracked — awesome in its age.

No wonder this abbey has become a focus for the community, and its ongoing restoration a spiritual bonding of old and young. No wonder it is called 'the abbey that refused to die'. The priests here have always had a practical bent, a hands-on involvement in the restoration. First Father Egan and then Father Fahey weave the historical and communal in with the spiritual. We see Father Fahey in an audio-visual leading a group along *Tochar Padraig (Patrick's Road) to Croagh Padraig*, twenty-two miles and eight walking hours away. He is no aesthete. We watch him passing the famine graves, where 300 dead from typhoid and fever were buried in 1842. He tells of Ballintubber's population dropping from 7000 to 3500 because of disease, death and emigration. He follows the old pagan druidic flagstone path where it once measured 12 feet wide so the two-wheeled King's chariot from Groghan could pass, and then, over the years, became a track of smaller flagstones along which Patrick walked to the mountain. The old pagan signs of the sun which he transformed into Celtic crosses are signposts on the way.

Going on Pilgrimage
Without change of heart
Brings no reward from God
For it is by practising virtue
And not mere motion of the feet
That we will be brought to heaven.

Book of Lismore

The audio-visual shows us a very old lady being interviewed on the abbey steps.

'Aye, she remembers right enough at Mass sitting on her coat on the damp grass with no roof above, exposed to cold wind and rain, and the candles never quenched. And aye, the place was full.'

A last look inside the abbey brings back memories of a similar atmosphere on the island of Iona in Scotland. There was another historic and spartan community built around an ancient church with Celtic crosses, and memories of another herioc saint—Columba (Colmcille).

A mile or so down the road an ambitious programme is under way. Gone is the ageless feel of the abbey, and in its place is a new story called 'The Celtic Furrow'. This is exciting stuff, dreamt up by a new wave of young enthusiasts. We are taken on a journey tracing the roots of Irish culture, exploring the festivals and cyclic seasons of Neolithic farmers and pagan Celtic cattlemen. Then it explains the difficult changeover to Christian values which Patrick and his followers introduced, down to eighty years ago. We are told it was a peaceful transition as he patiently exchanged the ways of the pagan gods for the Gospel, turned from the sun god to the Son of God — and the god of fire into the Pascal flame of resurrection.

The guide is a young history teacher on holiday, one of thirty new visionaries determined to understand their ancient roots as well as their Christianity and to meld them together. Why does the sun dance on a May morning? Why the wren boys on the day after Christmas? Why the Saint John's Night bonfire? Hallowe'en? Witches? Hags? Corn dollies? Why take down the clocks and mirrors at a wake? Why?

The Celtic Furrow experience is illustrated by artists, craftsmen and gardeners using wood, rock and dynamic artwork. Groups of schoolchildren, tourists and pilgrims are escorted through a dark tunnel of pagan Celtic beliefs, then step out into the enlightenment of Christianity, depicted by sculptures and emblems. An outside maze takes them on a walk signposted with Ireland's history and the meaning of each epoch:

> c9 & 10 vikings
> c11 danes
> c11 clontarf
> c12 normans
> c12 strongbow
> c14 black death — guilt
> c15 the pale — alienation
> c16 plantations
> c17 cromwell
> c18 penal laws 1720s
> c19 famine — population reduced by half

A notice hangs at the gate:

> a final choice has to made — devastation or hope?
> we are how we are today because of the choices that were made
> and the choices that we make now

'Why are you so keen on this project?' we ask the young guide.

'We have to fight the disillusionment in the Church and in our Irish roots. We want to teach people the history of their customs and legends and present them with a choice — to fill the growing hiatus of unbelief. The Ballintubber community and the EU are helping us.'

The spirit of the old abbey is here, but being translated for the new Ireland.

'Pop in to Mary Moran's thatched cottage next door and she'll give you a bowl of hot soup,' said the guide.

The community had restored this old relic too.

'Thar she iz on the warl.' A loud Irish brogue came at us from the simple restaraunt, a gnarled finger pointing to a photo. 'A cousin she iz of thus won.'

'Do you mean the first Mary Moran?' I asked him.

'That's herr!'

It was hard going holding a conversation with this old man, but he went on anyway, spelling out the village gossip and what he thought should be done around the place, while the 'cousin of thus won' found some apple pie and cream from somewhere. 'Made it missel' this morning, so I did.' Her 150-year-old kitchen was spotless.

'She made thut you're eatin herrsel'. Just fed a busful from America so she did.'

> For a while the path up Croagh Padraig follows a rushing brook. Then it gets very steep and rocky, climbing up an obvious and well-eroded track about 10 feet wide which leads to the centre col. Here the track turns west and the steep south-east face comes suddenly into focus. When I got to that point I stopped in my tracks, for the sight before me was awesome.
>
> Robin Neillands

A young American woman passed me on her way down.

'Have you been to the top?' I asked wearily.

'Naw, I haven't, and I ain't goin' up that rocky, muddy path. It's treacherous.'

A few of us lent on our sticks for a breather, looking out over the marvellous blues and greens of Clew Bay and the Partry Mountains. If only we could stop here — right here.

'Where do you come from?' I asked a friendly looking Irishman climbing up with his eight-year-old daughter.

'Donegal. We've been waiting for the weather to lift up for three days, so we have. So where do you two come from?'

'New Zealand.'

'New Zeeeland?' he gasped. 'Jaysus, what are you doing on this mountain and so far away? Jaysus, I can't believe what I'm seein'.'

The others came nearer.

'What she sayin'? New Zeeeland?'

'I'm trying to write a book about Ireland as it is today.' They looked incredulous. 'Well, most people think you're still in the

145

Angelas Ashes slums of Limerick and all that,' I prompted. The men looked at each other.

'There's no one hungry in Ireland today. If they are it's themselves to blame — the dhrink and all that. Ireland's *booming*. For the last two years we're really goin' ahead fast. Did ya see those new houses goin' up at Letterkenny? And . . .'

'And if the EU pulls the carpet out from under you, then what?'

'They won't. They're getting their share out of Ireland too, don't you worry.'

'A two-way street?'

'Aye, it's that all right.'

'The only ones of us getting a bad deal is the fisheries. I'm a fisherman at Kellybegs and Europe owns our waters now — that's the problem. The Spanish and them come and take what they like and don't throw back the wee ones neither.'

A few fit young people had passed us earlier heading for the top, but after an hour they were on the way down.

'Going back down,' they yelled. 'Too tough!'

It sure was. From where we were the way up to the summit looked incredibly steep and rough. No path, just a silver granite scree slope. Nothing to break a fall to the valley far below.

'But what about the thousands of pilgrims throughout the centuries who have walked on this stuff? Surely their feet would have made some path — some little dent at least?'

'Nothing touches granite like this,' David mumbled, 'and it's been raining for weeks. But we'll make it.'

Like so many ants, a line of black specks moved slowly up and down the scree. My mind whizzed into another gear. Better not look down. Better not be sick. Pull yourself together. Did helicopters land on holy mountains? What did Saint Patrick do up here? What did he live in? Did he bring gear up on his back? Disciples did that for him, I suppose. That story was starting to wear thin. And how could a woman come up here in high heels, and bring a dog under her arm? That was a porky. Ninety-year-olds had been known to make it. What a load of . . .

'You can't go back now,' some guys urged us on, smiling. 'Once you're over that rotten bit it's about half an hour to the top.'

Half an hour more of this? What for? I was no real pilgrim. It was then I saw the girl in bare feet next to me scratching on hands and knees. Bare feet? Face pale and sweaty, she looked heavenwards for help. Had she done her penance or whatever she had to do?

'I don't know any more,' she squeaked in a thready voice, and put sandshoes over her bloody scratches and black-lacquered toenails. Was she going to faint? Was she a nun? Not with toenails like that, I figured. I should do something to help her. Tell her she'd suffered enough to have her sins forgiven by now — surely. I'd tell her she didn't need to do anything to have her sins forgiven — just ask God to do it. My own voice sounded thready.

'Well what the hell are you doing up here breaking your neck?' she asked.

Saint Patrick wasn't there at the top like I'd imagined. Why not? The little chapel was shut, and the concrete steps outside wet on our bottoms. Didn't we get a blessing for nearly killing ourselves on this mountain? It didn't look like it. But exhilarated with success and near to heaven, we prayed. We prayed for peace in Ireland and for the elections next day; we prayed for our family in New Zealand and that David's 100-year-old mother would stay alive till we got home. It was good to be there. The air sparkled, and clouds drifted back and forwards across our faces. Some circled their stations while we ate our egg sandwiches.

Downhill is not a pilgrimage. There is no glory in a fight fought on the seat of one's pants, no feeling of triumph. Sir Edmund Hillary said, 'We knocked the bastard off' near the top of Everest, not the bottom. Yet there are people who break their legs or their heads or collapse going down mountains too. And David was about to break every bone in his body. Something in his Scottish genes made him *run* down the scree in spurts like a Highlander, using his stick as a crook. Dozens of loose rocks followed him, dropping over the precipice. He was crazy and made me feel sick.

'Do helicopters land on holy mountains?' I asked hesitantly.

'Oh sure, the choppers land,' our companions said. 'Crazy people try the Reek' — another term for Patrick's Mountain — 'and they can't even walk across the road. God bless them! They don't realise that it's 2510 feet above sea level, and you start climbing from the very bottom, not drive up halfway to a car park and cruise on up. You should be here at the Lughnasa feast on August 1 and see 60,000 start off! Americans fly in from the States to have a go. And the choppers are flying around from dawn, when everything starts. The stretcher guys are flat out, too, and the champagne flows, I can tell you. Look, there's someone being brought down by stretcher now. Is that your husband running down? God help us!'

'What's the real story about Saint Patrick and the bell?'

'You know Lent? Well, he stayed up there fasting and praying for forty days and forty nights. Then he flung his bell into space and it came back into his hand; and at each sound of the bell the toads and snakes fled from Ireland. That's the story.' He grinned. 'Good one, eh?'

Looking back up at this dramatic, dominating icon, I was struck by its magnetic majesty commanding the surrounding area of Mayo, Clew Harbour, the bog and the farmlands. It is perfect and awesome, and makes you want to cry.

A statue of Saint Patrick himself stands near the bottom of his holy hill, arms outstretched in a blessing. He had won that mountain for Christianity. I looked up at his face, feeling pleased to have made it to the top.

A very fit-looking American passed us on the last drag.

'You'll sleep good tonight, huh? Got to the top I hear.'

'Yes.' Barely audible.

'Got halfway myself but decided it's a bit late.'

'Oh yeah?' A load of bunkum.

He gave a salute and swung down with elastic gait. Elastic? The word had long since fallen from our vocabulary. It was one foot after another like a slow-motion movie.

A few Irish families were still waiting in the car park down below.

'There's an honest-to-God Irish pub just down the road,' they told us, grinning. 'See ya there!'

'You know, I love these people,' said David abruptly. 'They smile with their eyes.'

♣

148

It was goodbye to Moura.

'Mum's awa' havin' a coffee over the road. Sit down,' her daughter said.

'Howorya,' Moura sighed as she came hurtling in. 'I've just been having a cup of coffee and a croissant with a friend. She said I needed a break from this place for an hoor or so. Holy Mother, I wish I hadn't had that feckin' croissant now. I can taste the oil in it and I'm trying' to lose weight you know. Were yiz at Saint John's Night last night — the bonfire you know?'

'No, we were up at Croagh Padraig.'

'Blessed Virgin, you were too. Did yiz take a cam recorder with yiz?'

'No, I wouldn't want anyone to see my agony.'

'Look, ye want to go up when everyone goes — in the night with candles and thousands doin' it. The crack gets you there, so it does. Help each other along, we do. Take the Mass.'

'What did you do at the bonfire? What's it for?'

'Some pagan thing the Catholic church took over. I go for the crack. Every village has a bonfire. The midges ate us alive last night.' The lady in the next chair agreed. The midges had been brutal. She couldn't remember what the bonfire was for either.

'Supposed to clean out your wardrobes and car sheds as well,' she said.

'My kids collected all the old tyres and tried to get my hairspray cans to make a bang,' Moura nattered on. 'I stopped them doin' it so they threw in the cans of baked beans. Sacred Heart of God, ye can't stop these kids. I never ring in on them to their father tho', that's for sure. Seamus would blow up if they had their hair cut different, so he would. Better go to a coronary clinic, that Seamus.'

'I'm going home to look up about this bonfire night,' I told Moura and her friend.

'Come back with it on paper,' Moura said. 'Silly you knowin' about it and us not. My kids need to know too. All those baked beans an' all.'

On 21 June, when the sun reaches its highest altitude above

the horizon, many cultures celebrate the sun god. Some call the god Apollo or Hercules, but to the Irish he was Bran. In Celtic cultures, the oak was a sacred tree, so someone was selected to be the Oak King and sacrificed in Bran's honour. They were burned on the 'bone fire', and their ashes scattered on the land to appease Bran and in the hope of good crops. Their head was placed in a curragh, which was released on the river, so their spirit might be free to obtain immortality. It was a privilege to be chosen as Oak King. You were pampered for the year before you were sent down the river.

'Holy Mother of God, where on earth did you get that?' asks Moura.

'From the "Celtic Furrow" students in Ballintubber.'

'I'm for goin' to that place and I'll take the kids. We need to know what we're doin' these days. The crack's always good on Bonfire Night, anywa'.'

13. a lucky mistake

OUR HOUSE FOR HOME EXCHANGE
DONEGAL

A two-storey cottage, the last one on the edge of the village of Mountcharles, nestling in Donegal Bay five minutes drive from Donegal town, home of the famous 'Magees' Donegal tweed.

We have lovingly restored and renovated the house to a very high standard. On the ground floor there is an open-plan sitting room/dining room and a pine kitchen. The sitting room has a double settee which converts into a double bed.

A pine staircase leads to the first floor, which has two bedrooms, shower room and balcony.

Bedroom 1 has a double bed and is fully fitted with wardrobes and cupboards all along one wall. Bedroom 2 also has a (small) double bed, a dressing table and wardrobe hanging space.

The shower room has an instant electric shower, washbasin, toilet and bidet hose. All rooms have fitted carpet throughout, except the kitchen, which has vinyl floor covering.

The sitting area has a lovely pine fire surround with Victorian tiled insert, and an open fire.

The balcony is small but accommodates a table, chairs and a portable gas barbeque. The kitchen has an instant electric immersion water heater, and all rooms have electric heating.

As it is the last house on a side road off the village, it is quiet, yet the hotel, shops, pubs, P.O., butcher, etc. are literally round the corner.

Mountcharles is an unspoilt village with the beach about 10 minutes' walk away. It is an ideal location for easy access to all the beauty spots of Donegal, and indeed all of the north-west of Ireland.

Travel to Donegal either by flying to Dublin or Belfast or taking the ferry to Rosslare, Dublin, Cork or Larne.

WHAT A DREAM! We would take it for a month and ask some friends from England to share it with us. I would write every second day, and on the days in between alternate lying on the beach with touring Donegal. In return the owners could use our house in New Zealand for a month whenever they wished. After all those basic self-catering cottages it would be heaven.

What a mistake! What shattered dreams! This was no beachside cottage, but a tiny apartment squashed together with six others on a steep, narrow one-way track off the main road. Ours was the end one. Eye level for drunks to bang on the lounge window as they swayed up and down the hill to visit the six pubs. The balcony measured two metres by two metres and faced into the neglected back yards of our neighbours, or their broken windows. Two folding chairs took up the entire space; leg room for one person only. And washing facilities? A trip to Donegal town and the laundrette must be the trendy thing to do. No phone or TV!

'What about our guests?' I screamed in despair. 'We can't contact them now!'

Once upon a time Mountcharles was as posh as the name suggests. Some people even pronounced it 'Montycharlies' in an affected way. 'A pleasant hillside village a few miles from Donegal city.' It must have aged with time and become penniless and down-at-heel, a sanctuary for tramps, hitchhikers, tinkers and druggies. Old ladies ventured out in daylight to buy sausages from the butcher, then went running back inside for safety. God save us.

Vivienne and Peter Cox left Surrey in England to join us at our 'lovingly restored seaside cottage'. Two busy librarians on annual leave — she a New Zealander, he very English and precise.

'We couldn't find you anywhere,' they said, horrified. 'Then the lady in the supermarket said you'd bought some peat and left a message. What does *tra beach* mean? There's no beach, just a lot of rocks and slime and tinkers' caravans lining the road. What happened?'

'It's all one big mistake,' I blurted. 'Let's all get out of here now and look for something else. The four of us can't live in this "Coronation Street" together. It's a doll's house, and you've come all this way for a holiday. We can forget the deposit!'

Vivienne looked at the situation without emotion. She had been a Girl Guide leader in her day, been to world jamborees and all that.

'Look, half the world lives like this. Let's be huggy muggy and make do. Some people in the UK would call this outfit a cottage. New Zealanders wouldn't — that was the first mistake! Is the woman who owns it English?'

'She's from the North. Lives in Omagh.'

'No use attempting to write your book till we've gone. Tell her you'll pay for two weeks only, then move on. We'll explore Donegal in the daytime, rain or no rain.'

'I'll keep the peat fire going,' David offered.

'I'd rather we used my Renault,' Peter suggested very politely. 'Lock that Trixie thing up.'

'We'll make a roster about the bathroom,' I suggested. 'Mornings you two, nights us. Peter sleeps on the settee in the lounge.'

'Whew! That's good. The other one's no bigger than a single.' Vivienne glowed. 'I can read half the night, and listen to my ghetto blaster.'

That holiday was the best ever. Touring Donegal between showers and biting winds, driving through the most wild, rugged and beautiful land in Ireland, more suited to donkey and cart; thatched whitewashed cottages; stone-walled postage-stamp fields, where the hay is turned by hand and the cows are tethered. Donegal tweed shops and factories pepper the countryside with heather and honey coloured sweaters, shawls, hats and waistcoats. Saint Colmcille is the patron saint of this area. He follows the traveller up Slieve League Mountain, where Europe's highest sea cliffs plunge 233 metres into the water. He follows you down to Glencolmcille, where a devoted parish priest, Father James McDyer, lifted a village from poverty into a place where locals could be employed, a place with its own electricity and factories. A village folk museum takes you on that journey from hopelessness to prosperity.

'You may never have an opportunity like this again,' said Vivienne seriously as she left Mountcharles. 'Living in cramped spaces with no view is something New Zealanders don't understand, and looking at decrepit 200-year-old stone houses from the toilet seat is a unique experience.'

'What about those awful crows flying in and out the broken windows? That's not funny.'

'Go further north and look for something better,' she advised.

But there were nice people in Mountcharles too. Patsy Gallagher, the postmaster, liked a crack. Intrigued with jack points and e-mail technology, he watched patiently as David fiddled with the temperamental laptop.

'What are you planning to write about the North?' he asked me through the grille.

'I really don't know. I wish I did. All I want is peace up there, but it's very hard for visitors like me to understand. We don't have the sort of grudge memories they were born and brought up with. They don't seem to want to forget what happened three hundred years ago. But then, we've never had to live with the threat of IRA killings and bombs and thirty years of troubles. I keep all Nuala O'Faolin's articles from the *Irish Times*, you know. She lives in Belfast just now, trying to get her head round the situation. She's trying to understand too, in an objective way. We keep in touch.'

'You won't find a better columnist than Nuala, but it's really so sad. I've got good friends in Downpatrick, both Protestant and Catholic, but I never visit them, never.'

'Why?'

'Look, you can be in the wrong place at the wrong time up there, and me with a southern number plate. They all get on fine together in their little part of the village, but it might only need me to appear and things could turn nasty. I never think of visiting them. We go to the Canary Islands for our holidays.'

'How very sad this all is,' I whispered through the grille.

How many more times would I hear you could be 'in the wrong place at the wrong time'. It was the saddest phrase in Ireland.

Between customers, Patsy told me his story. Both parents with TB, shuttled from one grandparent to another — customer — and forced by poverty to leave school early, so studied at home. Held on to the belief that he had the brains to succeed — mother-in-law brings in morning tea — and the determination that his two boys would have the opportunities denied him. Why does mother-in-law bring in morning tea? He cuts her lawns and does other little things for her. Customer. Dozens of lads in Mountcharles with similar upbringing, and now drugs — customer — so better to live out of Mountcharles — customer — on the road to Kellybegs, which he does.

A neighbour, Tom, and his family lived at the back of the post office. We could use their jackpoint anytime the post office was shut.

'I'm trying to spend time with Tom this morning,' whispered Maeve, his pretty young wife. 'He's leaving for Lough Derg to do penance in an hour's time. You have to book this time of the year.'

'Lough Derg? I've heard of that.'

'Yerra, it's only half an hour from here. Saint Pat's Purgatory on Station Island's in the middle of the lough. I'll tell you all about it later.' She ran off, flushed.

'Do you want to go to Lough Derg yourself then?' Maeve asked later. 'It's a three-day ritual of penitence and self-denial. Walk barefoot round the remains of monastic cells and perform devotional exercises. One meal a day of bread and black tea and stay awake all the first night. The nuns see you do! About four hundred people can go at a time.'

'I'll give it a miss,' I said firmly. 'Not my thing, really, but I've heard some people feel a real cleansing from fasting and praying.'

'I've done it myself four times,' she said casually. 'After all, Saint Pat fasted forty days there himself.'

I popped next door to Patsy. 'You been to Lough Derg, Patsy?'

'No, and I'm not about to either,' he said, hiding his smiling face behind the grille. 'OK for some.'

'So, how's Tom today?' I asked after the ordeal.

'Asleep,' Maeve replied briskly. 'At least he'll appreciate the comforts he's got here,' she whispered behind her hand. Strong lady, Maeve. She'd see her Tom fronted up to his responsibilities.

At the crossroads, a few yards from our 'lovingly restored

cottage', stood an old green water pump — newly painted — with fresh flower boxes of pansies and alyssum. The plaque underneath read:

> SEAMUS McMANUS,
> AUTHOR AND SEANACHAI [STORYTELLER],
> WAS BORN NEAR HERE.
> 1869–1960

Thank you, Seamus. You gave me inspiration in this uninspiring town, and your books are lovingly preserved by your relatives in your home behind you. They say you saw nine provinces from there on a fine day. I haven't had one fine day in two months, and we can't see anything from our dump. I'm leaving here — so goodbye, my friend.

'Just ask as you go,' the tourist office girl suggested vaguely. 'We've got nothing, absolutely nothing, on our books in the whole of Donegal for the next six weeks. You should have booked a year ahead, and you coming all that way. It's high season now.'

Trixie bounced along the narrow unsealed road as if she, too, had been released from her prison in the back yards of low dives and pubs. What had she seen on those dark nights all alone? On the surface she had only lost her aerial — but what else?

Mountcharles to Ardara is mainly bogland interspersed with some large, new, naked houses without trees or gardens. No kids, toys or bicycles; no cars anywhere. A cold empty feeling hangs over the deserted expanse. Then it's back to peat again, some stacked already, covered with plastic bags like someone's shopping left out in the rain. It's lonely.

What would we find at Ardara? A heritage village in bank holiday mood: outside markets in full swing, cars parked up in twos and threes along the footpath, every second shop selling identical goods — Donegal tweed coats, hats and scarves, souvenirs and weather-worn postcards. In between, dozens of pubs offer Guinness and a snack, and there's a choice of five uninteresting-looking hair salons, two butchers and two small supermarkets. Out-of-town tourist buses park at the big factories, queuing up for Donegal tweed by the metre. Hundreds of metres rolling out for American and European markets. They love it and it's cheap. Free parking in the church grounds.

Farmers' trucks force their way through the tiny main street, clogging up the route south and north. It is bedlam in Ardara today.

A big notice tells the crowd that live Irish music would be on that night. When and where, we wonder? A farmer leans across the small bridge nearby, staring into space, so I ask him.

'See those birrds up therr?'

'On that building?'

'Aye. That's wherr.'

'What time does it start?'

'Half-ten around, but maybe they won't all come till half-eleven and go at one.'

'What do people around here do till half-ten then? Eat chips?'

He grinned broadly.

'Drink beer, that's what they be doin'.'

'We're full,' the B & B owners said. 'Why don't you try those chalets up the road? Run by chaps.'

'One spare — the small one. Do everything yourself. Peat extra. Washing machine out the back.'

We grabbed it, pleased to get out of the wind and weather. Country view, green hills, cows, fresh air. Did someone say 'run by chaps'?

'Excuse me, do you mind? A few things are missing in our chalet — towels, toilet paper, small plates, knives. And the taps are all red and back to front — turn L for hot, R for cold. The stove isn't working properly. And the bed . . .'

'Didn't ye bring towels then? I've a few wee ones. Dry yourselves off by the fire after.'

'But the bed! It sags badly in the middle. Could you swap it for another?'

'I'll think about it.' He doesn't.

David had a few ideas.

'A couple of slabs of wood would do the trick. That old mahogany door in the laundry. Rip out the handle and lie it on. I'll give you a hand.'

'That's foin. You'll need a bigger mattress to cover it, so you

157

will.' It never came.

'There's some as like to dump all their clothes at the laundry in town and they'll give it back dry in an hoor folded and all for a few poons. Saves ye drying it by the peat, like ye are.'

Oh yeah, man? A few poons?

One evening, after six weeks of rain and wind, the sun shone. Six o'clock exactly — Angelus time. Bells were ringing as we walked light-footed out into the wild Donegal countryside. A touch of heather appeared high up on the rocky hill, and small wild rasp-berries hid amongst the honeysuckle hedge. Down below, Loughross Point, stretching into the Atlantic, had dried out at low tide. Farmers yelled obscenities at their dogs as they made use of the few dry hours to separate sheep from lambs.

'Aye, the sheep are bigger 'n New Zealand, and plenty of 'em. But the weather's bin awful, jest awful. I've never seeen such rain in all m'life. Hard to get the silage dry or anythin' for that matter. The barley and oats — it's desperate.'

We walked on to the brow of the hill, where the Atlantic showed up in the distance. Not the crashing, bashing Atlantic, but a calm strip of inland sea, a thread of silver in the evening light.

'Has either of you got folks here?' asked a man walking by.

'My father came from near Ballycastle. His name was Magill.'

He stopped for only a second.

'Yeah, Magill from Antrim. Came here at the famine time be-cause he refused to become a Protestant just to get soup from 'em. Brought a flock of goats with him and took 'em to this high glen up here near the Glengesh Pass. Those Magills are so thick on the ground now you can't throw a stick between them. There were no Magills in Ardara before the famine. My name's Gallagher. We'd be second to Magills in numbers. The weather's lifted up — better be off. Had a heart operation and have to walk, they tell me.'

There are times when dreams come true! Ardara — full of Magills. Spelt in every possible way. And we'd landed right in the middle of them. Incredible! Who would have done any research on family trees round the place, we wondered?

I saw it first at the butcher's shop next day — a sticker on the door.

Patrick Macgill Summer School
Glenties

'Where's Glenties?' I asked the butcher.

'Just a step out of Ardara. Ten miles or so. Goin' there? Pretty place. They have that school there every year — same time. Magill country this is round here.'

Magill country? Donegal? A lost arm of the family.

It was late afternoon when we rounded the corner and entered Glenties main street for the first time. What a difference! After the annual Mary of Dungloe Festival, a competitive international event hosted by popular singer Daniel O'Donnell, Glenties burst on us like a song, lifting our spirits. Stretched before us were buildings washed in soft pink, yellow, white and blue. Flowers in window boxes relieved the severity of the traditional architecture.

'Look, there's a plaque to the memory of that poet, Patrick MacGill,' said David. 'Let's stop and take a photo. You never know.'

> patrick macgill
> 'the navvy poet'
> 1889–1963
>
> i'm going back to glenties
> when the harvest fields are brown
> and the autumn sunset lingers
> on my little irish town

The main street, bisected by a chuckling river, led to a large school set on the hillside. On the corner was a stone grotto with statues of Our Lady of Lourdes appearing to Saint Bernadette.

'There's a feeling about this place — a gentility. I see it's won the tidy town award a few times, too, and they're really promoting the summer school. Let's see if we can buy any books by this Patrick MacGill, just to see what he wrote about,' I suggested.

They had one volume left at the Co-op opposite the Highlands Hotel.

'That's *Children of the Dead End*. It's really his biography,' the girl said. 'But I can order more. The school's on this week, that's why we've run out of stock. He lived near here, you know.'

The Highlands Hotel had a feel about it too, the lobby shadowed and cool after the sun. To one side, a lounge, to the other, the pub. A casual sunroom also opened off to the left, friendly and inviting. For house guests. 'Irish coffees? Certainly madam.' Attractively served — in perfect taste. No loud talking here, or louts in singlets. Well-dressed and polite, customers spoke to each other in modulated voices. Visitors to the summer school. It must be special, this school, and we were strangely drawn to it. For a while we sat happily in the cosy atmosphere, pondering, then David spotted a watercolour near the lobby. He stared, spellbound.

'These are the best I've seen in Ireland so far. Are there any more, and do you know the artist?' he asked the receptionist.

Christine Boyle, the owner's wife, came to our table.

'My husband, Johnny, is the artist. He's opening his exhibition tonight before the paintings go to Soest in Germany for a one-man show. Look, here's an invitation. Why don't you both come and join us for the sneak preview. There are thirty-four paintings of Donegal in the back foyer.'

The Highlands Hotel was buzzing when we returned later in the evening. Not just with artists, but the literati of Donegal. So this was it — a meeting place for artists, writers, musicians and dancers. A tradition handed down from father to son. 'Old Johnny Boyle made sure his son ran this place when he died so it didn't lose the atmosphere. The young one would rather paint, but he's doing a good job and Christine's terrific.'

'Look everyone, here are those two from the antipodes. The doctor is the artist and his wife's the writer,' the terrific Christine called out. Then she took us round. 'Now, you must meet Lawson Birch, another artist . . . and Frank Harvey, a poet from Donegal town . . . and . . . ' David vanished to drool over the paintings.

I was drawn to Frank Harvey at once. He stood up to shake my hand, an elderly, white-haired gentleman — polite, gracious and quietly spoken — his every sentence a poem.

'You know, I've sat in this hotel and heard Brendan Behan and others reading. I can see Brendan still, sitting over there. Better sober than in his cups, you know. I took him to all the big houses in Donegal. He wanted to speak to the people and get the feel of them. I didn't have that desire, but Brendan needed a minder and I knew them all at the big houses — the Anglos, you know. Ascendancy stock.'

We could have talked forever, and I excused myself with regret. Frank needed to sit down and I had important business to do.

'Are Patrick MacGill's daughters in Glenties for the summer school?' I asked a few in the milling crowd.

'Of course they are. They're staying here at this hotel. Right now they're at a cross-border dialogue at the school, first ever of its kind in Donegal. There's MPs from the North and South. Should be over soon.'

Patrick MacGill's daughters here — from the States! I had to go now and see them.

'But it's after ten!' David gasped.

'Let's go! I have that gut feeling we could be related.'

The man at the door stared. Coming at ten for a cross-border dialogue? Photographers perhaps? Or journalists? But . . .

'Are the MacGills here?' I shot out in a rush.

'Yes, madam. Write me a note and I'll give it to Mrs Sheila. The meeting's nearly over. You can see her after. Sit in for the rest of the programme.'

The session was called 'A New Start for Northern Ireland', and the speakers were from all political parties in Northern Ireland, with the chairperson Mr Dinny McGinley TD.

'Some of these speakers have never crossed the border in their lives, not even to Donegal. Isn't it just incredible?' a lady whispered to me.

'Has it been a noisy meeting?' I asked. 'You know, these political dialogues can be bedlam. Everybody getting steamed up having their say.'

'You have no idea now sensible and committed to the peace agreement these people are. I do hope it holds.'

Sheila came out into the foyer. 'A Magill from *New Zealand*?' She gaped and clasped my hands. 'And a writer too? Get this down smartly in case I don't see you again.'

While she read from her notes I scribbled furiously.

161

What we have in Ireland is a genetic memory. An unusual force for good and bad.

1. The buoyant economy of Ireland is due not only to the EU but other factors also. A young, educated workforce is enthusiastic and competent. Big European companies are happy to open branches here and know they will be run efficiently. (As opposed to some European and American kids, who can leave school semi-literate.)

2. They have had no racial discrimination except the English, who are really speaking the same language, and many have English blood anyway.

3. No history of Industrial Revolution.

4. No pollution — clean water, air, etc.

5. While England was becoming industrialised, Ireland was treated as its market garden — its first colony, with easy access. They kept it as their back-yard farm deliberately. The plantation people's prime role was to produce for Britain, so the Industrial Revolution, with its polluting consequences, overcrowding and urbanisation, never really hit Ireland. As a consequence of this it is now one of the least polluted areas — land and sea — in the whole of Europe. Its education system has produced an abundance of young intelligent workers. The EU, recognising this, has jumped in to establish factories and major industries are confident they will be well managed.

Ireland — despite the Troubles, the penal times, the insurrections, the suppression of its natives and the actual process of colonisation — has its freedom, and has opened a pristine cornucopia to the EU.

'Look, it's after eleven. Can't you stay in the area for a few more days? What about lunch tomorrow at the Highland? We'll raise a few!'

'We *must* see more of them.' I jumped round excitedly. We did!

The two elderly American daughters of Patrick MacGill, Sheila and Patricia, and their husbands sat down with us to lunch. The past was very near. These two had done years of research on the family in the States.

'The first Magill was chased over the Antrim Hill by the planters, they told me in Ardara,' I started off, breaking the ice.

Sheila filled in the rest. 'MacGills, whatever their spelling, we're gallowglass — Highland mercenaries — sent over from Scotland to help the Irish fight their battles, long before the planters arrived. We're talking thirteenth century now. We're a sept of McDonalds of the Isles — an awful tartan. We're fighters!' And she clenched her fist at me, laughing.

'I hear your mother was the daughter of a cardinal,' I mouthed off without thinking.

The two professor husbands laughed into their drinks, almost choking.

'Oh, ha ha! The best I've heard yet!'

'Our mother was a niece of a cardinal,' corrected Patricia quietly.

'I'm so sorry,' I apologised lamely.

'Now, you two would be interested in the lectures Leo's giving on the 1798 rebellion as part of the bicentennial perspective. Why don't you join us here for those — and lunch after?'

Professor Leo Callahan of Iona College University in New York, Sheila's husband, gave two lectures on his favourite research topic. A masterly presentation to a crowded audience. We were favoured to be there to record it.

Patricia's husband — Professor Owen McGowan — had different interests. A quiet, gentle man, he seemed intrigued with his two new friends from the antipodes.

'What do you do in your spare time, Owen?' I asked over lunch.

'I teach lay people to do the work of priests,' he answered with a smile. 'We haven't nearly enough priests in the States these days, so I'm lecturing these men on the basics of priestly work.'

'Married men?'

'Oh yes, that's the idea, and a finer group of students it would be hard to find.'

'And women?'

'That will be a long time coming — if ever,' he said sadly. 'In the Catholic church anyway.'

Sheila and I exchanged some of the books we had written. Hers were detective yarns with an Irish flavour, and I passed over *Irish in the Blood*. Her father's book, *Children of the Dead End* took pride of place on the table.

'That book is so loved by Irish people — not so much by the priests, but that is a MacGill trait, with or without the C.'

'I suppose being fighters we don't take kindly to the clergy.'

'We never will.'

How sorry we were to part from our new-found relatives. Would we ever see them again?

'One of the American MacGills will always be at the summer school in Glenties each August,' Sheila said as we parted. 'We've attended every one since it started, and when we pass on our children will come over. You'll know one of us will be here. After all, he was our daddy.'

This is when New Zealand seems so far removed from Ireland. Popping over to the summer school from the States is not a big deal for them, but for us it is a world away.

It wasn't an issue that these MacGills were Catholics and we were Protestants. They were relatives and friends, and would be forever. Our pens would be busy.

GOING HOME

I'm going back to Glenties when the harvest fields are brown,
And the Autumn sunset lingers on my little Irish town,
When the gossamer is shining where the moorland blossoms blow,
I'll take the road across the hills I tramped so long ago —
'Tis far I am beyond the seas, but yearning voices call,
'Will you not come back to Glenties, and your wave-washed
    Donegal?'

I've seen the hopes of childhood stifled by the hand of time,
I've seen the hopes of innocence become the frown of crime,
I've seen the wrong rise high and strong, I've seen the fair betrayed,
Until the fluttering heart fell low, the brave became afraid —
But still the cry comes out to me, the homely voices call,
From the Glen among the highlands of my ancient Donegal.

Sure, I think I see them often, when the night is on the town,
The Braes of old Strasala, and the homes of Carrigdoun —

Patrick MacGill

MACGILL SUMMER SCHOOL
BELFAST PACT WILL BOOST DONEGAL, UNIONIST SAYS
By Frank McNally

Cross-border co-operation under the Belfast Agreement will have a dramatic impact on Co. Donegal, a leading Ulster Unionist has told the Patrick MacGill Summer School.

Mr Steven King, special adviser to the UUP deputy leader, Mr. John Taylor, said Donegal in particular had been ill-served by partition, which cut it off from the main commercial centre of west Ulster, Derry.

'Its population has declined dramatically, partly for that reason, partly because of peripherality, and partly because it bore the brunt of failed economic policies devised in Dublin,' he told the school in Glenties last night, during a debate entitled 'A New Start for Northern Ireland'.

The areas earmarked for cross-border co-operation would change all this, however, not least with regard to the fishing industry, but also the accident and emergency services, whereby people will be able to avail themselves of the services of Altnagelvin (Derry) and the Royal Victoria Hospital (Belfast) rather than travel to Dublin for a serious operation.

Transport would be increasingly considered in a cross-border context, he added, and he particularly welcomed a plan for a ferry between Magilligan in Derry and Greencastle in Donegal.

He admitted that co-operation had been limited in the past by the weakness of local government in Northern Ireland, with a single county council in Donegal facing 'many small and relatively ineffective authorities across the border.' Twenty-six local authorities were 'far too many for Northern Ireland, especially in the context of a new assembly,' he added.

But if the assembly was to work, he concluded, both unionists and nationalists had to be more realistic than they traditionally had been.

'Appealing to romantic visions of Ireland will not do,' he said. 'Equally, unionists have a duty not to pretend that Northern Ireland was an imperial idyll until someone invented the IRA.'

But a Democratic Unionist Party assembly member, Mr Jim Wells, said this phase of the peace process was another phase in the 'Sinn Fein/IRA strategy of the Armalite in one hand and the ballot box in the other . . . Once the present process of using the ballot box is exhausted, then they will return to what they do best and resume their terror campaign. That is why they will not give up their arsenal of weapons.'

But he added that the DUP was committed 'to holding Tony Blair and David Trimble to their pre-referendum promise that there would be no question of SinnFein/IRA in the government of Northern Ireland without the decommissioning of weapons.'

The debate was also addressed by the SDLP's Mr Alex Atwood, the PUP's Mr. Robin Stewart, and the editor of the Belfast News- *letter, Mr Geoff Martin. According to a supplied script, Mr Martin told the gathering that politicians in Nothern Ireland did not yet know how to build their future themselves, because they had had to be 'lectured, bullied and coerced' to move them as far as they had gone.*

'We have a peace process, we have commissions foisted upon us to adjudicate every issue we cannot sort out among ourselves, and we have a new administration, artificially constructed for us in a way that would insult our intelligence if we had achieved for ourselves the level of political maturity necessary to enable an egalitarian society to evolve and thrive.'

Few of the political leaders had voluntarily reached out to the people on the other side of the divide, he added, 'a process that is absolutely necessary if we are to heal divisions and build a new Northern Ireland'.

Irish Times

14. precious people of donegal

Rain poured down on Protestant and Catholic alike — no sectarian preference for the apprentice boys' march in Derry, or the annual Southwest Donegal Agricultural and Industrial Show in Ardara. Same day, same time, separated by only a few miles but three hundred years of history.

Judging livestock is not an Irish joke. The soggy field outside Ardara furrowed by tractors and trailers and drowned out from weeks of rain had turned into a sea of muddy slush. Trucks laden with hay drove in and out, scattering their loads on the flooded tracks in an effort to keep wheels moving, and despite the quagmire the show went on, as it always did — minus the band.

'It rains like this every year for the Ardara show,' they told us in town.

Gaily coloured stalls were offering the same old food known the world over — Coca-Cola and hot chips, pork sausages and pies — but in Ireland no show is fun without its dulse and yellowman. Guinness was just a step away, round the corner.

We hung over the fence in the driving rain watching cattle coming and going — magnificent specimens but breeds unheard of in New Zealand. Here were Charolais and many others. Sure they'd heard of our Jerseys and Friesians, but 'you keep them in the fields therr, don' yiz?' Earnest faces watched every movement as the judges poked and prodded the beasts, looking at them from every angle. No quick decisions and no crack today. Serious stuff this. Black-faced ewes, black-faced rams, wool tinted, carded and fluffed out like a blow wave, horns polished with CRC. Crossbreds, Texels ...

The loudspeaker yelled.

'What language is that?' I asked my neighbour at the fence.

'Just 'im.' He smiled. 'Just 'im. That's the way of 'im.' But how could 'ewes' be 'yoas'? 'Shouldn't have given that white 'un first,' the man said, shaking his head. 'That brown 'un should be first.' His face screwed up angrily, and he stomped off in a mood.

At a discreet distance from the cattle, horses with foals and ponies did their circles. A woman judging the ponies retained her feminine image. No gumboots or raincape for her, no umbrella even. Floral dress and high heels marked her out from the rest, her thin stockings already splattered with mud. She was the judge, regardless of rain and everyone else. Another neighbour said 'plah' when she entered the ring, and walked off.

No gumboots either in the élite horse section. We were in the aristocracy department here. In tweeds and riding boots, competitors showed their exhibits — Connemara brood mares — mares under 14.2 hands with foal at foot — and then the big stuff. Heavy and light hunters, Irish draughts. Two bowler-hatted judges, one very large, the other small, strutted their stuff. Smart men these, with twirling moustaches and the best in riding gear. Laurel and Hardy with riding stocks they were, performing to their rain-drenched audience. Round again, then again, stop, round again. Down to three now. Round again, again and again. The Irish know their horses and love them — you could feel it in the air.

Inside the big marquee people sheltered from the rain, running experienced eyes over the produce. Not much different from the women's division of Federated Farmers in New Zealand — just the local specials.

'Porter cake?' I asked the winner.

'I put half a bottle of Guinness in mine.'

'Baking powder?'

'Everything made with soda here — everything.'

Six hand-cut turf.

'I don't know why mine didn't win,' a despondent exhibitor moaned to me. 'It's darker and thinner. Look — it'd last longer than that pale stuff.'

'Aye, that mebbe so, but the pale stuff was textured and even,'

The clenched fist of a Protestant graveyard is a far cry from a fairy castle at the base of Mt Errigal.

Sitting on a sunny pier, having a drink and some crack, is a fine way to pass the time in Ballyhack, County Wexford.

Laughter, music and peat fires sustain the spirit of Lettermullen's tight-knit Gaelic-speaking people.

The Lambeg drum is a symbol of turbulent times in Northern Ireland.

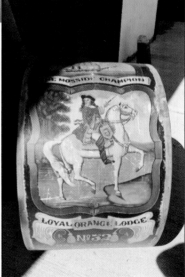

After 300 years, triumphant William of Orange remains the hero of Northern Ireland Protestants.

*'Give my head peace.' Beautiful Cushendun in the Glens of Antrim,
Northern Ireland.*

*The surprise 'view' from our 'beach cottage' in the once-glamorous
Mountcharles, Donegal.*

someone whispered behind his hand.

The home-made wine section.

'Here — try a drop!' called Paul Dunleavy. 'That's the winner!'

'De-lic-ious!' I drooled.

The makeshift trestle moved slightly under the weight of the bottles — and *crash!* Home-made wine spilled across the floor, trickling down to the floral displays. Broken bottles lay scattered about in a sorry mess. People stared in shocked silence, transfixed, their eyes misty. Paul Dunleavy sat down in a chair, head in hands. Many minutes went by before anyone rallied themselves to help.

'Desperate,' Paul mumbled, 'just desperate, but I know the winner — he wins everytime. It's just . . . Can yez smell it? Ah-ah-ah!'

And the names of the other organisers and entrants — ye couldn't throw a stick between the McGills and the Gallaghers!

Chairperson: Joseph Gallagher.

Directors: Nan McGill.

Patrons: F. Gallagher, Nan McGill.

Class 83: Three stalks rhubarb, Marie McGill, Scadaman, Ardara.

Class 11: Six brown hen eggs, Marie McGill, Scadaman, Ardara.

Photography Section: Best Colour Photograph, Animal or Wildlife (open): No. 2, Lochann McGill, Ardara; No. 19, Brid McGill, Macharie, Ard an Ratha.

And Lochann does the McGill research, they told me, but he was away just now!

I lost a kilo of beef sausages that day at the Ardara fair. The very day the local butcher had got round to making anything beef. It had been pork all the way in Ireland — pork, ham, bacon, pork, ham, rashers . . .

'Don't get a call for it,' the butchers always said. 'Gone off beef they have, since the mad cow. You know about that mad cow? And now it's eggs from the North that's bad. I wouldn't buy eggs from the North anyway so don't worry about them. Mine come from Sligo — always have. Always from Sligo.'

Butchers can go on and on if you let them, but this day he had made beef sausages for visitors in town, and I had lost mine.

'You *lost* those beef sausages? What a bugger! And I made them special for the fair.'

'Yes, it is a bugger. Any more?'

'Look, wait an hour or so and I'll make ye more, or just take this wee handful of mince for nothing. Make ye feel better.'

'I'll go back on my tracks first.'

'Aye, that's it — they'll have them. Sure they will.'

The text on his counter stopped me dead: O Lord, help my words to be gracious and tender today because tomorrow I may have to eat them.

'D'ye like that then? It's as true as I'm standin' here that is. God bless you.'

The man in the supermarket called his office loudly: 'A lady here's lost the beef sausages. Been handed in? Yoor sure? Sorry madam, they're not here. I'd give you every beef sausage from the shelves here if I had them, sure I would. Where did ye go from here then?'

'The laundrette.'

'Go there. He'll have them, that's for certain sure. He's always cleanin' up, he is.'

'Look, lady,' said the laundrette man, 'I've swept this place twice today and checked every bundle. No beef sausages, I've found. I'm always the last one to leave and tidy up. I would have seen them. Not like clothing, are they? No, they're not. Now, where did you go from here?'

'Upstairs to the coffee place.'

'Up therr? Go up then right now, that's where they'll be. Paul's sure to have them behind that coffee counter. Ye know it? Where they've got that big machine with all those wee beans in it. I can see them sittin' therr waitin' for ye.'

It was worth the hunt, even if the beef sausages were never found. Where would you get such a response to a simple question anywhere else in the world but Ireland?

The fascination of Donegal is its diversity. The wild uninhabited hills and glens, the pretty beaches and pre-Christian relics, all at a turn in the road.

Fort Doon (Fort O'Boyle) is a ring fort well hidden from the turn-off to Lough Doon. A weird, lonely road leads out through swampy marshes — a never-ending road, without a house in sight. Then, just when you're about to turn back, a drooping old sign directs you further inland. Dogs bark and rowing boats clutter the entrance to a small house.

'Five punts an hour to hire the boat,' the owner says matter-of-factly.

To us that's fifteen dollars. A huge decision to make.

'No other way to see it?' we ask hopefully.

'No.'

'A real ring fort on a lake,' David reads. 'Two thousand years BC, oval area enclosed by a massive stone fortification averaging four metres wide at the base and four point eight metres in height. All this for fifteen dollars. Let's go!'

It's quite a climb down the muddy, rocky hill to the heavy rowing boat, but all is dead calm on Lough Doon. Not a bird sings. Only the dip of our oars makes a slow, rhythmical noise in the dark water. Hard to believe rival O'Boyles galloped round these hills killing each other, then hid in this fort for months or years. Where is it?

Suddenly it's in your face. This huge fort in the middle of a lake. We leave a rock on the painter and walk round the uneven stone walls, looking down on high grass inside, unkempt and sinister. So people lived here, had a cow and chickens, made their home and — waited! O'Boyle was murdered here — it says on the wall. You can almost hear the clash of swords, see the blood. O'Boyle's blood. O'Boyle's head floating on the lough, face up. It's quiet now, too quiet, and you shiver.

> The nameless doon
> Who were the builders?
> Question not the silence
> That settles on the lake forevermore
> Save when the sea birds scream
> And to the island the answer echoes
> From the deep cliff shore.
>
> Wm. Lairime

The boat is back on land and an old man comes out of the small house, bent over his stick. He is 93. His name is O'Boyle.

'They got one of them, murdered at that fort, I know that. No one else has got us — those others — '

He's talking about his relative, Conor, in 1530, as if it was last year. He fastens his old pale blue eyes on us.

'Aye, you've got a woman with ye. I lost mine after sixty-four years.' He shakes his head. 'My mother was a hundred and two when she died here. I can remember everyone that's come in that door since the age of one year.'

I can believe him — his memory is uncanny, his eyes ancestral.

'I'm a Magill,' I prompted. He didn't hesitate a second.

'Chased over the hills of Antrim by the planters. Been here long ago. Fighters. Aye, I know them. But my woman, she's gone now,' he repeated sadly.

'You'll see her up above soon enough,' I pointed to heaven.

'Oh naw,' he squeaked. 'I don't believe in it.'

His son smiled wistfully as we left. These are the precious old men of Ireland.

On this first sunny day in six weeks we pass the White Flag beaches of Navin and Portnoo. Crowds of people stand waist deep in the calm water enjoying every ray of sunshine, every pleasant wisp of warm breeze. They don't swim much. Children play with buckets and spades on the white sand — it's heaven for them.

A long-haired youth and his buddies speed by in a flash car.

'Seen the dolmen?' they call to us.

'No. We're looking, too. They say if you're lucky you can see a huge stone mushroom in a field in Killclooney, back of the church. But you have to drive slowly and look.'

Suddenly, there it is. But it's just a small rock structure without any notice or fence or anything. How are we meant to get to it? Farm dogs bark madly as we approach the nearest bungalow and wait for a sign of life. After a while an old woman emerges and points to a muddy tractor road through wet bog and fresh cow dung.

The guide dog stops dead on the slushy track, his tongue lolling out. From this point the mushroom effect has changed into a

giant three-legged stool made up of a dome — an enormous flat rock — supported by three pillars two metres high, each a single massive boulder. Inside the legs, a deep, excavated grave is supported by huge slab rocks. We are looking at 2000 BC, and a strange hollow feeling hits us in the stomach. How did men lift these things, and what for? No one knows. They are there, that's all. We slush back through the muddy track, the dog barking madly at our heels. A precious dolmen stuck out in a derelict field? Put it in the States and people would be queuing up at a heritage park and paying the earth to see it. Put it in New Zealand and we would make a special room in a museum for it, under lock and key. Donegal is like this. It disguises its age and seems careless about preserving it. Perhaps one day the EU . . . ?

The lads are still racing up and down the road, looking. We point to the dolmen in the field and they stop. Up that bog is it?

Mount Errigal, 752 metres high, draws you like a magnet. It dominates the landscape for miles around and emanates a feeling of excitement when it appears round a corner. Like Mount Ruapehu in New Zealand, you love it. It does not demand a spiritual response like Croagh Padraig, just restful admiration.

Below it a road turns off to Poisoned Glen, and the remnants of an old village called Dunlewy (Dun Luiche). A beautiful Anglican

173

church sits in the sun facing the most magnificent view. On its left, the majestic cliffs of the glen; in front, Lough Dun Luiche; and the slopes of Errigal to the right. But it is empty and sightless, and sad. Made of pure white quartzite stone from the nearby hills, it exudes an atmosphere of extraordinary charm and beauty. But something has happened here in the past, and not just the ascendancy story. A large cardboard text of the Ten Commandments lies against the front entrance, looking totally out of place. It has been put there recently by someone in the Poisoned Glen. I started fossicking in my bag of books.

Quote from the Belfast nationalist newspaper the *Ulsterman*, editor Dennis Holland, 1858:

> Most of Dunlewy belonged to Mrs Jane Russell, who had a reputation for trying to convert her Catholic tenants. Holland remarked that she was a lady who tried to be a 'Good Samaritan' to the afflicted Celts of Dunlewy in a peculiar fashion — distributing among them cheap tracts and bibles, then quadrupling their rents. She was the owner of Dun Luiche House at the side of the Lough.

Perhaps her children's children had kept up the tradition and the Ten Commandments were there as a promise to their old grandma Jane to 'keep the witness alive'. They lived in the magnificent Dun Luiche House nearby, we heard.

In today's world, Jane Russell would have been loved more if she had given the 'afflicted Celts' some food and clothing instead of cheap tracts.

Returning to the long grass round the church I started looking for gravestones or clues, when an apparition over the stone wall caught my eye. A woman of about sixty, with a checked bonnet and blond plaits, was carrying water in a bucket. Was she trying to be Alice in Wonderland?

I called to her.

'Took the roof off in the 1950s to avoid taxes,' she called back. 'See the quartzite? Come over and see my place if you like — the oldest house in the village.'

I was looking straight at Jane Crane.

'The fairies told me to rebuild this stone house from an old ruin,' she explained artlessly, 'and they told me exactly how to do it too.' A peaked round brick tower on the side gave the appearance of a fairy castle even before we went in the door. How come she managed to get building permission for that and the low roof inside?

'I told them the fairies had instructed me to make it that way and they eventually agreed.' She had obviously arrived at a formula which confounded bureaucracy. Was she kidding?, I asked myself a dozen times. Was this all just a gimmick she tried out on gullible visitors? The magic tour went on inside — coloured candles, tarot cards, tree roots growing round wooden beams, murals of a haunted forest, owls, hares, deers, signs of the zodiac. And two black cats curled up sleepily by the peat fire. I knew they would be somewhere, for good luck. Pot plants rioted inside and out like scary cobwebs, all looking for fairies. Along one wall a huge library of books looked out of place. Fairies and leprechauns don't read.

'I don't usually invite people in here,' she explained. 'It's not finished. The workmen will tell you. I have two signs — one in English which says "Fuck off" in nice language, and the other in runic writing. See it here? *Those* people are welcome. I knew you were one of us when I called you from the church. You're fey, and yes — don't tell me — a writer like me. I was formerly a reporter for the *Sunday Times* in the UK, and Europe sometimes. I like Keri Hume and Shirley Grace and some others of your writers.'

We were outside now, with the lower slopes of Errigal running right down into her garden of gnomes and rock pools. The fairies certainly knew how to create a garden.

'Tell me your birth date,' she said.

I told her.

'Yes, that fits. And your visiting cards are the same colour as mine — Kerry green.'

'You're a fortune teller,' I suggested. 'And lots of other interesting things.'

'Yes, but the fairies said I was to finish this house before I started anything. I have to carry water for the men here, don't I? At first they thought I was crazy, but now they are happy to go along with the plan.'

We went out through an old green wrought-iron gate. It looked as if the fairies had given her that as a gift.

'I pick up every antique that suits this place. I look at all the sales in the newspapers and buy them. Send me your book, won't you?'

She stood at the gate — a quaint, plump Alice figure in pigtails. What would happen if I pulled one, I wondered? But who would want to destroy the magic she had created? There are too few characters in this world, and the trip to fairyland had been special.

Lucky it is when fairies have money!

15. a different drum

ORANGE DRUMS

The lambeg balloons at his belly, weighs
Him back on his haunches, lodging thunder
Grossly there between his chin and his knees
He is raised up by what he buckles under.

Each arm extended by a seasoned rod,
He parades behind it. And though the drummers
Are granted passage through the nodding crowd,
It is the drums preside, like giant tumours.

To every cocked ear, expert in its greed,
His battered signature subscribes 'No Pope.'
The goatskin's sometimes plastered with his blood.
The air is pounding like a stethoscope

Seamus Heaney

THERE ARE TIMES IN IRELAND when you wonder if the Second Coming of the Lord has already been and gone and you have been left behind on planet Earth. One such for us was on the road from Glenties to Commeen, where the mist-wreathed Blue Stack Mountains look down on desolate moorland. Not a house, not a sign of human life, only black-faced sheep and plastic bags full of peat left behind to tell the tale. What would the Lord want with those? There is a possibility we could be on the wrong road. Those tiny antique notices with Gaelic subtitles are suspect at times.

Trixie is jittery now and coughing nervously, knowing there is no one about to help her if she conks out. She should turn round, but something tells her she must go on. There is a curious-looking object in the distance beside a culvert, but it is not moving. At closer range it looks like a grotto. Maybe we could try a prayer or two to get us up to heaven with the rest of humanity. But surprisingly it is not a grotto, rather a carefully crafted cairn in sand-coloured granite, with a fiddle and bow above the Gaelic inscription in remembrance of a gifted man who gave music to a lonely community. That is Gaelic society — artists, musicians and writers are part of its life blood and held in high regard. 'Feckless layabouts' they may call them in the North. But nay — Mikey Jimmy O'Doherty was no layabout. Grateful people have erected this unique memorial for all to see, and his son, Jimmy, has carried on the magic, the name O'Doherty now being found on CDs and tapes, a byword in Ireland.

I gcuimhne ar mhici shimi o doehartaigh,
sar-fhidleir conallach.
ag an droichead seo rinne se an pandai a
shabhail a chraiceann.

In memory of mikey jimmy o'doherty, an outstanding
donegal fiddler.
at this bridge he made pandy [mashed potatoes with butter]
which saved his hide.

It is worth plugging on to Ballybofey now. We didn't understand the Gaelic then, but we had the feeling people were not far away. One small cottage appears, and another, then a small picturesque pub shows up round the next corner, baskets of flowers hanging from the verandah and a small stream running close by. What a picture! It is easy to imagine Mikey O'Doherty fiddling here in the evenings, the atmosphere charged with the magic of his bow. It would be nice to stay and chat in the sun outside this pub, and find out how making pandy at the bridge saved Mikey's hide, but it is to the North we are heading . . .

Some people imagine the border crossing between South and North to be a monstrous frontier of barbed wire and heavy guns. Others have no idea there is any difference at all — just six counties grouped together to make some place called Northern Ireland or Ulster. Something happened in the history of this island way back and they divided it up to keep people happy. That's all they know. To many New Zealanders it is simply like our North and South Island without Cook Strait.

It's a good kids' game to play 'spot the difference' as you travel south to north. The green *oifig an phoist* becomes the red post office; Union Jacks are mixed up with tricolours; punts go to pounds sterling; the Queen's head on stamps replaces Eire and the Tour de France; *priority aerphos* becomes *air mail; garda* becomes *police; yeild* is *stop.*

These are the outward signs any child can play at, but the real differences are complex and deep, going back hundreds of years. How can a visitor ever understand the minds of the people of the North? And the people of the North will never accept advice from 'strangers' from other parts of the world, the Republic included. They are always right — the Bible has said so. The result is confusion and anger, which can be *felt.* It takes a while to understand all that.

But I am back here to find out more about my father's birthplace, to get the real feel of Carvacloughan, and to meet my next of kin, Ivan McAllister. I want to set the old family tree straight and make a new one. I want to look for the villages and townlands from Linde Lunney's findings in Trinity College, and tell them about the other relatives we met in Glenties. It should be exciting, and I want to get on with it, but a certain heavy atmosphere pervades the place, damping my spirit. Are the people here Irish or not? Compared with New Zealand, where Union Jacks are flown on special occasions, they are flying here from all kinds of buildings and houses, as if a coronation was imminent. Another set of buildings is flying the tricolour of the Republic. Stickers on lampposts suggest someone works for M15, and graffiti is sending the Pope in a hurry to a hot place. Gerry Adams is responsible for all bad things and the IRA could creep up your drive or send one of its many baddies to ambush you. Paisley is a shite, and it seems so important that Orangemen must walk down this small piece of County Armagh called Garvaghy Road. Tension stares out from dull, unhappy eyes — in the shops, on the streets, everywhere.

Portadown township is sadder still, some of its buildings being repaired after recent bomb blasts. People tell you that with a curl of the lip. Along the country road where we live, many have gone abroad to miss the marching season — to Spain, France, Portugal, the Canary Islands, Switzerland. Even Scotland and England would be OK. And here we are, paying a visit to see the marching season as if it was some kind of circus. We obviously don't understand. We are curious and naive. That is an unspoken criticism.

'I've got all the freezers and fridges full this year,' says Chris, our hostess. 'I couldn't stand a repeat of last year's standoff when we couldn't leave the house for three days. You've got no idea what it's like here, and if the Orangemen get over that barbed wire fence at Drumcree this year, all hell will break loose, and with extra army over from England . . . Are you sure you want to stay? It might not be pleasant. But I'd wait till it's over before you head further north to Ballycastle.'

There is a siege mentality here. A tension from morning till night. The conversation is ominous, heavy, fraught with dark possiblities.

Houses are large and well maintained in our street, the gardens colourful, the people generous and hospitable. The view across the fields to the distant Mountains of Mourne is one which should bring peace and tranquillity, but somehow beauty goes unseen in the eyes of the people of Portadown.

Chris offers to drive us round the country area, and it is now I begin to get that closed-in feeling I experienced as a young girl in Napier. That claustrophobia of belonging to a group that considers itself right and everyone else wrong. You are one of us or one of them. Nothing in-between. That possessive mentality which claims God is their property alone, and to Hell with the rest.

We are getting a run-down now on the people in the area. Not a light-hearted overview of what people 'are' in life, like businessmen, tradesmen, farmers, professionals, artists or retired, but a run-down on their church affiliations. We're heavily into religion and politics again.

'Those in that house are Baptist, those Methodist, those Exclusive Brethren, those Catholics, those have a meeting in their garage, those in that huge white house are Cooneyites, those are Anglicans, those Presbyterians . . .' And so it went on. Dozens of groups.

'How come you know all that?' we asked, amazed. 'In our street in Auckland we haven't a clue who goes to what church, if any. Does it really matter?'

'They've got to have a tag round here, or else.'

'Or else what?'

'Or else they would be suspect. We have to know who they are for our own safety. You ask John. People are even asking about you guys.'

Oh yeah? We could be IRA spies, I suppose.

We turn into another road now, pass the Orange Hall waving a Union Jack and the Catholic church with a tricolour, and now Chris stops outside the small Brethren Hall. 'Prepare to meet thy God' is printed in large letters on one side and 'Ye must be born again' on the other. I am reliving a past life. This place has got to me already. Thirty years ago the Brethren in New Zealand had texts like that stuck all over their halls inside and out, and some on their cars. Not now.

'Like me, you were Open Brethren once, weren't you?' Chris is saying. 'If you're thinking of going into that shed on Sunday, don't! You'd need a hat and a letter of commendation — you know what I mean — and even then you'd be asked to sit at the back.'

No make-up or jeans. For a moment I think it would be 'good copy' and a bit of a laugh to pop in there, but it would be too painful and in poor taste to act a part, so I give it a miss.

'The Brethren have got a big Sunday school going there,' Chris continues. 'Give the kids hellfire then feed them up with sweeties. Keeps them out of their parents' hair for an hour or so.'

'Those Cooneyites you talked about. I remember as a kid they lived at the bottom of Cameron Road in Napier and wore long hair and black stockings and didn't mix with anyone. We were scared stiff of them. Very poor, they were.'

'Poor? You saw that huge white up-market house we passed? They're Cooneyites and run a big business. Not allowed radios or TVs in their houses but you see them looking at it in their shops or running out to their flash cars to get the news, then popping next door to watch the neighbour's TV. They love that programme *Keeping up Appearances* — you know, that Bucket woman. But they don't invite strangers into their houses — not allowed.'

'How do you know all this?'

'Everyone knows what people are doing round here.'

I was slowly sinking into a time warp. I'm back in Napier, surrounded by the same hypocritical mentality we lived with then. The only difference — they are affluent here.

'Where are you going this Sunday, then?' Chris asked, meaning to which church.

'We'll just go where you go — to that little Methodist church down the road. At least we could all pray for the political situation.'

The service dragged on, an unbelievable repitition of cliché and concepts belonging to a bygone era. How could such a young, enthusiastic minister be so out of date? He must have realised that a mile or so away thousands of Orangemen were marching to Drumcree at a crucial and historical time in the history of Northern Ireland. I was getting edgy and frustrated. David fiddled with his fingernails. Chris was bored.

'Takes you back, doesn't it?' she whispered laconically.

Barricades of steel surrounded the Drumcree church and the Royal Ulster Constabulary had descended on the countryside in its thousands. Helicopters buzzed overhead, and the pale faces of women looked up at the young pastor. Yet still we had to be born again and do all the things numbered from one to five he was pinning on the wall. Hey, Pastor! You're a nice young guy, but the helicopters are deafening. There's a mini war going on in your back yard, and the people have come here for prayer and comfort. I really don't want to hear about Nicodemus, thanks.

We sang two Charles Wesley hymns to the accompaniment of an old puffing organ. I thought of my mother, Jess, and decided not to walk out.

'If the Queen can listen to irrelevant messages, so can you,' she always said. 'You have a mind. Think about other interesting things.'

The helicopters droned, and the pastor spoke.

'After the service we will pray for the disturbing events bringing a heaviness to Portadown.'

'Heaviness' must be another word for 'danger' in his church lingo. It is amazing the Drumcree church doesn't shut its doors against these hooligans. They could have their annual church parade in some other church or hall. They don't need to use the Drumcree church kitchen to cook up a treat. There was an amazing kind of schizophrenia going on there.

A group of church men gathered by the hedge, chatting. Every now and then they looked over their shoulders in a furtive manner.

'They're trying to decide whether to go and support their fellow Orangemen at the field of Drumcree,' said Chris. 'Some of the women have rushed home to prepare food for them. They could be there for hours or days. Brave, aren't they?'

I did not answer.

We awoke to the news and went to bed with it. Politics and religion always at our elbows. TV and radio simultaneously. Big John came and went all hours of the night, his face grim. He knew more than we did.

The phone rang.

'We've got an invitation to see how Lambeg drums are made,' we said to Chris. 'A friend from New Zealand has jacked it up. Come for a breather.'

'If there are any roadblocks we'll have to turn back,' she said anxiously. 'Didn't you see that car burning at the end of the road? We'll take another street. John can't get home, by the way. Too dangerous.'

Jack Adams of Tandragee was the very personification of an Ulsterman and a Lambeg drummer. Tall, straight-backed, with a gentlemanly air and a tiny trimmed moustache, he was a former MP at Westminster who had served under prime minister Harold McMillan. I got the impression of an immoveable Rock of Gibraltar, a 'We are British or we are nothing' type of man. New Zealand is short on such characters.

We followed him into a special shed, expecting a modern version of our armed forces drums, or a sort of update of the bongos. But this is serious stuff, no laughing matter. The Lambeg drums came originally from Holland, and the Anglo-Irish have been banging them since 1690 to warn one another of raids by the native Irish. They can be heard eight kilometres away.

The drums are made of original materials, and every Orange lodge has its own drum and every drummer plays his own rhythm. It is not the soft rhythmical throb of a musical background, but harsh, ear-splitting cane on goatskin. And real goatskin it is, stretched across a shell of figured oak or walnut, at a ten hundred-weight tension. And each drum is big and heavy — over a metre in diameter.

'It takes two people to one drum, interchanging when on a march. Five hundred pounds wouldn't cover the cost,' Jack said, 'and I wouldn't sell my one for a thousand pounds.'

Although the drums were new, the painting and writing had that antique dark green/gold look with images of Orange heroes who died for the cause. Mottos stood out majestically: *Honi soit qui mal y pense* (Shamed be he who thinks evil of it), *Dieu et mon droit* (God and my right), *Quis separabis* (Who will separate us?) They were all there, adorning the drums of the loyal Orange Lodge.

Jack ended his demonstration with a profound statement. 'When the drums are silent, Ulster's finished!'

We stood around silently, not daring to contradict or question the old man. It would be like arguing with God, and anyway, we were visitors. Little did we know that in a few hours Orangemen

would be banging these monsters, demanding a seven-minute walk
to prove their right to use the Queen's highway, and they would be
prepared to stay there till the fortifications went down. All the while
the harsh beat would be pounding the message: 'No surrender!'

Hopefully, one day we would hear a different statement. 'When
the drums are silent, Ulster's at peace.'

How long would that take? Months? Years?

It is sad to listen to politics in this beautiful, mellow countryside
where everything seems peaceful on the surface and most people
live well. But talk about it they *must*, especially to strangers. Perhaps it is a catharsis, an outpouring of the hubris that eats at their
vitals. Tension mounts as 'the glorious twelfth of July' is imminent. If we make a statement, it will be wrong; if we are silent, that
is wrong too. People who believed reconciliation was the answer to
Ulster's problems most of the year and had voted for the peace
agreement, suddenly turned back to their roots for a few days round
12 July and yelled the slogans their parents and grandparents had
taught them. Them-against-us slogans, ugly in their bigotry.

'Put *that* in your book!' angry voices yelled.

'Don't dare put that word in your book — it's not true! yelled
another. 'We don't *hate* our neighbours. It's just the way it is here.
You wouldn't understand.'

And Ulstermen can yell when they want to.

'Don't go to your friends up north in Portstewart — you'll never
get back,' we were advised. 'If you *must* go, pack an overnight bag
and leave very early because of the roadblocks. Don't go anywhere
near Ballymoney — it's IRA territory.' We could hear the whispers
behind our backs: 'Those two are swanning around here as if nothing's going to happen. Casual, aren't they?'

'The referendum won't last. Tony Blair's a ... Mo Mowlam's a
... David Trimble's a ... Gerry Adams is a ... Bertie Ahern's a ...
The Orangemen are ... And there are eighty thousand, of them in
Northern Ireland. The RUC is caught in the crossfire.'

We would have to get out of here! There's no way an outsider
can understand or take sides in Ireland. It has been a dilemma for
centuries and only they can decide what to do. Talking to outsiders

about the Troubles seems to ease them in some way, but you cannot take too much of it. They can see no solution in sight, and all the talk dries out on the rock of intransigence. Enough, I say for now. Let's escape to Portstewart!

We drove through towns bedecked with flags, banners and shields portraying King Billy prancing about on his white horse speaking of the deliverance from papistry and barbarity he represented. Barbarity? It all makes you cringe. 'For God and country' and 'Remember the Battle of the Boyne and Drogheda'. The next town had Republican flags flying in the breeze! Sickmaking, the lot of it.

'You can't go back to Armagh tonight,' Toye and Sam Black greeted us on our arrival in Portstewart. 'Stay here. Plenty of beds. Have a gin and tonic. Trouble in Drumcree, it says on TV. Everything's quiet up here — no helicopters to wake you up. Go back early in the morning.'

The phone rang incessantly from all over the world — from New Zealand, from cousin Jo Cundy in Peterborough in the UK, from another cousin, Digger Magill, in Wales. 'What's going on there in Northern Ireland? The TV's full of it. We've been trying to get you in Portadown. What on earth are you doing up in Portstewart? Glad you're out of that Drumcree area. Stay out of trouble, you two. You could find yourselves in the wrong place at the wrong time.'

If only there were more women of Toye Black's calibre in Northern Ireland. Former mayor of Coleraine, now a councillor, she was known throughout County Antrim as a fair, caring, capable woman with nonsectarian beliefs. Easy to understand why her daughter, Linde Lunney in Dublin, upheld the same values.

Ulster needs more of these intelligent women — many more.

'When I was mayor I enjoyed being on the same stage as Sean McManus, the mayor of Sligo. I will always remember his words: "We live on a very small island. In fact, we live in a very small world, and we're only here a very short time."'

Toye Black kept those words as her talisman. She harboured no grudges, brooked no bigotry and got on with the job.

The Northern Ireland Hotel and Catering College in Portrush

was in full swing when we arrived for the Saturday-night meal, accompanied by Toye and Sam. Students waited on tables with the aplomb of European waiters, their French impeccable, the food delicious.

'Catering and entertaining don't come naturally to the northern character,' explained Toye. 'As people we're stiff and frugal — you know, "the hubris of the North compared with the élan of the South", so we have to actually teach these students how to make people relax and have a good time. If we're going to encourage tourists here, they've got to be up to standard. Up till now they've had to go over to Germany and Switzerland for the finesse. Now we'll teach them here.'

'They know how to serve wine now,' said Sam wryly. 'I'll come here anytime for a meal.' Renowned judge of Leicester sheep throughout the UK, he sat back in his chair, replete. 'You can thank Toye for all this,' he continued proudly, sweeping the restaurant with a gnarled hand. 'She's chairman of the board.'

I loved Sam — a rugged sheepfarmer of the North, happy to talk sheep rather than politics, preferring to whistle up a dog than bang a Lambeg drum. He and Toye restored my faith in Ulster.

'Let's go and have a drink with the director,' Toye suggested.

Professor Ciaran O Cathain couldn't have been more complimentary towards Toye. 'I would never have got this job if it hadn't been for her,' he told us. 'Despite having the best qualifications for the job, I was a Catholic. Toye fights for that everywhere. She demands efficiency, and gets it, despite religion.

'It's not easy living here,' he went on. 'We send our children to integrated schools and get stick from the priest for it, and a few Catholic friends look at us sideways, but like Toye and Sam, we have to take a stand on this. By the way, when Radio Pacific in New Zealand needs the latest on Northern Ireland, I get a call. Listen for it. I suppose I'm their foreign correspondent up here.'

Late in the night, we made our farewells to Professor O Cathain and his wife. We could have chatted with them for many more hours, but Sam was already asleep.

The media pounded Drumcree round the globe and tourism dropped to an all-time low. The ubiquitous B & Bs and classy hotels fell empty at their peak period while Drumcree soldiered on, trying to hurdle the barriers for a seven-minute walk. If there is one quality that the people on either side of the barriers at Drumcree share it is stubborness. Sometimes it can be a virtue, but when it comes to finding solutions to conflicts involving competing rights, it can be disastrous. Pride will have to be swallowed all round if a way out is to be found.

There seemed to be no way I could get to Carvacloughan to do my research. Back in Armagh, we watched the dark smoke of hijacked cars roll across the fields nearby, and the huge double-rotor planes bring hundreds of parachute troops in from England. 'It will be Tony Blair's Bloody Sunday,' someone smirked. 'It's his fault, all of this.' Poor Tony Blair doing his darndest, and Mo Mowlan putting all she had into this débâcle, and this was all they got from the locals. It wasn't fair.

'Look here, you two, I can't be responsible for what happens here in the next few days,' said Big John. 'We have to live here, you don't. Anyone with a car in Northern Ireland should get out before all hell breaks loose. It's not pretty just now, and we could be in for full-scale anarchy — but it's up to you.'

Chris begged us to stay, but we couldn't shrug off the warning from John. But where should we go?

The Glens of Antrim had always held a magic for me. What were these nine glens running down to the north coast? From childhood we had heard about them, and now maybe they could be a place of refuge. Didn't our relative Sir George White have property there? I could check up on that, and maybe take a trip along the coast to Ballintoy and hunt for graveyards. Self-catering cottages? Yes, one in Cushendun. A cancellation. Everyone cancelling, the man said.

> *The blue hills of Antrim, I see in my dreams*
> *The high hills of Antrim, the glens and the streams,*
> *In sunshine or shadow in weal or in woe*
> *The sweet vision haunts me whever I go.*

> Moira O'Neill, *Songs of the Glens of Antrim*

What a magnificent road is the coast road from Ballycastle to Glenariff. The hills lie backward to your right all the way; to your left is a blue sea, and on a clear day you can see Scotland over the water.

> There are hills that rise to the height of mountains, lowlands and highlands, glens and waterfalls, with slow rivers slipping through them, fairylike woodlands, broad pasturelands, sudden stretches of brown Irish bog, and always, either in sight or within hearing, the sea thundering on rocks or sweeping in long waves over yellow sands. Here all the beauty that Nature can crowd into two miles has been spread out in an Antrim glen. Two streams come singing down over the rocks. The trees form a green shade. There are wild flowers, a whisper of leaves, a roar of white water falling, green and brown mountains enclosing this beauty, and eastward the sea.

Sixty years ago Morton wrote this. The same magic is there today.

Eleven o'clock at night is the perfect time to walk the beach at Cushendun. Families were fishing together and cooking marshmallows over a bonfire. Twilight lingered over the sand and sea like a presence, the sky blush-pink. Little children ran about, excited with the catch of tiny plaice.

'D'ya see yon lights?' they chattered to us. 'That's Scotland, so it is, and them lights are the very street lights. Yous have to walk round the caves as well and sit aginst the wall. The sea pushes in therr — yous have to see it.' Their parents smiled.

'We've left Belfast for a break, y'know. The campin' ground's full of people doin' the same. Och! It's no place to be just now.'

We wandered home, glad to be in Cushendun, far from Portadown, and away with the fairies. Strange to read about fairies in these glens. Every book hinted at it, some seriously.

> Onest before the morning light
> The horsemen will come ridin'
> Roun' and roun' the Fairy Lough,
> And no one there to see.

Would we see any 'little people' in Cushendun? Or find one of their caps, as big as a thimble? The glen rioted with stories. Rosemary Garrett tells many stories about the little people of the glens:

> A woman in her eighties living near Lurigedan, told of the visit of a fairy man or grogah to her home when she was a young wife with a baby in the wooden cradle. Her cottage had the usual 'halfdoor' and this was closed, and she was baking farls of bread over the fire when she heard a step outside and a knock. She looked over at the door but saw no one. Then she heard another knock and went to the door and looked over it and there outside she saw a wee man with a tassel on the point of his cap and a blackthorn over his shoulder with a red handkerchief tying up a bundle at the end of it. He looked at her and said 'Good day, fair maid, could I have a bite and sup, for I have far to go?' She told him she had no bread but had farls baking on the griddle at the time, and would he come in and wait till it was done, and 'I'll be giving you some.' He came in and sat on the hob at the side of the fire and never spoke. The woman was trembling with fear for the baby was in the cradle, and she had forgotten to lay the iron tongs across it. [This was done to protect babies from the fairies.] She kept her eye on him while she finished the baking and then she gave him a wee mug of milk and buttered a farl of bread for him. He ate it and rose to leave the house, and then he said to her. 'While you live you will never want milk or bread.'
>
> She watched him walk away and he took a path that led between two tall trees. When he reached these trees he disappeared. A neighbour came in soon after and seeing the woman looked scared and unwell, asked if there was anything wrong. When she was told what had happened she didn't believe it and said 'You've been dreaming,' but the woman of the house showed her the empty mug and the cake of bread with only three farls instead of four, and the neighbour was convinced she spoke the truth. This woman is still alive and a most sincere and truthful person.
>
> Rosemary Garrett, *The Glens of Antrim*

'Do you know of any Whites in this area?' I asked at the local store.

'Whites?' The young boy scratched his head. 'There's a book at home but I can't remember too much about it. Something to do with those big houses round about.'

'Well get it for the lady,' the bossy fat woman said. And to me, 'Come back tomorrow.'

Our neighbour knew more. 'Whites? You mean the Whites of Whitehall in Broughshane? That lot? They gave half this glen to the people.'

'Do they live near here?'

'Go down the drive next but one to you and you'll see a big house near the church. That's Glendun, and it belongs to the Whites. Mrs Patricia isn't there at the moment, but the people staying there will give you her address.'

Next but one to us? The Whites of Sir George White fame? Our relatives?

We walked slowly down the drive, savouring the thought of being related to the Whites of Whitehall and knowing the owners of a 'big house' in Cushendun.

'Mrs Patricia and her husband live in London, but I'll give you her address. She comes down from time to time.'

I started the correspondence immediately. How amazing to land in Cushendun and find Glendun next door. And our neighbour had *Five Big Homes of Cushendun*, by H.E. Brett, on his bookshelf. It was all there. Would Mrs Patricia reply? The family would be over the moon when I came up with the facts. At last, another addition to the old family tree. How long would I have to wait for a reply?

In the next glen, Cushendall, a busy little street hummed with visitors escaping the mounting dangers of the marching season. The tricolour waved bravely from the tallest building. This was Gaelic territory from long ago. IRA territory, some said. And then, like a cheeky greeting from an old friend, a small pub appeared at the roadside.

BAR-A-HOOLEY
p. magill

It was too much of a laugh to pass by. With only half a dozen tables in the small room, it seemed cramped with people having predinner drinks. I ordered a couple and told the boy attendant my name was Magill and we were from New Zealand. He smiled and said, 'I'll tell Dad. He'll be back in a while.' Out of nowhere Pat Magill emerged — outgoing, friendly, with a quick walk and smile like his New Zealand namesake. They could have been brothers.

'I'll show you round downstairs. I've got a beer garden down there. If it wasn't such a wind we'd be out there tonight having a barbeque, and you'd be welcome.'

What a great set-up. Dark beams inside gave the place a ranchy atmosphere, and outside solid tables surrounded the barbeque. Pat was proud of his Bar-a-hooley, and I bet the crack was good on fine nights. We had a drink together with this Magill from Larne, near Belfast.

'I tell you what though,' he said. 'I keep my day job as a builder — this is a hobby. I'm not being caught that way.'

We left then, the young Paddy at the bar refusing any payment. We might even come back for another visit.

There is nothing more beautiful than driving through the Glens of Antrim. No wonder people came every year to stay — from England, Scotland, Belfast and further south. The atmosphere is so far removed from the grizzly reality of life, and no one talks politics as a daily diet. 'It gives my head peace,' one lady told me. But time was running out for us, and no research done. We must try to find the graves at Ballintoy further along the north coast.

Ballycastle, usually so gay and colourful, looked sad, deserted by its local friends and tourists. 'People just cancelled out,' the B & B owners said. 'There's no one in the big hotels either. That's the end of the summer vacation now for us. They won't come back. Ballintoy's the same.'

At last — Ballintoy. A quaint village set on a hill overlooking the sea and the island of Rathlin. And, yes, Scotland in the distance and the Mull of Kintyre calling like a song.

How come the olds were buried here in this village, we wonder? It's a tidy step from Carvacloughan. Maybe we should move on round the corner and look for the main churches? That old one down below on the cliff seemed just one of those antiques dreaming in the sun, a few gravestones keeping it company. But what a marvellous photo. A simple stone church perched precariously on the edge of nothing.

We wandered round the gravestones nonchalantly, looking at the little harbour below and the quaint limestone cliffs, when *there they were*. The original Magills as far back as paper took us. Archibald, James, Mary. Lead lettering set in sandstone. One and a half metres high. There was no mistake — they were there lying below this stone, and two hundred years later one of their family had come back from New Zealand and found them!

So — do you like my visit? I speak to the dead ones. In reply I read the text, still clear and vivid: 'BE YE ALSO READY Matt. 24.44.' Were they like that too? The same as Uncle John in the Napier graveyard with his message 'READER IS YOUR SOUL SAVED?' Were they all like that then? I would like you to have approved of me — Archie, Mary and James — and if I lived nearer I would tend your graves and visit you often. The grass is high and the place unkempt. I would clear that off and plant some flowers. But I live on the other side of the world. Would you have been austere or loving? I get out my pad and pencil and write down everything there is. Next time I'll bring you flowers. What else can I do? I say a wee prayer and leave them to sleep, tears running down my cheeks. Why do I live so far away?

The little Church of Ireland nearby is open for visitors, a historic place full of memories, simple and uncluttered. It had been a refuge for Protestants during the 1641 rebellion, and the Catholic priest kept them supplied with food. Then the rebels killed him for it. My God, what next in this place? A priest helping needy people of a different religion in time of need and getting killed for it by his own kind?

But there's more. Just inside the door, on a plaque:

pause ere thou enter, traveller,
and bethink thee.
how holy, yet how homelike is this place.

time that thou spendest humbly here will link thee
with men unknown who once were of thy race.
this is the father's house, to him address thee,
whom here his children worship face to face.
he at thy coming in this place will bless thee,
thy going out make joyful with his grace.

Thank you, little church at Ballintoy. You have restored my shattered faith.

Neither the beautiful glens nor the friendly people can stop the work of hooligans and bigots in Northern Ireland. How was it possible to wake on Sunday morning and hear that three innocent boys had been burnt in their beds? A petrol bomb thrown into a small house as the family slept. What sort of lowlife terrorised the streets of Ballymoney at 4.30 a.m.?

Political and church leaders pleaded with Orangemen to leave Drumcree and go home. But drums continued to beat, tin whistles peeped, and piano accordions pumped the tune across Ulster — 'No surrender!' The 308th anniversary of the Battle of the Boyne must continue, and unresolved resentments rot the spirit of Northern Ireland.

'Not our fault,' the Orangemen said. 'Blame Breandan MacCionnath and Brid Rogers — those who speak for the people of Garvaghy Road. Anyone but us!'

How are we to forget the misery of yesterday? Three small white coffins lifted into a church at Ballymoney, a few miles distant.

'What bloody man is that?'

Only the people of Northern Ireland can answer this question. Only they have the answer in their own hearts, if they will but look inside.

MARK LEFT BY SECTARIANISM IS STRONGEST IMPRESSION OF THE NORTH

An independent production company in Belfast is making a series of television programmes called As Others See Us for showing in Northern Ireland. It is about the way outsiders see the place — people who have left it, people who have moved in, southerners, tourists and movie-makers.

And journalists, who have chosen this or that way to report the place to the world. I was one of the people the television programme talked to. The task concentrated the mind. What is different about the North? That's to say, what is worth talking about?

Because you could always fob a serious inquiry off with a list of small differences, such as, for instance, the way Belfast people add the suffix 'so it is' to 'it is' statements, thus — together with the lavish use of the adjective 'were' — lending a charming air of the infantile to their speech. Or talk about the marvellous bakeries, the standard of home hospitality, the care for neat and spotless and respectable apparel.

I could have talked about the presence of the Bible. I could have talked about the sense of imploded genius — or a trapped, black intelligence — you pick up in some company in some pubs. But none of those is the really important thing. The really important thing about Northern Ireland is the underlying, omnipresent sectarianism.

That's what I'll take away as my main impression, now that I am finishing my little stay in the North. When I came there was snow on the hills. Now the montbretia is coming out, the flame-coloured wildflower that children so sadly call the back-to-school flower.

I think I've lived in Belfast long enough to get a taste of the place. But I know now that I'd need a lot more time to really get back into it. I feel more and more that I want to get back south, to home. On the other hand, by any standards Northern Ireland is a very interesting place, and it has been a privilege to learn how to move around in it.

I was very lucky in my half-year. Soon after I came there was a period when Catholics were being randomly killed in the city. Everyone was waiting for retaliation from the Catholic side, and then for the familiar cycle of violence to resume. But that didn't happen.

Instead the paramilitaries have stayed quiet and there has been a flowering of creative, political and constitutional ideas, all of them eventually backed by the majority here, if not yet by an overwhelming majority. For all the trouble there has been and will be, the Northern scene has utterly changed in this very year.

Though I imagine it will take a very long time for any ordinary kind of mutuality to take hold. Nearly everywhere in this rich and beautiful province looks normal, and nearly all its pleasant people behave absolutely normally nearly all of the time. But it isn't a normal place. That's what is worth saying.

It is a place that is suffering in the working-out of its modern identity. The South has become extraordinarily complacent. The big debates about social legislation seem to have ended debate. But in Northern Ireland, everything is up for reconsideration.

Well — not quite everything. The Roman Catholic Church doesn't seem to take the blame for anything, or have any intention of changing anything. But other institutions — Republican, Unionist, Orange — have all scrutinised themselves deeply. Northern Ireland is in the making as the Republic is not.

The fact remains that it is a very odd place. The first thing people do with each other when they meet a stranger is to suss out, from a thousand signals, whether the new person is a Catholic or a Protestant.

You can be denied a job or hunted from your home or simply killed for being a Catholic — or, much less often, a Protestant. There are whole social circles, from birth to death, which are exclusively Catholic or Protestant, even though it is a tiny place with a mixed population.

Because this is so, the whole society is infected by extreme sectarian self-consciousness. In polite society, when person A realises that person B is not 'one of us', a barrage of empty smalltalk is hastily erected. The art of giving absolutely nothing away in conversation, while appearing to be conversing normally, has been perfected.

This is the social and human gulf that matters. The two cultures as represented by individuals are always on the brink of suspicion and hostility.

There are many many ecumenicists, but on the whole, people believe the worst of the other side. Why wouldn't they, when three little boys can be burned to death because they're Catholic, or people gathering to commemorate their dead at the war memorial in Enniskillen can be blown to bits for being Protestant?

I haven't found a way in to an understanding of Northern society. Perhaps I needed a workplace, or children going to school, or a leisure pursuit that involved a wide circle of acquaintances. But I'm still trying to learn.

Over the next few weeks I'm going to meet the Apprentice Boys in Derry — because everything in Derry is different from in Belfast — and then to end with, I'm going to go back to the one place I've been in Northern Ireland that seemed to me a little bit of paradise.

There is no single topic or place or event that sums up the place. But as impressions go, there is just that one strong one — of the marks left by sectarianism. Westminster has put in place a great deal of antisectarian legislation. But the past is very near.

I haven't met any Catholic in Northern Ireland who has not been wounded in themselves or their community by the exercise of superior Protestant power.

And I haven't met any Protestant who really understands those wounds. The only exceptions to the polarisation whereby you have to think of people as Catholic or Protestant are a few middle-ground liberals and the handful of strenuously indifferent people who say 'a plague on both their houses'. And even the exceptions revert to the sympathies of their origins when it comes to the tribal crunch, as it does around the Twelfth.

I tried to say more than that, or other than that, to As Others See Us. But basically, after seven attentive months, that's what I have to say.

Nuala O'Faolain, *Irish Times*

16. a step too far

IVAN MCALLISTER WAS IN HIS OFFICE at the Department of Health in Ballymena. It would be another week before we could get together on the farm at Carvacloughan. Did he know how much I was relying on his memories, I wondered, or on any letters and papers he had tucked away? Surely he would know by now he was the last of the Magill line in Ireland — and that time was running out. Like Tantalus I seemed to be running for the fruit but it was never there.

'I haven't found anything on Kathleen Magill and Randal McAllister yet,' I told him on the phone. 'And yet they had sixteen children.'

'Who told you that?'

'A Mrs Frances Glass near the Drumtullagh church — your aunt, I think. A very old lady. Remembers Randal dying when she was at school.'

'Hum,' he said vaguely.

'The graves of Archibald and the others are at the old church in Ballintoy — the one on the cliff.'

'Did ye see them then?'

'Yes, I'll bring the sketch on Sunday. But I can't find anything about Mary White — supposed to be buried at Ramoan. Been to both graveyards, Presbyterian and Anglican.'

'Hum,' Ivan mumbled again. 'Good then, see ye Sunday.'

We left Ballintoy and passed the old farm at Carvacloughan again en route south. The whole area was becoming familiar now as we travelled back and forwards escaping the standoff at Drumcree. We gave it a wave each time, slowing down to watch where the cows were grazing and how the light was playing on Knocklayd. The family could have been happy here, I thought each time. And then the size of the whole farm came into focus. On its own it was very small, like a home paddock in New Zealand. Not a chance for all those children to make a living.

Linde Lunney's detailed map had mentioned Manister and Skehoge and Moycraig as possible alternatives to the fabled Archibald being descended from the Kings of Munster and his wife, Alis, being born in Craig-in-a-she-oak in Giant's Causeway.

'Don't forget you are descendants of the Kings of Munster,' the aunts in New Zealand used to say, in hushed tones. Craig-in-a-she-oak had them confused though. Nothing aristocratic about that gobbledegook. Linde knew this area well — her last assignment had been focused here, and she had an uncanny historian's ear for name sounds.

'I'm almost certain the old gentleman who wrote these notes didn't really hear properly,' she suggested politely.

'"Kings of Munster" could well be "Manister", and "Craig-in-a-she-oak" could well be Skehoge with Moycraig nearby. They are all within a mile or so of Carvacloughan. It makes a lot of sense. Add Mullaghduff to all those hamlets and you've got a fair bit of land to farm. The little Drumtullagh church looks down on them all, too — they're within walking distance of that.'

'Our cousin Reynold was apt to make swans out of ducks, we've heard. And that Sir George White business — we're still waiting to hear about it,' we told her.

We had the feeling Linde Lunney had it right, but we'd check with Ivan. How much did Ivan know? I was beginning to feel less sure about Ivan's memory. We drove on through the rich and beautiful land crisscrossed by all those little hamlets — Skehoge, Moycraig and Manister. Add that to Carvacloughan and Patrick's own farm at Mullaghduff, and it became workable for the family. The jigsaw seemed to be filling in.

Shocked by the death of the three small boys, Drumcree had sobered up. Orangemen had gone home in hundreds, sickened with the outcome of their seige. Only the hard-nosed bigots were still camping out, waiting for a break in the defences so they could walk that Garvaghy Road, and at last the Drumcree church closed its doors. About time, too. Even some other churches were making a stand against the Orangemen.

'Give my head peace,' the woman in the Glens said.

Meantime we would look at Derry.

Derry for some, Londonderry for others. It is said if you utter the word Derry in the Protestant pubs of the Fountain, you will certainly suffer physical assault. In the Catholic pubs of Bogside and Creggan the utterance of Londonderry will produce the same result. I wish I hadn't read that before coming to Derry. That statement colours your thinking before you even start. Better try to forget it.

The wonderful seventeenth-century walls had always intrigued me, as had the story of the Seige of Londonderry — how thirteen Protestant apprentice boys shut the town gates against King James' army while the city fathers waffled in indecision. If only you could just enjoy that story and walk round the walls admiring the unique city within a city, the magnificent Saint Columba's Cathedral with its seventeenth-century spire soaring heavenwards. But the past is too near, and reality hits you right in the face, like it or not.

From a distance you can see how the pretty town lies in the bend of the River Foyle, and across to the western escarpment, where solid Victorian villas stand. Further on the view takes you to the new suburbs north and east across the Foyle. It is very pleasant out there away from the loud graffiti of both Loyalist and Republican, which damn the inner city. Women can do their power walking and socialise freely amongst their own kind, do their shopping and push their children along clean streets and green parks. That's the pretty Ulster they know about — out there.

Down below the city walls, houses are stacked up together as if for protection, grey stone under grey skies, back yards and dreary washing visible from above. We move on reluctantly. A large British Army and RUC fortress, barricaded and equipped with closed-circuit TV cameras and steel-enforced walls, is the ugliest reminder of today's tension. Slits in its turrets look down upon activities in the Fountain and in the Bogside. Looking over the barbed-wire walls straight at the miles upon miles of small houses jam-packed together, however, is a shock to New Zealand eyes. We are not used to the great industrial cities of the world and the housing estates that go with them; not used to people living so close together in thousands; not used to a graveyard on a hillside nearby waiting to receive the next undernourished or unwanted child, or someone caught in a fight or cross fire. We are not used to any of it. We are naive. Bogside — Bloody Sunday Bogside. How do you marry this with the affluence over the Foyle?

Inside the city walls markets have been trading for hundreds of years on exactly the same spot — fish, clothing, trinkets, bric-a-brac, books. Caravans have replaced tents for cover, clothing has changed its style, books and magazines have become more colourful and revealing, but the atmosphere is the same and the smart-talking salesmen use the same old spiel.

Outside the walls, remnants of the last 12 July bonfire still sit in the street. Two old armchairs have escaped the flames and lie on their sides; old cardboard, empty wooden boxes and charred rubble add to the untidy clutter. A Union Jack hangs limply from a nearby house, its cobblestoned path painted red, white and blue. Working girls are flat out doing their jazzercise to loud music in an upstairs room. All this we can see from the wall.

It is not surprising that London was tacked onto the old name of Derry. To look down at the red-sandstone Gothic guildhall with its elaborate stained-glass windows is to look back on the city's historic association with the trade guilds of London in the seventeenth century. The guilds, with their many skills, which founded towns like Coleraine, Limavady, Dongiven, Draperstown, Moneymore, Magherafelt and many others. Clothworkers, tailors, ironmongers, mercers, vintners, salters, drapers, skinners, haberdashers, fishmongers, grocers, goldsmiths, tallow chandlers — the list goes on.

The skills of these trade guilds were taken by the Irish of Ulster to the new colony of New Zealand. Drapers were mainly Irish in our small town of Napier, and they knew their trade. We had a haberdashery department in our shop, and no one really knew what on earth it was. We called it 'habby', and had to watch it for petty thieving. It had ribbons, pins, tape and small items which could easily drop into a shopping bag. Fancy finding the origins of the humble habby right here in Derry.

'You be kind to your fether. Your fether's been a good fether to you. He's given you arl a thrade.' So said the Irish drapers to their sons. To have a 'thrade' meant to have everything.

Considered one of the top ten museums in the UK, the Tower Museum, housed in a medieval fort, deserves every bit of that accolade. Derry's history is depicted in every art and craft form from the sixth century. It is superbly arranged, researched and promoted. It is clever, humorous, painful and gut-wrenching. Up to a certain point the visitor could go out smiling, impressed with the whole innovative creation. It is the audio-visual at the end which touches the soul. Somehow Derry becomes alive on that screen — today's Derry. The narrator has captured a melancholy, a haunting, hopeless Derry caught between yesterday and tomorrow. 'And what of the future?' he asks. 'What is the future for this "place of the oaks"?' Does anyone know? The atmosphere is poignant. We are trying not to snivel. Some people stay seated, others walk out without looking at each other or speaking.

Shops are closing their heavy doors with a loud crash. Wooden window shutters swing into place with a bang. It is exactly 5.30 p.m. Anxious faces pass each other on the street without a greeting, their tired bodies in a hurry to get home. No little inviting cafés for a quick meal, or a cute warm pub. The girl in the chemist hasn't heard of Calomine lotion, nor cotton wool, and fumbles under the counter aimlessly. Her boss looks at her watch. I make a little joke to relieve the tension, but neither seems to understand. Then it dawns on me. We are in the North.

We say goodbye to Derry at the great Stone-Age fort six kilometres out above the Foyle valley — Griannan of Ailleach. Its massive walls are four metres thick, five metres high and twenty metres in internal diameter, and are shaped like a Roman amphitheatre with stepped platforms. Could this have been used in pre-Christian times for druidic rituals? Some say so. What is certain is the 360° view, from the River Swilly to Lough Foyle and ahead to Inch Island and Inishowen. Nothing could be so perfect in the setting sun. How sweet is Ulster from this distance.

Children played on the clean white beach at Rathmullan on the shores of Lake Swilly, and old men fished from the pier. A far cry from the drama enacted here in 1607. Someone has said the Irish earls didn't need an exhibition or an 'X marks the spot' display. They were too big for that, larger-than-life soldiers whose very lives spoke for themselves. That is true, but maybe the modern generation needs a concrete reminder of Ireland's most traumatic historical episodes, which put an end to the centuries-old rule of the Irish chieftans and saw the loss of their ancestral lands. Tourists and school parties need an actual place to visit and see replicas of their mighty chiefs.

The Flight of the Earls would make a great book and a marvellous movie. I wish someone would do it. Even the name is exciting, and the two chieftans would show up as tremendous Irish figures on the big screen, handsome and commanding in their distinctive Celtic gear.

A converted old fort near the beach houses the heritage centre, which tells the story, in documents and waxwork tableaux, of the flight of the earls O'Donnell and O'Neill. It takes some fortitude to stand and read the long history of negotiations between England and Spain, including the letters to King Phillip, and his replies — memorabilia so carefully documented. Contrary to popular opinion it has only recently been discovered that the flight of the earls was not the journey of despairing men into voluntary exile, dragging their friends and families behind them, despondent and defeated. No. Even in exile O'Neill was unbroken in spirit, politically minded, active and astute.

The Spanish ambassador in Rome wrote to King Phillip: 'The Earl is a great nobleman. Your Majesty owes much to his loyalty and devotion.' Pity the King of Spain preferred his devious political alliance with England to assisting the earl, but that is history and it suited Spain at the time.

Ireland's politics today have much to do with 'a small fishing vessel of 60 to 80 tons sailing away from Lough Swilly in the early days of September 1607'. To all appearances the earl was preparing for a journey to London, but he was privy to what lay ahead there — trial and possible execution. So, 'after a stormy voyage he landed in France and, later, Rome.' He wasn't silly.

Among the immediate results of the flight of the earls was the vacuum they left behind. Who would take over the power and authority of those large ancestral estates in Derry and elsewhere? Some were granted to the Twelve Companies of the City of London — hence Londonderry.

Over the border at Strabane we stopped to watch the River Strule flow by and to eat a sandwich or two.

'You guys going to Omagh?' A friendly face leaned out of a car window and gave the thumbs up. 'I've been to Australia.'

'New Zealand!' we both called back. He grinned and headed off in the direction of Omagh. We followed later, oblivious to the danger ahead.

I remember Omagh vividly on that disastrous day. It was just after lunch. Looking at the church spires clustered together near the little township, I wondered where Caroline of the 'Monty-charlies restored cottage' lived? Her address was The Old Rectory. It shouldn't be hard to find, and I could return a book I'd borrowed. A little parade was starting up — a small town festival. It would be good to stay around a bit and have a look.

'You're just nosey,' David said. 'We'd better get going to the Navan fort, near Armagh.'

'I *am* nosey, but Caroline lives in a restored mansion near those churches and had the nerve to plonk *us* in Coro Street. I'd like to tell her . . . '

'Forget it. You'll be fiddling round Omagh all afternoon sussing out everything. The audio-visual in Navan is meant to be terrific. Celtic folk tales on the big screen — the lot. Come *on*.'

I didn't want to move on. Little children were dressed up and giggling with anticipation, babies in prams being wheeled along for an outing. There was a feeling of small-village gaiety about the place. We could go for a coffee and watch the fun.

It wasn't till later that evening the full impact hit us. Devilish deeds were being hatched as we half-lingered in Omagh. That bloody red Vauxhall Cavalier parked by the curb, its occupants fiddling with a plastic lunch box full of a deadly substance. And that woman we passed in the phone box giving a message that would kill and maim. We were there and didn't know.

My watch said 2.30 p.m. at the Navan fort 60 kilometres further on. For some reason I looked up at the big clock on the wall too. It also said 2.30. Should I phone Chris now to tell her we'd be a bit late? Maybe later on — people were filing into the theatre, and then there was the Exhibition to see afterwards. Better go. A wonderful place this, but somehow, after half an hour, I suddenly had to get out.

'How do you get out of here?' I asked in a panic.

'Use that emergency red telephone and they'll come and take you out a back way. There's no other exit except the one through the audio-visual room, and there's a show on. Feel sick?'

'Yes — um — sort of. What's the time, do you know?'

'Ten minutes past three.'

'*What?*'

'Why? What's the matter?'

I didn't answer. To say something terrible was happening would sound crazy. She'd think I was a nutter.

A helicopter hovered low over Armagh.

'There's trouble here,' I mumbled to David.

'Probably routine flights,' he murmured. 'There's a helipad near here. RUC I think.'

But I knew by now it wasn't 'routine flights'. Something dreadful had happened. We drove up to Chris and John's home. The doors were open, the TV blaring. Chris rushed down the steps, yelling.

'A bomb's gone off in Omagh! I've been ringing the hospital and the police looking for you. Where *were* you at ten past three? You're late!' She flopped into a chair, ashen-faced.The TV screen flashed pictures of a war zone in Omagh. Dead bodies, dismembered limbs, crying children, bits of babies — *bits!* Ambulances, stretchers, blood and bandages. Someone was yelling out under a pile of rubble. Find her, please! And the long, long line waiting at the morgue to find a loved one — dead or alive, maimed or broken.

'A bomb in Omagh! Who did *that*?' I asked John.

'Not the Salvation Army anywa' was it now?' he said in my face.

Two hundred people injured.

Twenty-nine dead.

Many had lost their sight or limbs. Others had lost the very faces they saw in the mirror. Years of plastic surgery ahead.

'Don't anyone say that the Prods did it to the Catholics or vice versa. Omagh is a mixed town. It did not need tragedy to bring them together, for they insist they were never apart — and they were right.'

So why was Omagh bombed? The excuse given by the Real IRA was an insult to the intelligence of those who were expected to follow it.

'It was a commercial target . . . part of an ongoing war against the Brits . . . it was not our intention at any time to kill any civilians.'

And the second announcement was as pretentious as the first: 'In response to appeals from Bertie Ahern and others the Real IRA is embarking on a process of consultation on its future direction. In the meantime, all military operations have been suspended.'

You'd never have guessed that what they'd done was murder twenty-nine people and land seventy-five in hospital — shoppers, shop workers and children — by planting a 500 lb car bomb in a busy street and giving a callously inadequate warning.

To claim this was a strike against 'a commercial target' or 'part of an ongoing war' was so much guff, as obscene as the bomb itself, or the way in which the Real IRA would no doubt write off Omagh's terrible loss as 'collateral damage'.

Journalist Nuala O'Faolain wrote:

> Maybe we'll have to pay harder for our history than we imagined. We thought to get out of it with ceasefires, referendums, diplomatic and political and beaurocratic initiatives. But maybe we've been left with an untreatable psychosis. If you can look at a street full of humans, detonate the bomb, well then, psychosis is what politics has become. Things in Ireland have never been better in my lifetime. I say it now though . . . there has never never been a blacker day. It will take every bit of faith to go on hoping for peace now.
>
> I take what I've learnt about Northern Ireland, good and

bad, with me with thanks, now as I go on extended leave. I'm going to see if I can write something that is not an opinion column, something with people in it and a plot. All around me there is change. I'm going to try to change myself. It may not work but the thing about trying is that at least you move on. You start again.

I wrote to Nuala O'Faolain thanking her for the columns she had written while I was visiting Ireland. I told her that although I came from New Zealand I could empathise with her feelings, and understood so much more of the country having seen it through her eyes. I wished her well with her book and her future life. After noting my address in a village outside Omagh, she replied, in her own handwriting:

> Why are you where you are? I couldn't have borne it. Thank you very very much for going to the trouble of sending me your generous note. And every best wish. Nuala O'F.

It was only when I read her autobiography, *Are You Somebody?*, back in New Zealand that I realised what she had gone through in her own life. That is why she can write from the heart. That is why she is such a brilliant journalist and TV interviewer. That is why she understands Northern Ireland and the feelings of people there. She had studied in Oxford and lived in the UK for many years. It gave her a much wider picture than those who had lived all their lives in the south. That's how she knew. *Are you Somebody?* is the Irish number one bestseller. It deserves to be. Thank you again, Nuala. Go well.

17. the search for irish blood

'Gosh! You met him at last.' I knew what the family in New Zealand would be saying, eyes bright, all agog. 'Did you feel as if you'd known him for years? All your life? Was he just as you expected? Like another brother? Did he have the answers?'

Ivan McAllister ambled casually into the house in his work clothes. He could have just come in from milking before going out again to fix a fence. Just like that. But he wasn't a farmer, so maybe he had been tying the dogs up or mending a tyre. He looked like 'the chap next door' — neither short nor tall, fortyish, thickening round the waist, dark hair thinning, and with a kind smile which could throw a twinkle occasionally.

'Sorry I wasn't in when you came by last time,' he said casually. 'Mary should have given you a cup of tea that time but she had the place filled with handicapped people. Really difficult ones — making a row in the lounge an' all. Anyway, how's it going?'

'Well, great really. We met another branch of the family in Glenties. They come from the States.'

'Donegal, eh? Haven't heard of them.'

'And the graves in Ballintoy — that was a find. Did you know about those, Ivan?'

'I guess I did drive past there one day. Old church isn't it, on the cliff?'

'Here's the sketch anyway. We can't go back any further on paper.' He didn't put out his hand so I placed it on the mantelpiece.

'Yeah, thanks.'

'Now, Ivan, these townlands — Skehoge, Manister, Moycraig.

Have you heard of them? This could explain all those strange words in the family tree.' He looked puzzled and called Mary.

'Phone up one of the uncles,' he ordered. 'Ask them about all this.'

Mary obeyed readily. The tone of his voice echoed back over the years. That bossy voice of an Irishman to his wife. God help us, how did they put up with it? I could even hear Da ordering me about.

'So, what did he say?'

'Wants to speak to the lady from New Zealand.'

I went to the phone.

'So you're the lady from New Zealand who wants to know about those places, eh? Know them all. Always have. Remember as a kid some of the family walking over from there. Not far from where you are now. A couple of miles maybe.'

'Do you know anything about Kathleen Magill who married Randal McAllister? The only Magill left here in Carvacloughan when the rest went to New Zealand. My great aunt, your uncle.'

'Before my time,' he replied huskily. 'I'm over eighty now.'

'But there must be graves. And your sister, Frances, remembers Randal dying when she was at school. Said they had sixteen children.'

'Did they now? Well, well, you should have come before Bob died — that's Ivan's father. He knew about all that. Anyway, good talking to ye.'

We were getting nowhere.

'What did he say?' Ivan wanted to know.

'He knew the names Skehoge, Moycraig and Manister all right. Always known them. Not far from here, he said. That's all.'

'I wish Mary would raise a cup of tea like I asked. I was on duty all yesterday with these patients, you know, all on my own. The others went over to Scotland on the ferry for a family picnic.'

'Why didn't you go too, Ivan?'

'The girl who helps out let me down at the last minute. Sick or something. Doesn't matter. I'll go over another time. I like the ferry trip, and I missed being with the family, ye know? Now, while Mary's raising that tea, I'll go up to the loft and bring down a photo — and something else.'

He came down covered in dust clutching an aerial photo of his old farm with the Magill property adjacent. Now we were getting somewhere. But nothing had changed next door. The house had already gone, leaving only a pile of stones. Ivan's old house had been pulled down and made into a respite house.

'Sold a bit of land to put that up,' he said. 'Took two years to do it. Hard work that. See this patchwork? That's old. My mother's.' He handled the simple quilt carefully and with great respect. 'The children have all got one, and this one I keep in this bag.'

'You were an only child, Ivan?' I asked tentatively. 'And close to your mother?'

'That's right. Um, er, Mum died when I was a boy at school — only Dad and me left in the old house. We didn't go out and about, and didn't have folks come here. Just the two of us mostly. Dad could have told you more, but he didn't discuss much with me after Mum died. Didn't say anything much about the family. Kids don't listen anywa'.'

'What was your mother's name then?'

'White. Mary White. Plenty of Whites round here . . . '

'Do you think, then, that old James married a White from around here?'

'Oh, surely. They didn't go a far distance to find their wives. She would be from a farm nearby, like Mary-Anne McGowan in your book. Her uncle lived just down the road here. They'd be visiting each other on Sundays and Patrick would have seen her. Clever in the head, the McGowans, always. Too clever to just potter on the farms. That's how they were — in their books all the time. I remember that.'

'I got a letter from Mrs Patricia English, who was a White of Broughshane. Owns the big house in Cushendun. Mary White who married old James Magill doesn't fit into their family tree. She traced the whole thing back.'

''Course not. That man from Harley Street was dreaming. He came here about fifteen years ago. The Magill house next door was still standing then — a bit broken down it was, but I don't think he heard right what people told him. I think I'll go and tell Mary to hurry up with that tea. I'm tired from yesterday.'

I took out an 1861 Griffiths valuation map of the old farm and handed it to him. His eyes lit up then — the whole layout, as far as Moyarget Road.

'We'll walk it over,' he said promptly. 'No sign of tea yet, is there, by the look of things?'

Mt Knocklayd had disappeared under a cloud, and a fine misty rain blew in our faces as we walked the fields in gumboots and coats. Ivan didn't bother with a coat — his old jersey looked used to all weathers.

'It's just rizzle so it is.' He smiled. A few heifers grazed on the lower field, with a randy old bull looking for fun and games.

'You're walking on the drive that was, and the old house was here, facing that way,' he said without hesitation. 'Looking towards Knocklayd it was. Feel the rocks under ye? There's a bit of bogland across the road. Some of that was theirs too, surely. We'll go over.'

Looking at the same bog which warmed their bodies and cooked their food for generations triggered a strange feeling in the pit of my stomach. All the uncles would have had a turn digging into that turf and bringing it home. Easy to imagine them all lined up against the cliff, and my own da picking up a few pieces in his boyish arms. The old stories came alive on these fields.

I said, 'My father used to tell us he was sent across the fields to a neighbour to ask for "a hapeth of tea till the hen laid".'

'Was it as grim as that?' Ivan asked, astonished. 'Waiting for the hen to lay an egg to pay for tea? I didn't know about that. He'd be walking that way, maybe to the Davidson's. They weren't so poor. No drink.'

'And then not knowing where the pants started and patches ended.'

'"Subsistence farming" is today's name for their lifestyle then, with a brick kiln and linen-making to help out. The old pond for soaking the flax is still down there by the stream. You can see it at the bottom of the fence. A communal pond it was, surely. No one's as poor as that these days.'

We walked along the lonely road bordering the two farms which once hummed with activity. Back then cows would be standing in their sheds waiting to be milked, the uncles clanking cans and loading carts. Patrick would have been walking across from the McGowans at Armoy and Mary, their mother, making do with potatoes and buttermilk to feed the large family. Today that earthy smell of cows and hot dung no longer came to meet us; no farmer appeared along the road stopping for a bit of a crack; no little lads ran across the fields with a message. It was all over — just a memory left in our minds.

One thing was clear — Ivan and his boys had no interest in farming. A large, disused, old stone shed told its own story. Once humming with life, the plastered and whitewashed walls stood dingy with neglect, slate roof rich with lichen. Inside was worse. Ivan unlocked the heavy door to reveal old farm gear left exactly as if the previous farmer had just walked across the road for lunch. Five chains hung from the walls waiting for cows; space for a few pigs, and a stable for the horses, their harnesses hanging on the crossbeams. Dusty cobwebs wreathed a sad path across the silent fowl house. The only sound of life came from behind a wall where the frantic jumping and barking of imprisoned dogs pierced the silence.

Without any emotion Ivan shut it up mechanically as if it all belonged to another era. Was his father, old Bob McAllister, the last to use the shed? Did Ivan not 'have the mind' to pull the whole thing down? Too many memories, Ivan? Memories of mother, too, collecting the eggs. You were close to your mother, we know that. Broke your heart when she died. They say you wanted to go to heaven to be with her. But we won't intrude too much on the past, nor ask too many questions. The little room was crowded with unspoken words anyway.

Mary had been able to 'raise a cup of tea' by the time we came in. Ivan seemed delighted.

'I need this,' he said bluntly. 'Here, have a cake or two, and a scone there. Mary's mother makes them.' They were pikelets with jam.

'Let's have a drive to Mullaghduff,' Ivan then suggested suddenly. 'I've a feeling . . .'

What was he saying? Mull-agh-doo? Oh, so that was it! Said with that throaty Celtic click on the 'agh'. We'd been saying it wrongly for years. His little daughter, Sarah, jumped into the car with us, obviously intrigued by our New Zealand accents.

'You'd better teach me as we go along,' I told her. 'We don't know how to pronounce things properly round here.' She laughed her head off. Fancy grown-up people not knowing the right way to say things.

Assuming we were in for a long drive to this Mull-agh-doo, I gazed dreamily out of the window at the now familiar fields, but we were there in five minutes. Walking distance! So Patrick and Mary-Anne lived 'just down the road a step'. Well, well.

'The Davidsons live over the road there. You mentioned them in your book. Jackson was in Melbourne.'

'You don't mean . . . Are some of them still there?'

'Surely, they didn't all go.' Ivan was warming to the subject. 'Now, that railway line. Let's all get out and look.'

We leant over an old gate and followed his directions.

'It would follow the valley down there right through the field — that'll be Mull-agh-doo farm, surely. The old railway station is just nearby, so it is. I wouldn't be surprised if Pat's old house was just behind that hedge . . . ' Ivan was at last in gear.

Patrick and Mary-Anne had left this lovely green land to come to swampy Napier? But the misty rain off Knocklayd blew in our faces as if to mock the thought. As if to say 'This is July you're in, not December. And remember the first Annie who died. Remember the icy wind whipping at the windows, little babies and old people dying with the bad chests. The consumption. People spitting blood. Try to remember all that.'

'About that horse of old James being brought upstairs?' I questioned. 'Is that just one of those family jokes about the old boy?'

Ivan swerved off the Armoy road. There, crumbling on the corner, were the ruins of an old farmhouse with outside stone stairs going up to a loft or bedroom.

'It's no fable.' He smiled. 'Plenty of those outside stairs about. Easy for a horse to be taken up there.'

Imagery turned at last to reality, fiction to fact, hearsay to actuality.

The car stopped again, outside Armoy village.

'Any idea where John MacGowan's big house was?' He turned to me. I shook my head.

'Over there, I think. Pulled down just a year or two ago. As a kid I remember going up the big avenue. Yes, up there it was.'

Ivan's memory was working overtime now. The whole picture clicked into perspective. Mary-Anne riding her horse across the fields and round the lower slopes of Knocklayd; Patrick walking across from Carvacloughan to take her to Ballymena. Not far at all. The past was very near. A complete backdrop on an empty stage. The actors had moved on and we were as shadow puppets play-acting their parts.

'We'll go to Ballycastle the back way,' suggested Ivan.

With Glenshesk on our right and Glentasi on our left, we climbed the mountain road between the two. Without the sun Glenshesk looked heavily wooded and dark — not a place to be alone at night. The mountain retreat of Corrymeela went off into the distance.

'We've seen a few of those Corrymeela reconciliation centres in our trip round Ireland,' we said. 'They must do some good. After all, Protestants and Catholics have to talk together some time, don't they, and try to understand each other? This grudge memory can't go on forever.'

Ivan just shrugged, his silence too heavy to penetrate.

We were on the road now from Ballycastle to Carvacloughan — a mere 10 kilometres.

'Do you consider yourself an Irishman, Ivan?' I asked straight out.

'No,' he replied without hesitation. 'I'm British living on Irish soil.'

It was that ambivalence again. All the relatives who had left here last century were proud to call themselves Irish. That's what they were in New Zealand. Here they were clinging to Mother England to prop up a certain lack of self-esteem which seemed to have affected most Protestant Irish in the North. We knew Northern Ireland had been part of Britain since the partition in 1922, but Ivan and his ancestors had been born here in Ireland, of Irish stock. Surely that made them Irish? Strange. We left the words unsaid. No use blowing up a storm of discussion right now.

> The psychology of the Protestant Ulsterman is too difficult
> for the casual observer to understand. Partition is a tragedy
> and a unified Ireland is a reasonable aspiration but every-
> thing in Irish history shows that the worst way to achieve
> unification is to force the issue. The Northern Protestants
> are Ulstermen first, Irishmen second. In their anxiety to re-
> tain their connection with Britain, and as the unfortunates
> of a perpetual crisis of identity, they insist that they are, above
> all, British.
>
> *Irish Times*

And the aunts in New Zealand had told us we were related to
the kings of Munster!

'Well, Ivan, you've made me feel as if what I wrote in *Irish in the
Blood* wasn't a load of fiction. Sometimes I wondered if I'd dreamt
it all up.'

'Oh, surely,' he said, suddenly tired again. 'It's all true, what
you wrote. It's just a pity my father isn't still alive — you missed
him by only two years. He had a good memory for family, but as
you said in your book, they never tell you anything. That's why I
can't help you about Randal and your great-aunt Kathleen.'

'And no graves either. Should be at least sixteen McAllister
graves somewhere around here. Maybe next time we come you'll
have found them. Write me a letter if you ever do, Ivan, and look
for Mary White too — in Ramoan.' Write a letter. Famous last
words.

'You can come and stay here anytime you want,' said Ivan as we
left. 'No point in going all the way down to Armagh when you
come to Ireland again. Come straight here — eh, Mary?'

Mary smiled happily, her bonny face glowing. I felt a certain
elation. We had moved from 'visitors' to 'family'.

'Put your false teeth in when David takes your photo.' Ivan
grinned at her, pleased with his own simple joke. As if a woman of
Mary's calibre would be without her teeth. A radiographer who'd
given up her job to nurse the handicapped.

We left Mountain View Respite Home wondering how long Ivan
and Mary could keep up the demanding challenge of caring for

handicapped patients. Would strength keep up with devotion? They needed a holiday, for sure.

We hadn't got all the information we'd hoped for, but was that so important? Leaving a few mysteries to nut out was something for the future — and we'd met the last of the family and been invited to stay.

'Magill — planter or Gael?' I asked Linde Lunney in Dublin.

'In that area and with that surname it would be hard to call. I think I would come down on an uninterrupted native Irish/Highland Gaelic background, with influence from Lowland traditions.'

She was right! That fitted with the gallowglass.

We had been in Ireland for many many years. That felt grand. *Sláinte*!

18. washed by the Irish sea

'YOU MUSN'T MISS THE WICKLOW HILLS,' people said, 'and the fascinating southeast coast round Wexford and Waterford. The climate's kinder there. None of those brutal Atlantic gales. You'll be washed by the Irish Sea.' The very words were soft and compelling, like a song. We would follow the tune.

Dublin was in one of its crazy moods that day. 'Quare' they call it. Round and round went the arrows to Dun Laoghaire harbour — round and round and back again, up narrow streets, cars moving by inches, bumper to bumper. Then we saw them — the tall ships in Dublin Bay! Trixie stopped dead. Mad motorists piled up behind, angry as hell. But Trixie refused to move.

David sat trancelike, eyes glued to this piece of heaven on earth, this fleeting glimpse of another world. As if propelled by an inner desperation, he crossed the road to photograph the majestic creatures. Horns blasted, fingers were lifted in rude signs, until, unable to cope with mounting pressure and garda uniforms bearing down from behind, Trixie moved inexorably into the merciless network of humanity flowing out of Dublin.

'One moment of glory,' sighed David, slumping over the wheel.

'Let's stay overnight,' I pleaded. But he shook his head.

'They wouldn't let me get near enough,' he sighed. 'I can't bear just *looking*.'

But Wicklow had glory too. The great hills lay fold on fold, some long and gentle, others sharp and conical; and in their hollows deep lakes glittered like patches of fallen sky. Someone lived way down there in all that beauty right at the edge of Lough Tay.

A mansion hid amongst huge shady trees, sheep grazed in green fields, paths led seductively into woodlands, and a pretty little gazebo perched by the lake edge conjured up visions of skinny dippers and all that. A waterfall dripping diamonds completed the magical vision.

'Jeeze,' a man said from the car nearby. 'Americans.'

It was near evening when we drove through Sally's Gap. Little brown streams trickled through the dark chocolate peat with patches of heather awaiting their last touch of sun. Slowly the hills turned blue, and apart from a lone cyclist pushing his way into the vast spaces beyond all was still and sleepy, waiting for the night to cast its spell.

Once the stopover for horses after a long journey from Dublin, or weary pilgrims on their way to pay homage to Saint Kevin, the quaint village of Roundhead has become today's Mecca for trampers and tourists. Youth hostels, caravans, hotels, B & Bs, reconciliation centres and restaurants lined the narrow roads. Outside the Coachman's Inn, bicycles and backpacks lay in disarray, their weary owners lounging inside, chatting in a fascinating mix of French, Dutch, German and Irish. A mountain of coffee beans was being sucked through a giant grinder, its enticing aroma pervading the old-fashioned bar. No 'instant' for the European clientele here. Wine flowed like water, loosening aching limbs and inhibitions, until tiredness gave way to indiscretion and even the couple next to us became wrapped round each other in a passionate embrace, lifting their heads occasionally for a gasp of air and a long kiss. At the next table two Irish women were chatting seriously eye to eye, nose to nose. Refill after refill of Guinness put a red flush on their cheeks and a mounting gaiety in their loud laughter. It was good crack in the Coachman tonight! Then it was ten o'clock, and dinner. Salmon, fresh trout, cheese board . . .

The village drunk took his leave from the bar, valiantly walking a straight line to the door. He still had his legs and therefore his dignity. They all bid him goodnight till tomorrow.

Next morning we meet Saint Kevin in the beautiful and historical valley of Glendalough, where he founded his monastery 1400 years ago. He joins Saints Patrick and Columcille, who have travelled with us throughout Ireland.

'The bells rang for Mass in Glendalough when there was no sound in England but the meeting of sword on sword and the cries of the Vikings beaching their ships.'

So, we are in a holy place — centuries before England was a Christian country.

The earthy story comes first. How Saint Kevin made his bed in a cave in the rock face and gave his would-be admirer the brush-off by throwing nettles at her until 'the pleasure of her love became extinct'. Another version recalls him pushing her into the lake.

But Glendalough is much more than legend. Remains of an ancient round tower, churches, stone slabs and crosses are there to help piece together what the monastery would have been in its heyday — numerous dwellings, workshops, areas for manuscript writing and copying, guest houses, an infirmary and farm build-ings. There is nothing more lovely than this heavenly little valley with its two small lakes lying cupped in a hollow of the hills. So high are the hills, so deep the lakes, that even on a sunny day the waters are still and black. The monks knew what they were doing when they chose this site for their home.

Large buses full of students and tourists drew up at the herit-age centre as we entered, Europeans and Asians with little English.

'Please come back in half an hour,' the guide pleaded. 'I'll take an English-speaking group round later on.'

In the toilet an Italian girl was learning to say 'thank you' in English. She repeated the two simple words over and over again, until, elated with success, she smiled at me and tried them out for the first time. Her friends sniggered. They knew more than I did about bus-trip romances.

No one prepares you for the sight of morning sun on the heather in bloom — that purple haze which spreads across the hills and sends a thrill up your spine at every turn of the road.

'You may get a peep at it in August,' they say offhandedly, as if it was no big deal, this magenta-coloured blanket of brush. Cars whizz by without much thought, wondering what two people could be doing taking a photo of gorse. Too common; too simple. But take any Irishman or Scotsman to another land without the heather and their eyes will fill at the sight of a photo. That 'bonnie purple heather' is part of their heritage. It was part of ours, that morning in the Wicklow Hills, and we kept a bunch with us all the way back to New Zealand.

Trixie's radio splutters. Surely she won't let us down at this momentous time. We want to join in Ireland's vigil for the dead at Omagh. It is exactly a week to the minute since the bomb exploded. The clock on the court house in Omagh says ten past three, and the entire island of Ireland is frozen into silence. We will stop in a minute to listen. But round the next corner a crowd is gathering at the village of Tullow. Miraculously one parking space is empty and we can join the five hundred or more who have gathered to sing and pray. Ministers of all religions, Catholic, Church of Ireland and Methodist, together with civic leaders, read the scriptures. We sing 'Amazing Grace' and 'Make Me a Channel of your Peace', and at precisely ten past three a hushed silence falls over the village. Not a car or truck moves, not a voice is heard. It is a humbling experience. The message of Omagh is clear: good must triumph over evil.

Those who have witnessed the worst of the Troubles are the most convinced that a corner has been irredeemably turned. This was the watershed. The sight of Mary McAleese, President of Ireland, sitting in the sunshine outside that court house alongside Bertie Ahern, her country's prime minister, and nobody finding their presence in Northern Ireland in any sense unusual or objectionable, is one slim strand of evidence of change. The two traditions and the two communities have been merging in encouraging and enlightened fashion ever since the Good Friday agreement. The week has been full of such cameos, and none more significant than the sight of Mary McAleese grasping the hand of David Trimble for consolation as they watched the coffin of a lad in his Celtic Football Club shirt being borne to the graveyard.

The President of the Republic finding strength in the First Minister of the Assembly, who was until quite recently the favourite son of the Orange Order.

As we sat on the steps of a monument in the centre of this village in County Carlow, surrounded by caring Irishmen and women, we prayed with them that Ireland would no longer be subjected to the murderer's bomb. Our tears mixed with theirs, our hearts ached with theirs. This would be the most poignant moment of our whole time in Ireland. Something told us that.

We looked more closely at the fine monument. It was of a priest, Father John Murphy, and his faithful follower, John Gallagher, who were murdered fighting for the United Irishmen in 1798. Two hundred years ago. How far had Ireland come since then? Not far, if the IRA was still throwing bombs and the Orangemen still marched.

'Did anyone tell you the story of Father John Murphy?' the little lady next to me asked. 'Well, it's arful, just arful. They whipped him nearly dead to make him speak and give vital information to the English, and then when he wouldn't they half hanged him and still he wouldn't. So they hanged him proper. Did ye know he didn't utter a cry of pain? He was protecting us — his flock. Then they beheaded him and put his head up here on a stake.' She pointed up to the top of the monument. 'They burnt his body in a barrel of tar and the people all round here were made to open all their doors and windows so the "holy incense" would smoke them out and teach them a lesson. I live in that house over in the corner — the yellow one. We've always lived there. I've sat on these steps of Father Murphy's statue since I was a kid.' She could have been talking about yesterday.

'That's a terrible story,' I answered, nearly sick. 'Reminds me of Easter.'

'Aye, it is, it is, and what are yez doing here?'

'We missed the Omagh bomb by an hour,' I told her. 'That's why we feel close to the people who lost their lives there. We are thankful to be alive.'

She covered my hand with hers. 'Jesus, Mary, Joseph,' she sighed. 'I thought all this was over. Where do yez come from then?'

'New Zealand'

'Dear God, and they nearly . . .' She bowed her head in another prayer.

We would never forget the vigil in Tallow, sitting beneath Father Murphy's statue and joining all Ireland in a service with both Protestants and Catholics.

A last look at the monument said it all. In large letters:

GOD SAVE IRELAND

'Welcome to the South-East, where the sun shines' a notice says. It is certainly warmer. Hay bales are already rolled into balls of yellow ochre on the fields, and the barley has a silken sheen on the straw. Our self-catering cottage is at Arthurstown on Waterford Harbour. It is a converted farm building, tarted up with carpet and lace curtains. Cattle are gone now and the old yard is a car park.

Kathleen came out to meet us. I wanted to laugh and hug her like a sister, this tall, red-headed Irish woman of about forty. I'd known her for years, it seemed. Even her silky brown dress was familiar. She started talking immediately.

'Paddy went to glory five years ago. Five years dead he is and the children don't want to be farmers. Just look at their pictures on the wall in those gown things. They want to be doctors, nurses, computer buffs. You name it, they want to be that, and not be here helping their ma. In Dublin they are. Come home and sit around at the weekends. That's them. Can't even take my phone messages right. Nearly mucked you up didn't they, love? But, do ye like it — the place — the two of yiz?' Kathleen was in one big flap.

'Just look at the kitchen floor. Isn't it just awful now? Something's coming up from under it making it dirty like. But it's not dirty, Mary luv, I tell ye. I'm getting tiles on it when you've gone. You're from a flash hotel in Belfast aren't you now and ye see this floor . . . '

'Look, we're from no flash hotel, Kathleen,' I told her. 'We're Gipsies, writing and painting and living on a shoestring.'

'I knew it! You can see breeding shining out of cat's eyes. Not like that Canadian just gone. Walked out and never paid. Reported me to the *Borde Failte*, he did. Jesus, didn't even tell me first like. Decent people are not exact, Mary. Have ye heard that? Look, I'll say it in Irish.' She did. Then, again, 'Decent people are not exact. People like him are just "Johnny come oops". That's all they are. Now, are yiz going to like it?'

'We'll love it,' I said honestly. 'No worries. We'll heat up the peat fire and make it do. Where's the washing line?'

'Half way to Duncannon,' she laughed.

Sure it was — two hundred metres out in the fields, but it was fun having a walk to peg out the 'smalls'. The whole field had been a tennis court in the good old days with Paddy about, ornate pillars gracing the entrance. Outside our front door a huge iron pot took pride of place. Painted black, it was over a metre in diameter and one metre deep. A small, spindly phoenix palm spiked awkwardly up from the middle.

Did they boil whale blubber here once upon a time?'

'Och, no,' Kathleen answers. 'If Paddy was here he'd tell ye right. They cooked potatoes and turnips in it for the pigs, they did. Put a fire onder it.'

The old pot took on a bit of class after that. Pig food seemed somehow better than whale blubber.

'I've found a wee place for ye to be private now, Mary pet, for the writing. Come with me.' We went behind an old hedge. 'It's just perrfect for ye, so it is.'

'You've got a table and chair somewhere?' I asked hesitantly.

'You'll be needin' something like that too, I suppose now. I'll be looking up in the loft for somethin' to suit ye just.'

Kathleen never ever brought the table and chair, so she didn't, but she made up for it. Her soda bread would win a prize anywhere.

All TVs were switched on in the farmyard. RTE had full coverage. In New Zealand it would be an easy miss, but who could resist the 40th anniversary of the Rose of Tralee in Ireland?

'Are ye watchin' it, Mary pet? The Rose? Live from Tralee?'

'Hope it's better than the coverage of the tall ships,' David moaned. 'All that nostalgia and singing and flag waving, and no real stuff. They don't know how to handle it here — live from the water.'

Kathleen sniffed. She wasn't into tall ships, not at all.

But this *was* real stuff in Tralee, and the roses were not just dancing dollies with pink cheeks and shamrocks on their socks. They were intellectuals — graduates from universities, law students, sophisticated speakers who could sing and dance as a sideline. They were the new women of Ireland, and the winner, Luzveminda O'Sullivan from Galway, would gain a place in Miss World any day. We were proud of her, so was Kathleen.

'Did yez see her? The tall one from Galway? I picked her first off, so I did. Clever an' all.'

What a mixture Ireland is. One minute we're looking at the roses, the next it's heavy politics and Bill Clinton's imminent visit. There were only two TV channels at Kathleen's — RTE 1 and 2, English and Gaelic — which left us with just one.

Gerry Adams' bearded face appeared, his throaty Irish voice giving the country some hope. 'There is a shared responsibility to removing the causes and to achieving an end to all conflict. Sinn Fein believe the violence we have seen must be for all of us now a thing of the past, over, done with, and gone!' Surely he would keep to that statement? 'Past, over, done with, and gone'? The other architects of the peace agreement were winding up too for Clinton's visit, their vibrant, determined faces and passionate voices spelling hope for the future. Fatigue dimmed their eyes in their pursuit of peace.

In our small farmhouse there were no negative voices or whining bigots to dissuade us from believing what we were seeing was for the good of future generations. In the North they would be muttering, 'Gerry Adams is a *murderer*, and Tony Blair and Bill Clinton are *do-gooders* who should mind their own business. Bertie Ahern has no business interfering either.' None of that talk down here. They were anxious for peace.

So what *did* they want up there in the North? Thirty more years of IRA bombing and a repeat of Omagh? Or peace?

Once out of Kathleen's big homely farm gates in County Wexford, it was better to be quick off the mark and establish our identity.

'We're from New Zealand,' we said smartly, aware that the history of this area didn't give the English top marks. A big minus in fact. What better place for invaders to cross the Irish Sea and sneak into the perfect little harbours opening up all along the coast from Wexford to Waterford. Dozens of old forts and tower houses tell the story dating back to the Vikings, the Normans, that bastard Cromwell, and Vinegar Hill. It's not pretty. Neither are the stories of the Knights Templar castle at Ballyhack. Young guides repeat the gruesome tales of war without a blink — hot oil and rocks raining down from the second floor through a hole in the ceiling of the entrance lobby, called a murder hole, giving unwanted guests a warm reception. Nowadays as the car ferry crosses the narrow harbour, there is no need to be on the alert for warlike enemies.

'The only enemy here is someone making big bucks out of a geographical situation — saving a long trip of sixty miles by car and charging the earth. Bastards!'

Wexford has tried to piece together a silted-up harbour and an old fishing village into a go-ahead town. Empty old buildings look sadly at the pier, blaming it for their down-at-heel appearance. Owners long dead still retain a living presence, their names in paint on rotting wood. Up from the harbour a 3.5-metre-wide street hums with business. Room only for one horse at a gallop. Today's customers leave their cars in the old fish market and elbow themselves into banks, pubs, cafés, hot-bread shops, high-class crystal and china stores and the best bookshop ever. A huge girl sat on this main street singing 'Amazing Grace' for a cent or two, while people pushed by in single file to avoid her. Such is the quaintness of Wexford town, without the glamour and notoriety of its harbour, but making money still with today's merchandise, in the same old shops and market places once inhabited by the Vikings.

The town might be a jumble and a cluttered old dump, but once out into the countryside large houses raise their heads in pride, and gardens flourish in the warm sunshine. New wide roads take us down towards the coast and, hey, what's happening in Piercetown? Huge new housing estates are growing up on both sides of the road. Not the boring old bungalow bonanza, but two-storeyed wooden town houses well laid out in spacious grounds. Old stone houses of a past era are being made over and new farm sheds lie happily next to the ruins of churches and castles. That aristocratic feeling of the Anglos lingers here in the names on a few gates and in a few graveyards. The perfect setting for them to picnic in a foreign land amidst golden hay and silken straw grain.

Then a sudden change takes place in the countryside. One thatched cottage after another appears on this south road to the coast. They are beautiful, with colourful baskets of flowers on window ledges, quaint letter boxes, grinning ornaments. And then a group of six together. They are trendy up-market buildings, some B & Bs. We turn the corner and find the beach at Kilmore, where cafés, restaurants, pubs and townhouses, are overrun by the 'beautiful people' at the weekend. They walk jauntily about the quay eating ice creams with a chocolate bar sticking out of the side. Trixie looks pathetic beside the gleaming monsters alongside, but she is not embarrassed. David examines a maritime museum while I join the fashionable promenading along the quay. I watch a group of rough fishermen unloading their catches of enormous crabs, and hear them speaking in the Gaelic to each other. But they are polite enough to answer my simple questions in English, while the glamorous ladies walk past me without looking back.

'The Spanish are taking all they can, even undersized crabs and fish. No one is able to stop them in a four-mile limit. We don't need the Spanish,' they tell me forcibly, in colourful language. 'We used to catch twice this before they came.' Yes — the downside of the EU.

The beach is a tiny curve of sand, and a few children are playing with buckets and spades. Room for half a dozen families crammed together. No shady trees or shrubs. It is low tide and the sea is two hundred metres away now. Green slimey rocks separate sand from water.

I feel sad for the kids, and wonder what they would think of New Zealand's huge beaches with all-tide swimming and endless clean sand. But they are happy to wait for the next high tide, six hours away, and their parents are happy to be in designer clothes, drinking at the seaside café.

All is peaceful out in the bay, and the Saltee Islands make a shelter for small yachts and rare birds. Two Wexford rebel leaders were found hiding there before they were brought to Wexford to be hanged and beheaded in the 1798 rising. A brand new plaque on the quayside commemorates the bicentennial. I put my hand on the fresh plaster and shudder. It could have happened yesterday. That certain melancholy blows in from the sea — you can feel it whispering against your face. It is the melancholy of unfinished battles and unforgiven feuds that only the Irish living here can really understand. I can only sense it as an ache in my stomach and a feeling of sadness in my heart.

Cromwell follows you round the long tapering finger of Hook Peninsula jutting out into Waterford Harbour. The hungry glint in his eye flashes against the still water in the perfect anchorages opening up on each side.

'I'll get in there by Hook or Crooke,' he warned. 'Here, on the peninsula, or at Crooke, in County Waterford.' And he did, the rotten scoundrel. And one of the oldest lighthouses in Europe, built by kindly monks in the fifth century, gave him a guiding light right up the harbour. Little did the monks know their good works would lead to the overthrow of Ireland. Today, families picnic nearby on black slabs of rock sloping down to the sea, and fathers throw out a line to catch a fish or two.

Further down the Hook another of Cromwell's perfect anchorages has turned into the village of Fethard-on-Sea, where tourists and Dubliners enjoy swimming, golf, horse-riding or Irish football. Restaurants, pubs and outdoor cafés line the picturesque main street, and you could rent a modern apartment or a smart B & B but you would be paying for the pleasure. 'It's not a place for scruffs or riffraff, no it's not,' sniffed Kathleen, 'but I send some of my guests there for an evening meal if it's glamour they're after.'

Not many remember that the Anglo-Normans made their first landings in Ireland just a mile south of Fethard in 1169. It's too far back now, and the grisly past doesn't always make for good conversation under candelight. Following a small road leading down to overgrown earthern ramparts overlooking Baginbun Beach, it is easy enough to picture the drama enacted here when a herd of cattle was made to stampede into the disorganised Irish-Norse defenders, throwing them into disarray. Then, to teach the enemy more warfare skills, the Anglo-Normans broke the legs of seventy soldiers and tossed them over the cliff. The precipitous rocks look daunting still, high above the beautiful beach, and it takes some nerve to peep over the top. Down below small children dance about in the sunshine, oblivious to the bones of their ancestors lying underneath. The sobering reality of this place is aptly summarised by a locally sited plaque:

> at the creek of baginbun
> ireland was lost and won

Thus began eight-hundred years of English involvement in Ireland. It is a useless pastime to wonder what would have happened if the Irish had won this battle. Useless, but interesting. Certainly there would have been no Troubles or Omagh.

It is not easy to find a church in Dungannon. The postmaster scratched his head.

'Try the pub on the corner. They open at half-ten.'

'Ask the shop over the way,' the barman said.

A busy woman baking bread rolls pushed trays in and out of the oven.

'Protestant or Catholic?' she asked matter-of-factly, one eye on the rolls.

'Protestant if possible. Doesn't really matter,' I said, as if choosing ice-cream flavours.

''Course it don't, but wait till I fix these buns and I'll ring a friend. Changes every Sunday I know that. Times an' all. Buns first, God second. Don't sound right does it? The "God second" bit.'

The phone conversation wasn't whispered, allowing half a dozen customers to listen in with interest. All eyes turned my way.

'Right, now,' she said, 'I've got it. It's nine o'clock at Fethard-on-Sea, ten-fifteen at Black Hill. Say one for me, won't ye?'

'Black Hill?'

'Up the road.'

Bells chimed at All Saints' Church, Killest. Ten people found their way into the old Church of Ireland. Two Germans, two New Zealanders, the rest local. Magnificent stained-glass windows added their colourful figures to the lonely worshippers, and Jesus looked down sadly from his statue way up near the rafters. An aristocratic middle-aged man played readings, prayers and hymns on an old gramophone with 45s, trying to beef up the thready, self-conscious voices of the ten worshippers. How pathetic is this, O God?, I questioned the Almighty. Behind us the Germans fiddled with their prayer book, as did the Kiwis. Wouldn't you think the vicar could have spelt out the page numbers? But no! Every good churchman should know the sequence of the church calendar, and who said what where. After all, the prayer books had been in those pews since 1914. Leather-bound and gold-leafed as befitted the lord of the manor in the nearby demesne. But the manor house was a hotel now, and featured in Ireland's famous *Blue Book* for the best cuisine. The Chichester family was just a polished bronze memorial plaque on the wall.

Handsome church, exquisite marble pulpit, hand-embroidered linen, but the glory had long since departed — people glory, that is. Shekinah glory too. And the very elderly vicar and his reader had lost their own marbles long since. We were listening to a children's talk to adults. Even the marble pulpit failed to transform the few halting sentences into a sermon. Goodbye Anglos. You have gone from ascendancy to oblivion. A pity about the handsome building on Black Hill and the lovely memories. Without the visitors you would have six people here. So now what?

A few miles up the road at Ramsgrange an old teaching convent had transformed its buildings into the Shielbaggan Outdoor Education Centre. Once a home-science school for prospective farmers' wives to learn culinary skills, the beautifully tiled kitchens and bathrooms had become self-service or catered units for today's outdoor students. The would-be farmers' wives had gone to Dublin to become doctors and lawyers and computer experts in the new Ireland. Two old Catholic churches at Ramsgrange had become community centres, crèches and meals-on-wheels depots. That's what!

The peninsula across the harbour looked uninteresting from Duncannon, despite the cunning Cromwell's determination to get there. Was it worth paying that car ferry for a look at a fishing dump called Crooke? And beyond that — scruffy farmlands?

The first notice said we were entering the Barony of Gaultier. Surely a leftover from the good old days? It was plain old East Waterford on our map, and we'd seen nothing yet to warrant such a classy name.

Already overseas tourists had found their way to these secluded, untouched beaches with new traditional thatched cottages and splendid hotels. Just fly over from Europe, buy up the crystal at Waterford, then taxi to the playground of Tramore or smaller intimate seaside villages further north.

A smart young lady emerged from her glamorous thatched cottage on Dunmore Beach, batik beach gown covering a perfectly bronzed figure, large white beach towel hung nonchalantly over one arm. With firm steps she took her morning walk on the untouched sand, then plunged into pristine blue waves. Alone in her private bay, washed by the Irish Sea, she struck out for six perfect strokes, then waded ashore to sit basking in the adoration of the passers-by.

Tonight she would be served . . .

pan-fried cockles in garlic butter

monkfish or cod

peel estate chenin blanc 1997. golden yellow in colour,
pungent wild-flower nose. dry with a firm acidity.

Whoever said Ireland was backward?

Assisted by government grants, these brand-new cottages thatched in reeds would cost $NZ90,000. And inside? Not peat on the hearth, but a colour-coordinated en suite for my lady of the beach, plus air conditioning or central heating.

If being cut-glass makers to the world is Waterford's pride, so is East Waterford's Ring of Gaultier. No fishing dump, this — and Cromwell knew that. We passed Crooke Head as a 40-foot keeler headed off on a cruise up the harbour. That's what the old devil was after — a perfect harbour.

Time to leave Kathleen of the 'dacent people' and move — again. There were tears in her eyes — and ours.

'Jesus, Mary, Joseph,' she whispered, and crossed herself. 'And these two missed Omagh by an hour. They did too. Tell them about me in New Zealand. Tell them they'd like it here, now. You'll do that won't yiz?'

Of course we would. They'd like it even to meet Kathleen just and walk the fields to peg out washing or collect blackberries from the hedgerows.

19. the fun of cork

The road that runs due south from Cashel through Cahir and Clogheen over the mountains to Lismore is one of the most beautiful I have ever travelled. You have the Plain of Tipperary round you for miles and facing you are the Knockmealdown Mountains. Just behond Clogheen the road rises and you mount quickly into the wild hills. You come to a hairpin bend, and when you can safely do so, stop and look back. This is one of the grandest views in the British Isles. Below you lies the great Plain of Tipperary with the little white roads criss-crossing through the greenness of fields and the darker green of woods. West of Cahir are the Galtee Mountains and on the east is Slievenamon. On a good day you can see the Rock of Cashel rising up from the green plain twenty miles to the north.

H.V. Morton

'THE BEAUTY OF IRELAND MAKES you weep. Sometimes I wake up nearly crying with it.'

Grabbing his camera David started running towards the hills to catch the sun on the heather, his words echoing my own thoughts.

Heading up Knockmealdown Mountains we stopped to pick blackberries and gaze at the huge rowan trees. Within minutes a farmer appeared out of nowhere, stopping his tractor when he saw us, his jaunty cap and jerkin reminiscent of the other farmers we'd met and loved.

'Morrissey's the name. Andy Morrissey. I've got a brother somewhere over your way. On a ranch way up in Kaitaia. Been there for years, he has. Nothing in his pocket when he left here.'

A *ranch* in Kaitaia?

'Why don't you go over and see him?'

'Oh naw, this here will do me. You'd best be hurrying on. You'll be getting the hurricane before me. Get to where you're going before it comes.'

'You don't mind us picking these blackberries.'

'Wouldn't touch them meself. The taste's kind of bitter, but yous take as many as you want.'

We left Andy leaning against his tractor watching us until we turned the corner and were out of sight. Another friend, another character, another parting. Each becoming more painful than the last.

Despite the hurricane warning we stopped at the pass. Who could miss the view over Tipperary spread out below, which Morton described so beautifully sixty years ago. Today the simple farms are crisscrossed with huge country estates and riding stables set in picturesque parks, limestone land producing studs of international fame.

On a small hill behind, a well-worn path led up to a statue of Our Lady of Knock looking down on the scene below as if in contemplation and wonderment. Beside her a weather-beaten stone hut sheltered a simple Communion table. Here modern pilgrims gather to remember and worship, their devotion enriched with beauty. (The original vision at Knock was first seen by poor peasants at a time when the people of Ireland needed something to strengthen their faith. Today, Knock has an international airport bringing streams of pilgrims from around the world to witness the hallowed place.) There is mystery here.

Somewhere in County Cork the last self-catering experience awaited. Days were precious now as the thought of leaving Ireland gave added impetus to every adventure, every meeting, every twist of road. We followed directions — Kilconnor, Shanballymore, Doneraile, Mallow, Graigue. We could have been cruising backblocks style in Hawke's Bay, winding in and out the small hills and valleys of Te Aute, Otane, Waipawa and the old farm at Argyll. And — suddenly — there it was.

'Do you want to stay then?' a pleasant, rosy-cheeked woman asked. 'Take a look about you. We left it just as it was after Seamus' father died. Not a thing touched. You'll be quiet for your writing.'

We were looking at a 200-year-old cottage set in a field, surrounded by hedges choked with blackberries, stinging nettles and hawthorn bushes. Chestnut, sycamore, oak and beech trees lined the entrance and vines grew into the wall, with thatch peeping from under the iron roof like hair growing out of an old man's nose. Crisscross plasters patched up the broken windows. Whitewashed stone farm buildings faced the back door, their dark gaping mouths a home for . . . rats? Ghosts?

'Go in then,' Ina invited.

The basic simplicity of it all appeared strangely familiar. I had seen this before in my dreams. The place where my father lived in Ireland. An old parlour with a turf fire; a mantelpiece with a three-metre-wide facade; bellows worked by a hand wheel; a hinged frame for hanging pots; a multitude of memorabilia — saints, crucifixes, clay dogs, holy water in a small, chipped container near the door; old chairs draped with woollen crochet squares; mats over a concrete floor. And a loft.

'It's a no-no area,' Ina said.

A no-no area? God help us. I wouldn't go up there if someone

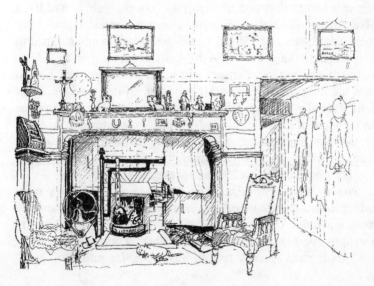

233

paid me. Two hundred years of feet had struggled up those ancient stairs to that bedroom, every child born in this house, their bare feet leaving dents in the aged wood. In that small loft bodies had slept together keeping each other warm, while their parents slept underneath in a room big enough only for a bed and table. Another generation had added two more rooms, but later. Much later.

'You can sleep here — or there,' I heard Ina saying from far away. 'More blankets in the loft, and a hot electric overblanket Seamus' mother had before she died. See?'

I did see.

A lean-to to the left — the bathroom and a tin bath; a lean-to to the right — the kitchen with a gas cooker. Twenty tin teapots lined the shelves, large to small. Electric cables cobwebbed the walls and ceilings, while the heating pipes, connected to the wetback over the fireplace, snaked about the floors threatening to strangle the place like ivy round an old stump. Two doors shut properly, the rest hung half-open in limbo.

I could see David mouthing the words behind Ina: 'Are we staying?'

I nodded, almost against my will. This would be the closest I could get to Carvacloughan, the closest to Da's way of life. Holy pictures looked down on us with pity. 'Dacent' people had lived here, worked hard, paid their bills, been to church, looked after their neighbours and old folks, said their rosaries and stopped to pray when the Angelus rang. A different colour religion from Da's — but the same God. Farmers and gardeners, who knew how to turn the soil and gather peat. He would have liked these people of Cork with the name of Lillis, would have liked Ina and Seamus and the 'cut of their cloth'. 'God-fearing,' he would have said.

'Not much of a marriage bed,' David said jokingly as he examined the thin plastic foam mattress.

'The power came in 1950,' announced Ina.

Power? Maybe . . . ? And there it was, an old 1940 HMV radio sitting above a grandfather chair; and tucked in the corner of another room, a portable TV. An old-style telephone had been left attached to a wall, its numbers sunken and yellow. Another museum piece?

'I got it when Seamus' mother was dying,' Ina said. 'Still goes.'

♣

The famous Irish author Brendan Behan defined the Anglo-Irishman as 'a Protestant on a horse', and somehow we had found our way to this cottage near a village called Doneraile — the last bastion of the Anglo-Irish ascendancy. Lining one side of the road for miles, high stone walls had been built to keep Irish peasants out of the large domain, ending with a wide circle into the main street. Grand gates opened up into a wildlife park, formerly the estate of Saint Leger, the Doneraile family name. Many and varied are the stories of Lord Doneraile, and the people of Cork knew them and repeated them. I'd read the stories before in *Picnic in a Foreign Land* by Anne Morrow, but now I found myself accidentally in a place where all these tales had been played out.

An elderly woman who had been a dairymaid at Doneraile from the age of thirteen remembered how the servants had to line up at the gates as he drove about in a coach and four, allegedly inspecting his estate each morning, but actually eyeing something sweet for after lunch. He was rather partial to a post-prandial walk and enjoying the company of pretty local village girls in the summer-house on the estate.

This 'taking one's pleasure on the county' was not limited to hunting and shooting but included other outdoor sports, and was fairly common practice even for rather bleak Evangelical landowners. William Ponsonby Barker, who had an estate in the rich farmlands on the borders of Tipperary, would make his selection as he presided at family prayers, taking a maid up to bed, justifying it on the grounds that he needed a 'human hot water bottle', though what he said in the summer is not known. If the girl, eyes downcast, was not too fresh after a day hauling coal and wood, he would sprinkle her with eau-de-Cologne. Once mistakenly picking up an inkwell in the dark, he claimed that he had been teaching the poor creature to write.

Not all the girls in the village were shy of Lord Doneraile; some were happy enough to catch his eye, glad to while away the afternoons with him dallying in the conservatory. It was one of the earliest in Ireland, with its stained glass and ornate tiled floor. Or they might be taken for a stroll by the charming Awbeg River, and wooed under a willow tree or by

the lily pond. It was better than making soda bread in a
thatched cottage, shouted at by a crabby grandmother to bring
in the turf. A close Doneraile relative suggested: 'So many of
us were born on the wrong side of the blanket.'

Anne Morrow, *Picnic in a Foreign Land*

Today the Saint Leger church still stands opposite the old estate, its name changed now to Saint Mary's. With all that *droit de
seigneur* going on over the road it was probably better so. In a country where the horse is king, racing by keeping the steeples in sight
enabled the riders to steer cross-country — an activity they called
steeplechasing for the Saint Leger stakes.

Dozens of castles rise up unexpectedly out of the landscape in
County Cork, and no one seems to care a toss, or bother to remove
the ruins. They like them. Driving through an ancient archway in
the middle of the main street of a village is commonplace. Children kick about among the stones of old castles, while their mothers
push prams proudly on narrow paths out of bounds to their serv-
ant-class grandmothers.

The magnificent cast-iron gates of Creagh Castle stand open
facing the main road from Doneraile to Mallow, hiding a gatekeeper's cottage in the bushes behind.

At the end of a drive a 'big house' appeared next to the remains of a Norman tower house. The two didn't marry well in the
surroundings, their ages too diverse, their appearance incongruous. A sporty young woman appeared, hesitant at first, but at the
mention of New Zealand and our connections with the Creagh
family, she opened the doors and we walked in with an entourage
of dogs.

'My uncle married Kathleen Creagh,' I heard myself sounding
off in a silly name-dropping voice. 'Her father was a sea captain
from here.'

'We're only renting this place,' the friendly woman said. 'We're
from Scotland, but Julian Humphries, the owner, wants every
Creagh connection written down in this book. He's planning a reunion sometime.'

What a pity Willie Magill (with the watch) of *Irish in the Blood*
and his lovely Kathleen Creagh weren't able to see their castle in

County Cork, nor their dignified ancestor in the life-sized painting above the stairs. They could have taken back photos to show
the proud family at Armoy in Napier. No pulling of blinds or hushed
voices over *that* piece of news. All Carlyle Street would know that
Willie's Kathleen had come from a castle in Cork with its own
private graveyard in a small grove nearby, and a large estate of
rolling fields. But how could they have left this for swampy Napier
and a small house at Port Ahuriri? Like all the ascendancy élite,
they had known their glory days were over with the advent of Irish
independence and heavy taxes on their lands and buildings. An
end to their picnic in a foreign land. An end to running big estates
from England and paying their workers a pittance.

Church bells were ringing for Sunday worship at Saint Mary's
in Doneraile, and news of our visit had spread in the small community. Pub talk, no doubt. 'Rellies of the Creaghs from New
Zealand, staying in that old cottage of Seamus and Ina in Graigue,
so they are. Strange stayin' there, wouldn't you be thinking?'

Sitting in this seventeenth-century church listening to David
read the lesson from Jeremiah seemed unreal, like a re-enactment
from another era. David became Jeremiah and vice-versa. A blur,
their voices as one. But on the wall directly above my pew a white
marble tombstone spelt out the words 'Arthur Creagh — well-loved
and respected in the town of Doneraile'. More unreal — creepy
even. I hadn't chosen that seat because of Arthur Creagh's plaque
— no one had mentioned its existence.

There was something different about this Saint Mary's church.
It was a leftover from the ascendancy days, but still living and
vibrant.

'It's because of that little lady, Nora, there,' they all said. 'It's
her that does it.' Even seasoned old farmers gathered round to shake
her hand. 'And see these young people here? Nora brought them
all to faith in a Sunday school she ran in Mallow, and never lets up
on them. Keeps tabs on them all. They adore her.'

'If I hadn't broken my leg weeding the graveyard you would
have come home with me to Sunday lunch,' seventy-year-old Nora
said to us from her wheelchair.

♣

237

I was looking forward to a day in Cork, Ireland's second largest city, with the River Lee flowing through the middle of the shopping centre. It sounded attractive and I expected an old harbour city, colourful and bristling with interest. Instead it appeared a jumble of quays and bridges, of spires and Georgian houses, bustling markets, derelict pubs and hidden alleys, dark in the daytime, dangerous at night. Unfinished building sites added to the clutter and heaviness of the place. But the atmosphere, too, was different. There was a clannishness about the people that excluded the visitor — one could almost be in a foreign country. The girl on the tour bus had a distant, bored air about her, quite different from any other guide we had encountered in Ireland. We were intruders in Cork, it seemed.

'Those two church spires you see there. One was donated by Guinness, the other by Murphy's. But when in Cork you must drink Murphy's. Never ask for Guinness in the pubs here. That's the tower of Saint Anne's Shandon ringing the quarters.' She didn't smile, and tourists left the bus uninspired and somewhat bewildered.

I shall remember Cork by day if only for the gentleman in the second-hand book shop. Dressed in a tweed suit, he sat nonchalantly behind a desk chatting to customers, the smoke from his pipe sending out an aroma of amiability. He glanced at the books I had chosen, then at me. One of my choices was *Now and in Time to Be*.

'Tom Keneally wrote that book in too much of a hurry,' he said. 'Parts of it are good, but . . . '

I interrupted. 'It's difficult to write about today's Ireland when there's so much of the old mystique lingering about, and so many books have already been written about the old times. Perhaps Keneally wanted to get away from the sentimental and supernatural.'

'Don't ever leave the mystique of Ireland out of *your* book,' he said knowingly, 'and send me a copy when you've done with it. Here, have you got a card with your name on it?'

How did he guess I was writing a book?

At night Cork city takes on a different mood. People suddenly come alive, drab buildings turn on their neon lights to advertise glamorous girls and massage parlours. Cinemas and pubs stay open to enjoy the crack peculiar to the Cork culture. No wonder the shops are slow to open and the place is tired and listless by day. Cork people are night people.

Friends drove us through the floodlit city, heading for the British Legion headquarters, then in and out of dark back streets and hidden alleys to finally arrive at a scruffy basement filled with old soldiers and their wives winding up for a night of nostalgia. A large portrait of the Queen looked down with dignity on the crowded revellers. The English queen in a Cork basement? Surely not! The mind boggled. But these old soldiers were preparing to leave for a pilgrimage to France and the Somme. Many Irishmen fought with the English in the Second World War and took the King's shilling, and they were proud of that. Murphy's and Guinness set their eighty-year-old bones moving in old waltzes and foxtrots, and voices boomed into old songs that made all our tears flow. 'Faded Coat of Blue', 'Christmas in the Trenches', and then Eric Bogle's 'The Green Fields of France':

> *Did they beat the drums slowly?*
> *Did they play the fife lowly?*
> *Did they sound the Dead March as they lowered you down?*
> *Did the band play the Last Post and chorus?*
> *Did the pipes play the Flowers of the Forest?*

It is at such times that you know what this pilgrimage is all about, and what memories are being revived in the old soldiers' minds.

Our host, Cliff O'Hanlon, called on David for a haka. Was this a song or a dance? The clever guitarist fiddled with his strings, then gave up. This was no song.

'Oh, yeah, All Blacks,' one old boy squeaked. 'New Zealand.' They liked it.

The dark mysterious waters of the Lee reflected Cork's twinkling lights as we headed home past Mallow and Shanballymore with our friends. Cliff was an Englishman who had fought in the Second World War, but had spent most of his life in Ireland. His wife, Anna, was an Irish schoolteacher. She had been a nun once upon a time and given it away. What a lot I wanted to ask her, but the British Legion was the last place to converse — we both knew that. It wasn't her scene, nor mine, but we silently enjoyed each other's company. There was a certain wistfulness about her, an inner strength that made her special. I did not want to part from this new friend. Why was New Zealand so far away?

For tourists who wish to escape the heavy, secretive atmosphere of Cork, the coastal town of Kinsale is only 25 kilometres south. Here there is style and character. Yacht-filled harbours, brightly painted cottages, art galleries and antique shops by the dozen, hotels and B & Bs catering for the beautiful people of the world. Small cobbled malls wind about outdoor cafés, and coloured umbrellas throw an almost Mediterranean shadow on the cappuccino-drinking tourists. I ventured into one antique shop in Kinsale. A figure reclined nonchalantly on a raised stage, long cheroot matching a sinuous body clothed in a smart tweed suit, black felt hat shading today's popular white matt make-up and black eyelashes. It did not move an inch. A plastic model perhaps, to enhance the up-market antiques? Then it blew a spiral of smoke heavenwards from parted red lips and I retreated, freaked out.

'Haloo,' it called after me.

Further along on the cobbles, an artist sat on his little stool, palette open, busily sketching the outline of an old building. No one cared. There were more round the corner.

Trixie looked quite out of place parked on the boulevard. We could have walked past her with our heads in the air, pretending she didn't belong to us. We could have become part of the parade of fashionable tourists from the continent taking an afternoon stroll by the harbour. But maybe our clothes gave us away — and anyway, Trixie was our friend.

A few miles from Cork is the saddest spot in Ireland — Cobh, pronounced Cove. This place has heard, and will hear again, the keening of mothers lamenting as if for the dead. Here immigrants and convicts departed for America, Australia and New Zealand — millions of them, a constant stream of Ireland's best and youngest blood. I thought I had shed all my tears about the awful goodbyes, heard all the gut-wrenching stories, but the melancholy can still be sensed in the atmosphere of Cobh today. An ocean liner waited in deep water just outside the railway station, but instead of immigrants bent over with grief, American tourists walked the gangplank seemingly unaffected by the drama of the past. As if to reawaken old memories, a vivid exhibition spanned part of the old railway station, with static displays and films depicting the hell of life in Ireland — famine, starvation, typhoid, coffins, partings — then the awful escape on the cruel sea to a new life of uncertainty and dread. Screaming winds, broken masts, shipwrecks, death. As if that wasn't enough, a poignant bronze statue of three children commanded a corner of the wharf, commemorating the first girl and her two brothers to land on Ellis Island in America. Young and defenceless, they stand as a reminder of Ireland's pain, and England's shame. It is a most beautiful statue, and even the sun's rays could not quench the intense sadness in those faces. The stories, the stories — the grief.

> The father came into the room, dressed in his best clothes. He wore a new frieze waistcoat, with a grey and black front and a white back. He held his soft felt hat in one hand and in the other hand he had a bottle of holy water. He coughed and said in a weak, gentle voice that was strange to him, as he touched his son: 'Come now, it is time.'
>
> Mary and Michael got to their feet. The father sprinkled them with holy water and they crossed themselves. Then, without looking at their mother, who lay in the chair with her hands clasped on her lap, looking at the ground in a silent, tearless stupor, they left the room. Each hurriedly kissed little Thomas, who was not going, and then, hand in hand, they left the house. As Michael was going out of the door he picked a piece of loose whitewash from the wall and put it in his pocket.
>
> Liam O'Flaherty, *Going into Exile*

Steep, narrow streets climb the hill above Cobh's natural harbour, giving wide views across the bay. Towering over it all is a magnificent Gothic-style cathedral, built in 1868. One has the feeling that Cobh needs this protection of God as its ships sail out into the fickle Atlantic. It was the last vision of home for the immigrants and the last church the passengers on the mighty *Titanic* ever saw. Cobh was their last anchorage, too.

It was all of half-nine when our neighbour Seamus paid a visit. Cork farmers wait till dark before they call.

'The fairies are not about till then,' he half joked.

'They tell us Murphy's is the only thing to drink in Cork,' I joked back. 'Never the opposition.'

'I'd never touch Murphy's in a hundred years — dreadful stuff,' he flashed back, heading for his father's chair.

The crack would be good tonight. Seamus was sparking already. Even the sight of this big man sitting in the house of his birth gave the small parlour an atmosphere of timelessness. The mood was on him. His eyes looked darker in the semilight; his long hair curled into the nape of his neck, and now and then he twisted it round his finger in an endearing gesture. How often had he run up those old stairs to the loft to join the rest of his brothers squashed in old iron beds and sagging mattresses.

His arm reached up to turn on the radio above, exactly as his father and uncle had before him. He laughed at the memory of his father and uncle following the BBC.

'That's what they did. I can see them now, reaching up without looking to turn on the news. Farmers or not, they knew what was going on in the world,' he said in his thick Cork accent. 'They were readers, too. Anything they could lay their hands on. And religious — in the best sense. Not like today — phoney stuff. Well, that's another story.

'I'm off to do business next week, buying up more veterinary supplies,' he told us.

'To the North?'

'I wouldn't go near that place — ever. A man like me with long hair, a Cork accent and southern number plates, carrying a briefcase, would be under suspicion. Even in England they'd look at me sideways. I do my business in Spain or France. They have a laugh with us there. They like the Irish. Keep the Yanks. Why, that Starr has had eleven years to pull Clinton down and given his lawyers barely twenty-four hours to reply. Is that democracy? Anywa', no chance around here to think about that sort of carry-on with women and the like. Everyone knows what the other's doing every minute of the day, and the colour of his car.'

'And the Celtic Tiger?' we asked.

'I couldn't go to Dublin for a drink now. Wouldn't show m' nose there. Turned into yuppies those in Dublin. They'd hear my voice and say "Here's a fuckin' joker from fuckin' Cork." And I'm not changing my accent for anyone. The Celtic Tiger can roar in the cities, but we're getting no spin-off here in the country, with the falling livestock prices. And they're trying to turn the Irish into Yanks. Putting money before the real values we stand for. Instead of church it's shopping they're after. Forget the graveyards and Sunday dinner together and drive round in those flash cars — to nowhere. Who's going to look after the neighbour next ye? Not the Celtic Tiger. We'll lose the friendliness we're noted for. By the way, I hear you were in Maurice McCarthy's pub yesterday. I wouldn't drink in Maurice's pub much. Nice man, Maurice, but too depressed. Sits around his pub depressed and passes it on. Had a depression once a time back. Should have been a historian or something, not a publican. Anywa', what were you doing in there?'

'His dog ran out in front of us on the street in Doneraile and we took him back. Found he was an uncle of Tim and Neil Finn of Crowded House from New Zealand. They played one night in his Glenaneen pub he reckons.'

'Sure they did, and did you see the gold disk they gave him? Got it up in the pub has Maurice.'

Maurice had told us the story:

'Thought Tim would be giving me a T-shirt or some little thing after the Cork concert, and then came this gold disk and I said to Francis, "Jesus, it's the real thing," and Tim said, "Hang it in your pub" and there it is. Come inside and see it for yourselves. They played in here y'know and it was desperate. Didn't invite anyone, but by two o'clock the place was packed like sausages. Tim and Neil and his parents. They were all here. 'Twas a night, I'll tell you that!'

'Yeah, that's right,' said Seamus, rising to go. 'But Maurice can do with Francis about. She runs the pub and does the good talking.'

The parlour felt empty when he had left. We'd had a great night together.

'So many questions I wanted to ask him,' David sighed. 'He's been talking for four hours and I haven't been able to get one in.'

They made up for it 'out the back' when Seamus came along each morning to fix his farm equipment. Fifty acres of land and forty-one beef cattle didn't bring in much — neither did the vet business. No EU trickle-down here.

Seamus and Ina Lillis were the most interesting and loveable neighbours we could have found in the whole of County Cork. He a Catholic, she a Protestant high-school teacher with two degrees. 'Mixed marriages in Shanballymore are no big deal,' she said. 'No great, dark cloud hangs over us. Socialising isn't a problem with the neighbours or anyone. Only being left out of some of my family get-togethers. "Forgot to send you an invitation," they use as an excuse. Anyway, Seamus wouldn't want to go. Not his fancy. He takes the two boys to Mass, and I'm on the vestry at Saint Mary's. On special ecumenical occasions we join together as a family either in his church or mine. I wish there were more of those, especially in the Catholic church. By the way, do all the holy things in this house bother you?'

I assured her we were interested rather than bothered.

'They've never bothered me since I married Seamus either, and I nursed his father and mother in this house till they died. Seamus and I agree on many spiritual values which have nothing really to do with churches or *things*, but he has that ingrained tradition and I understand that. It's the tradition rather than the reality of faith that keeps him going. He knows that.'

Where the N20 motorway between Cork and Mallow cuts through a high ridge, a huge stag with immense antlers stands defiantly on the crest. An Irish joke, we wonder? But it demands closer inspection. A 30 metre scramble up the face of the cutting reveals a bronze, life-sized replica of the Great Irish Deer (10,000–8000 BC), standing two metres high to the shoulder with a three-metre-wide spread of antlers. It thrived along with the mammoths of the last ice age, and many specimens have been preserved in the Irish bogs.

Two complete skeletons flank the
entrance door of the geology
department of Trinity College,
Dublin, while a skull with antlers is mounted proudly in the
dining hall of Cahir Castle, re-
minding man of his mortality.

'Well, we've seen the rest of
them, let's look at the one in
Cahir Castle,' David said, over-
come by the immense size and
antiquity of the great animal.

There is a limit to how much you can look at old castles,
churches and ruins in Ireland. Would Cahir be just another lesson
in Anglo-Normans, barons, earls and that bastard Cromwell? I
sighed. At least there was a concert of traditional Irish music later
on, so why not look around?

Cahir Castle was indeed different. It does not fall readily into
any category of Irish castle. It is larger and more complicated in
plan than most of them. Its shape is conditioned by the rocky island in the River Suir on which it stands, and from its high towers
one can look down on a pretty bridge and the water winding its
way through picturesque woodlands. That was special, and I
couldn't wait to see it lit up at night.

As the competent Irish guide explained about murder holes,
boiling fat and other medieval atrocities used to ward off intruders, there were features of this well-preserved castle that were
inspiring, and you wondered all over again at the complexity of
the building and its inner courts, early privies and keeps, how
many courses of meat the Butler family ate their way through in
the hall, and why Cromwell agreed to leave this particular castle
undisturbed if the occupants moved out for a while — a rare
occurence. Was he really related in some way to the Butler family
in England? The guide hinted at the possibility, and a small pam-
phlet gave it a few lines in fine print, lending credence to the
castle's preservation. A secret pact between Cromwell and the
Butlers saved Cahir Castle? I looked down at the River Suir and

245

wondered. The word Cromwell was distateful even here.

> There is a perfect hall in this castle which is sometimes used
> for dances and other functions. If I owned this castle and
> had the money to indulge a fancy, I would restore it and fur-
> nish the finer rooms with armour, furniture of the period . . .

Just wait, H.V.M.

> I like to stand at an upstairs window of the excellent homely
> hotel in Cahir, which was once a private house, and watch
> the slow life of the wide main street. There is often nothing
> in it but a few old people mysteriously congregated with their
> donkey carts . . .

It was difficult finding a park in this slow main street of Morton's day. Cars and trucks swerved round and round the square
heading to Dublin, Cork or Cashel. Pubs and shops were coming
alive at the hint of darkness, and people crowded the footpaths.
We purposefully chose the 'excellent homely hotel' and looked at a
photo fitting Morton's description hanging near the door.

'Although Cahir is often empty it is never asleep,' he says. He
was right on that count. I doubt if Cahir ever sleeps even today. On
our way home at 11.30 p.m. we would pass little old men dressed
in black heading off for an 'evening ramble' or a 'wee strolly'.

Darkness had fallen quietly while we were eating, and we
stepped out now into a different world where bustling outdoor traffic had given way to a cosy hum indoors. At the bottom of the little
hill, Cahir Castle faced us, floodlit and mysterious. Joining with
the crowd we moved steadily into the old hall with its magnificent
acoustics to hear the 'Best of Irish Traditional Music' — Niall Valley, Niall Keegan, Mel Mercer and John Spillane. Concertina, flute,
percussion and song — a band of incredibly skilled and passionate
young men, filled with the new spirit of Ireland, sounding a new
optimism to replace the haunting melancholy of the past. Elegant
women of the Cahir Castle Arts Society lifted high heels to beat
out the rhythm. How could they have remained still when the jigs
stirred every fibre of one's being? And the great deer looked down
impassively, its antlers spread wide in welcome.

'See you across the road at the Manhattan pub for a drink,' the lady next to me invited. 'Local musicians will be there too.' But the little Manhattan was already packed out and spilling on to the streets, so we headed to a spot out of Cahir where we could see Cashel of the Kings.

> So deep a hush lay over the plain of Tipperary that I could hear the dogs barking as far away as Rosegreen and Cahir. The setting sun was almost warm over the plain, and not one whisper of wind moved the grass.
>
> Before me, in the centre of the Golden Vale, rose Cashel of the Kings, that mighty rock, lonely as a great ship at sea lifted above the flat lands as Ely lifts herself above the fenlands of Cambridgeshire. If you visit Ireland only to see this astonishing building you will not have crossed the sea in vain. It is the strangest sight to one accustomed to Norman churches in England to see this great piece of Norman architecture not built by Normans. It was built half a century before the Normans invaded Ireland by those much-travelled Irish monks, who went out from their monasteries to every part of Europe, and copied something they admired . . . If I were an Irishman I would haunt Cashel of the Kings, for there and there alone is visible a link with the Gaelic Ireland which, subjected to invasion and oppression, has stubbornly survived; the Ireland of the *Book of Kells*, the Ardagh Chalice, the Cross of Cong, and the Tara Brooch . . .
>
> When it grew dark a great yellow moon swung up over the Tipperary plain and hung in the sky above Cashel. Little knots of young men idled and talked at the street corners, laughing and joking and speaking English woven on a Gaelic loom. And on the hill I looked up at the ancient ruins of Cashel of the Kings, rising darkly against the stars. It was silent, empty, and the moon's light was over it, falling down on it like a green rain.
>
> It rode in moonlight over Tipperary like a haunted ship.
>
> H.V. Morton

'When we think of going for a picnic on Sunday afternoons I can think of only one place and that is Lough Gur,' said Ina Lillis, 'so we always find ourselves there.'

No wonder. More than twenty tombs, stone circles, hut foundations, forts and lakeside dwellings have been excavated beside Lough Gur, one of the most complete Stone Age and Bronze Age sites in northwestern Europe. But amidst all that history, children are swimming in the lake, and families open their picnic baskets on the green lawn nearby. They are sitting on a site which was a meeting place for social gatherings or religious ceremonies 4000 years ago. For New Zealanders this is an incredible thought, and we do not know what to do with ourselves. A strange feeling of tapu, or sacredness, engulfs us, and we stare at the mysterious lake in awe. Some other relic could be dragged up any time, they tell us. A few miles down the road the Grange Stone Circle sits in a field as if children had been playing there and placed the boulders in a circle just for fun, like playing sandcastles. But these are huge stones, too heavy even for adults to lift. They are waiting for the dawn of Midsummer's Day, when the first rays of sunlight shine directly through the narrow entrance and into the centre of the circle. We wonder, what happened here? There are mysteries as yet unsolved.

We must say goodbye to Shanballymore tomorrow and head north. We must say goodbye to Seamus and Ina, Anna and Cliff. It is time to leave the South.

Where better to say farewell to Ireland than in this little old cottage queerly alive with memories of Da and the kind of world he lived in. We had been given everything in such cottages throughout Ireland, and we would remember them all — the kindness, the laughter, the tears, the smell of turf fires, the long chats, the openness, the acceptance. We had come as strangers amongst the people and left as friends. I had found in Ireland what I had searched for — that minor note which sounds through every Irish thing, poignant and melancholy, yet full of joy and laughter. I had found a place of antiquity, and a spirituality which had nothing to do with religion, and a certain magic which you have to listen and wait for. It cannot be described, but it is there.

20. OVER AND OUT

FRIENDS IN THE NORTH HAD BEEN so hospitable and generous, opening their spacious homes and listening to our questions.

'No one can understand our problems unless they live here,' they said. 'It's too complicated and deep-seated, but I must say you two seem to have a grip of what's going on. How come?'

'We've read every book we could find, and kept every important page of the *Irish Times*,' I told them. 'You should see the huge pile we're taking home. We're *trying* to understand.'

We came here at Easter as the peace agreement was being signed. Hope was born. A tenuous delivery fraught with pain and anxiety, but the peace child breathed its first breath nevertheless. Now we were leaving this frail six-month-old, still struggling desperately for life. The majority of people in Ireland wanted peace — they had voted for it. They wanted an end to the bombs, and a safe place where their children could grow up without fear. It could happen but for the bigotry and suspicion fostered by insecurity. Maybe it would take another generation to rid the country of this deadly poison which eats into the very fabric of life. But a start had been made.

We made our farewells to Trixie. A polished and glowing Trixie, who had served us well. It would have been fun to take her back to New Zealand, but she was too old for that. Sadly, we watched her being driven away by the dubious-looking car dealer. The money would come later, he assured us. It never did.

We made our farewells to the Emerald Isle too, one Sunday afternoon up in the Mountains of Mourne, with the warm sun bathing them as they lay against one another in soft and gentle lines. They are different from the blue hills of Donegal, different from the weird peaks of Kerry or the wild highlands of the west; yet they are linked to all these by that unearthly quality of the Irish landscape which I can describe only as something which seems half in this world and half in the next. If only this beautiful country could live in peace.

If only the people in the South would stop looking towards Dublin, and the people in the North stop looking towards London, and both turn and face each other. Then there would be peace.

THE CURE AT TROY

Chorus
Human beings suffer,
They torture one another.
They get hurt and get hard.
No poem or play or song
Can fully right a wrong
Inflicted and endured.

History says, Don't hope
On this side of the grave,
But then, once in a lifetime
The longed-for tidal wave
Of justice can rise up
And hope and history rhyme.

So hope for a great sea-change
On the far side of revenge.
Believe that a farther shore
Is reachable from here.
Believe in miracles
And cures and healing wells.

Call miracle self-healing,
The utter self-revealing
Double-take of feeling.
If there's fire on the mountain
And lightning and storm
And a god speaks from the sky

That means someone is hearing
The outcry and the birth-cry

Of new life at its term.
It means once in a lifetime
That justice can rise up
And hope and history rhyme.

Seamus Heaney

After six months in Ireland it was time to go. New Zealand is a very long way from my father's homeland, a long way from the people I had learned to love. The country was going through one of the most historic periods of its life and I was leaving it. News would be sketchy in newspapers and TV, and I would be relying on the Internet. What must our families have felt as they left Ireland's shores last century? No Internet for them, and no return. Only heartache for the loved ones left behind and a gut longing for their beloved country.

> W.B. Yeats said that 'peace comes dropping slow. Trust comes even slower.' But on Thursday, 2 December 1999 the setting up of the Northern Ireland Executive will be remembered as the day the conflict ended. A conflict which has lasted for almost a millennium has finally been settled with the main participants learning to live and work together in peace, understanding and trust.
>
> Former Taoiseach (prime minister) Albert Reynolds
> http://www.irish.times.com   2/12/99

'You guys been away? Where did ya go?'

'Ireland.'

'What did ya go *there* for? Rotten weather, wasn't it?'

'Yes. No summer at all.'

'Hey, that peat stuff they talk about. What's it like? Do you eat it or what?'

'No. It's like coal. You put it on the fire.'

'Oh yeah? You mean they don't have electricity there — sort of backward? Lots of kids and poverty?'

'That's the *old* Ireland. They're really far more advanced than we are these days.'

'You're kidding.'

'When I get this book written you can read about it.'

251

'Hurry up then.'

The new generation of Irish New Zealanders seem to be unaware that life has moved on in the land of their forebears. Their memories have stopped at the famine, and the times when leprechauns danced on the fields at sunrise.

epilogue

I HAD NEVER MET MY RELATIVES in England and Wales. Someone from the Magill family in New Zealand had sent over a copy of *Irish in the Blood*, sparking a spirited correspondence and interest, adding extra stories, extra information. In a casual note I had told them I was coming over to Ireland to actually see the places I had written about, and check out a few strange names on the family tree. I hoped to see them before returning to New Zealand.

Without the research of cousin Reynold Harold Boyd, the family tree would never have been constructed, nor the notes accompanying it compiled. But even Harley Street specialists have been known to make wrong diagnoses, and Reynold's visit to Ireland had been in the misty past of twenty years previously, and his visits to New Zealand fleeting.

It was to Reynold's cousin Graham 'Digger' Magill in Wales that I paid my first visit, and just in time, for he was to die a few months later. Air Vice-Marshal G.R. Magill CB, CBE, DFC and Bar, always wanted to be known as a Kiwi with Irish ancestry. We found him living quietly with his pilot son, Peter, and wife, Pat, in the Vale of Glamorgan. Short and nuggety in stature, he radiated a strength and charisma which masked his debilitating illness. Sharp and alert, and up to date with the politics of both New Zealand and Ireland, he wanted to help with our questions and fire off some of his own.

'What's this about Mary White being an aunt of Field Marshall Sir George White of Ladysmith fame?' I started.

'Most of Reynold's geese were swans when it suited him,' he laughed. 'Always like that.'

'And the bit about the Magills being descended from the Kings of Munster?' I persisted.

'The old boy was deaf when he went over there — you know that, don't you? Mixed up a few things. I knew that. Wished I could have come over to the auld sod and travelled around with you. Tell me about it. Going ahead, eh, in the South? And that old shit Paisley. Why didn't you kill him while you were there?'

Then the doctor came and it was time for us to go. It was hard to leave this man we had come to admire in such a short time. Why did it have to be this way? A meeting, and a leaving . . .

We stood outside the lovely old home, autumn leaves falling from the bare branches of windswept trees. Digger stood to attention with a salute as we drove away. There have not been many moments as poignant.

Digger Magill made newspaper headlines at the start of the 1960s when he was identified as 'the officer who would press the nuclear button'. It followed his appearance in No. 1 court at the Old Bailey, where a number of ban-the-bomb demonstrators were accused of breaching national security at a US air force base in East Anglia.

Then an air commodore serving in the air ministry as director of operations, Magill was indeed the officer who would have launched Britain's V-bomber force, armed with the country's strategic nuclear deterrent, if the world had been facing Armageddon. His obituary in the *Times* summarised his life thus:

> Graham Reese Magill was born in Cambridge, New Zealand, the son of a draper whose parents had emigrated from County Antrim. Although he did well at Te Aroha High School he declined to go to university, opting instead to train as an electrical engineer at Hamilton Technical College, after which he worked for a while as a journalist before deciding he wanted to fly. He scraped together enough money to pay for his passage to Britain in order to try for an RAF short-service commission, intending to return to New Zealand as a civil pilot. When the RAF accepted him in 1936, he was down to his last few shillings.

♣

The city of Peterborough is new, with a cathedral 750 years old. Whether you enter the city from the railway line or the ring road, this magnificent building hits you with awe and wonder. The huge sturdiness of the Norman structure makes its impact immediately.

Trixie spluttered in disbelief as she made her way through the Norman arch in Cathedral Square and into the forecourt. The bishop of the diocese of Peterborough is Ian Cundy, and his wife, Josephine, my cousin. We were to be their guests for a family reunion. The venue — the Bishop's Palace at the back of the cathedral — was in the traditional English episcopal style — large, spacious and without pretence. Simply a home for bishops to live, entertain and work. A small chapel for private worship led off the foyer, its walls permeated with the prayers and hymns of devout Christians down the centuries. The clatter of our shoes on the hard tiles felt out of place and irreverent.

We turned on cobbled stones through Prior's Gate (ca. 1510), with symbols engraved in its walls by an old abbot to flatter the Tudors.

Would we have time to wander through this historic cathedral, or would the Magill family antics engage our attention? How could we bother with such trivia when the building next door had not only been built on the site of a 655 abbey, but had a long history of sackings by the Danes, fires and destruction, and was the burial place of Katherine of Aragon (1536) and Mary Queen of Scots (1587). The mind boggled. Did her head come with her? Of course!

Our enormous bedroom in the Bishop's Palace overlooked ancient cloisters and flower gardens, where, in 655, monks with bowed heads prayed silently as they walked. The vegetable garden was just out of sight, but we walked along its paths and ate vegetables and fruit from the same patch tended by those early monastic gardeners. To me this garden was as holy as the cathedral itself.

'Bit of topsoil needed since then,' the cousins laughed, 'but not much more.'

We were a strange group descended from Irish Magill stock. Watered down now by distance and marriage, but clannish enough to come together for a brief weekend. The bond was there, the understanding, the mutual admiration for forebears who braved that three months of hell on an emigrant ship from Ireland to Napier so their families could have a decent life in the colonies. Some of their children died on that voyage, some perished a few months later. We were indebted to them for so much — their love of education, their work ethic, their God-fearing genes. They were no slugs. But all that didn't prevent us from rattling a few skeletons and laughing at their idiosyncrasies.

We sat round one of the tables in a corner of the enormous dining room, with an art gallery of bishops looking down from behind gilt frames. Dozens of ecclesiastical dignitaries spanning the centuries. Bearded, bespectacled, solemn, and dressed in dark gowns and white fur stoles of the period, they could have had a crushing effect on us if we had let them. They may have been boring old boys from a bygone era but they did not have that effect on the present company — quite the reverse. The Irish are noted for a certain disdain for authority.

'How do you live with these gents?' I asked Jo.

'It took me a while to get used to them.' She smiled. 'Now I forget they are there. But there are those demanding days when my diary is so full, and I'm exhausted, and I look up and hope they approve of what I'm doing around here. I wouldn't like them to disapprove, if you understand.'

And so we shuffled papers across the table and swapped stories. Maps and photos were expertly duplicated on site. Uncle John looked at us severely. We all knew what he was thinking — and Jo voiced our thoughts.

'Wouldn't some of our Plymouth Brethren forebears turn in their graves if they could see us all now in the precincts of this ecclesiastical grandeur they so despised?'

We all laughed.

Our fingers ran over the names of the original emigrants:

> Descendants of three older Magill brothers — James, John and Patrick — are here today. The younger boys — Frank and Robert — died young and without offspring. Mary-Jane is caught up with her husband's — the Campbells' — family tree, but we have her photo. Archie is lying near the sea in Ballintoy, in Ireland and . . .

Kathleen? Where are you and Randal, your husband? Can someone tell us that?

We have the feeling of a great cloud of witnesses hovering over our heads, but we are unfazed. It is to the Boyds and Cundys we must look for any old material as yet uncovered. Had it not been for their father, Dr Reynold Boyd, and his aunt, Annie, there would be no family tree, no precious notes, no will. They were the first to visit Carvacloughan, twenty years ago, and provide the basis for my research.

So it is to Reynold we address our remarks — in absentia — and we dare to ask his permission to alter ' a few wee things'. I am sure he will accept the alterations from historian Dr Linde Lunney of Trinity College, Dublin.

To Reynold
Pity about Field Marshall Sir George White. You tried to inject a little bit of class into our family tree, but there are no Magills in the White lineage. I have that from Patricia English née White, who sent me her family tree. Never mind. It was wonderful to visit Cushendun in the Glens of Antrim and see their great house, called Glendun.

Then, Reynold, we must give the 'Kings of Munster' a miss and change the word to 'Manister', a small townland not far from Carvacloughan. The Magill aunts will not like this change — their little claim to Irish royalty quashed forever. But they have passed on and will not feel the pain.

'In-a-she-oak' changes to 'Skehoge', which makes a lot of sense, and explains the clue to the crossword puzzle we have worked on for years.

Wonderful to find the old graves of Archie and James and Alis in Ballintoy. But where is Mary White? Randal McAllister and our Kathleen Magill must be somewhere, too, and I have 'the feeling' they are resting in the old graveyard at Derrykeighan, not far from Carvacloughan. It is easy to walk a mile or two south along Moyarget Road and find it, and we did that, Reynold, but many of the names are obliterated now with age, and the soldiers documenting the inscriptions many years ago listed only the surname Magill on their notes. One day they promise to use a modern substance in an attempt to restore the details on those old gravestones. In the meantime, we must let them lie unnamed.

I met an old lady called Mrs Frances Glass down the road from the 'wee church on the hill' in Kilmahamogue. She was once a McAllister.

'Aye, I was a wee girrl in the school when Randal died,' she said. 'I don't remember awful much. But between he and Kathleen they had seventeen children, so they did. Brought them up awful decent.'

'Where do you think they are buried then?' I asked her.

'I do know they didn't like the old Ramoan graveyard at Ballycastle. Said it was too wet. Didn't want the wet. I remember them saying that. Did ye look therr?'

'Yes, we did, but they weren't there. It's damp and the writing is faded.'

'Aye, I knaw.'

Frances Glass — a charming old lady of over eighty — sat quietly by the peat fire, watched over by her granddaughter. Her lovely grey hair had just been permed and she was proud of that.

'Aye, they wanted me to have that done,' she said simply. 'D'ya know they're turning the potatoes just across the road? 'Tis a good day for it. Can't help ye with the graves. Must be dozens of them somewhere.'

Your name was always spoken of with pride, Reynold. You should know that. You had finished reading medicine and agriculture by the time you were 22, and Wanganui Collegiate awarded you their honours tie for services to medicine and as long-time secretary of the London branch of the Wanganui Collegiate School Old Boys' Association. Congratulations! Being so far away from you all in England, it gave us a special feeling to say our uncle was a Harley Street specialist. Most New Zealanders know what that means!

What have we to show in worldly goods? This group sitting round the big table?

Uncle John's Bible. Battered and heavily annotated, it is inscribed: 'John Magill, Napier, August 11, 1907. Born again 15th December 1868 in 54 Upper Sacville Street, Dublin.'

Annie's dark leather-covered portable school box from Napier.

A pewter tea pot, and a blue and white bowl used for eggs — both from Carvacloughan.

That's all!

So what was Uncle John's Bible doing way over here in England when his four daughters were still living in New Zealand? Why didn't he leave it with his eldest, Mary — the matriarch — the one my dad declined to marry?

'Mary was probably trying to convert Reynold and gave him that as a hurry-up momento,' Jo Cundy suggested. 'She and Uncle John were always trying to convert my father.'

We haven't any paintings of Mount Knocklayd or Ballycastle, yet some of the women were accomplished artists. We could ask a hundred questions of our forebears. But they have left us their 'Living Will'. That's why we're here, together.

We have the Griffiths' valuation map of the exact farm, showing townland boundaries, farm boundaries and roads. We know the valuation of tenements in the parish of the grange of Drumtullagh. We have sketches of the graves of Archibald and James in Ballintoy. Old photos peer back at us; some are new to us, some are new to our cousins in England, so we promise to swap and send.

Our lunch together in the palace grounds is momentous. At last the sun is shining after weeks of rain, and an unspoken feeling is in the air — we will never again be together like this. We know our roots, and we know each other now. That is the miracle of the Magill family reunion at the Bishop's Palace in Peterborough.

We are chatting about Ireland. I say in good faith and with absolute sincerity: 'Well, now you know exactly where to go when you visit Ireland — straight to the farm in Carvacloughan and the old graves at Ballintoy.'

A pregnant silence ensues.

'We value our lives too much to go over there. We'll probably leave it to our children to make the visit.'

I am too shocked and dumfounded to say the obvious, and decide to accept it as a joke. What I want to say is: 'Well, we've just come from there — and all the way from the antipodes. You only have to fly across the Irish Sea and you'll be there in a hour or so.'

Were they waiting for the peace agreement to work, or the IRA to decommision their guns? There are many things we cannot answer, and many things we don't understand. We live too far away from the day-to-day action in our insular islands at the bottom of the world. Our memories are uncluttered by bigotry. We are New Zealanders.

BIBLIOGRAPHY

Adamson, Ian, *The Identity of Ulster*, Pretani Press, Bangor, 1987.

Bardon, Jonathan, *A History of Ulster*, Blackstaff Press, U.K., 1997.

Carleton, William, *Traits and Stories of the Irish Peasantry, Vol.1*, reprinted by Colin Smythe, Buckinghamshire, 1990 (original 1844).

Foster, R.F., *The Oxford History of Ireland*, Oxford University Press, Oxford, 1989.

Garrett, Rosemary, *The Glens of Antrim*, Alexander & Sons, Bangor, 1968.

Graham, Brendan, *The Whitest Flower*, HarperCollins, London, 1998.

Gray, Marie, *Irish in the Blood*, Hodder Moa Beckett, Auckland, 1997.

Harbison, Peter, *Ancient Irish Monuments*, Gill & Macmillan, Dublin, 1997.

Heaney, Seamus, *Opened Ground, Poems 1966–1996*, Faber & Faber, London, 1998.

Illustrated Guide to Ireland, Reader's Digest, London, 1992.

Keneally, Thomas, *Now and in Time to Be: Ireland and the Irish*, Flamingo, London, 1992.

Lunney, Linde, *Bellett, John Gifford*, research paper, personal communication, 1998.

MacGill, Patrick, *Children of the Dead End*, Caliban Books, London, 1985 (original 1914).

MacGill, Patrick, *The Rat Pit*, NEL Books, London, 1971 (original 1915).

Moorhouse, Geoffrey, *Sun Dancing*, Weidenfeld & Nicolson, London, 1997.

Morrow, Ann, *Picnic in a Foreign Land*, Grafton Books, London, 1989.

Morton, H.V., *In Search of Ireland*, Methuen & Co., London, 1930.

Neillands, Robin, *Walking Through Ireland*, Little, Brown & Co., London, 1993.

O'Faolain, Nuala, *Are You Somebody?*, Hodder & Stoughton, London, 1997.

Quigg, L.F., *The Wee Church on The Hill,* self-published, Ballycastle, 1991.

Sheehan, Jeremiah, *Beneath the Shadow of Uisneach,* Boher & Co., Westmeath, 1996.

Walsh, Michael and William, *Along My Father's Hills,* Patrick Walsh, Dublin, 1997.

Walsh, Micheline Kerney, *Hugh O'Neill and the Flight of the Earls,* Flight of the Earls Heritage Centre, Rathmullen, Co. Donegal, Ireland, 1991.

Wood, James, *Annals of Westmeath, ancient and modern*, James Woods Memorial Committee, Ballymore, 1977.